Global Politics as if
People Mattered

NEW MILLENNIUM BOOKS
IN INTERNATIONAL STUDIES

Series Editors

Deborah J. Gerner, University of Kansas
Eric Selbin, Southwestern University and Umeå University

NEW MILLENNIUM BOOKS issue out of the unique position of the global system at the beginning of a new millennium in which our understandings about war, peace, terrorism, identity, sovereignty, security, and sustainability—whether economic, environmental, or ethical—are likely to be challenged. In the new millennium of international relations, new theories, new actors, and new policies and processes are all bound to be engaged. Books in the series are of three types: compact core texts, supplementary texts, and readers.

Titles in the Series

Global Politics as if People Mattered
Mary Ann Tétreault and Ronnie D. Lipschutz

International Law in the 21st Century
Christopher C. Joyner

Military-Civilian Interactions, Second Edition
Thomas G. Weiss

Globalization and Belonging
Sheila Croucher

The Global New Deal
William F. Felice

The New Foreign Policy
Laura Neack

Global Backlash
Edited by Robin Broad

Negotiating a Complex World, Second Edition
Brigid Starkey, Mark A. Boyer, and Jonathan Wilkenfeld

Forthcoming in the Series

Liberals and Criminals
H. Richard Friman

Law in International Politics
B. Welling Hall

The Information Revolution and World Politics
Elizabeth C. Hanson

The Peace Puzzle
George A. Lopez

Elusive Security
Laura Neack

Political Violence
Philip A. Schrodt

Global Politics as if People Mattered

Mary Ann Tétreault
and
Ronnie D. Lipschutz

ROWMAN & LITTLEFIELD PUBLISHERS, INC.
Lanham • Boulder • New York • Toronto • Oxford

ROWMAN & LITTLEFIELD PUBLISHERS, INC.

Published in the United States of America
by Rowman & Littlefield Publishers, Inc.
A wholly owned subsidary of The Rowman & Littlefield Publishing Group, Inc.
4501 Forbes Boulevard, Suite 200, Lanham, MD 20706
www.rowmanlittlefield.com

P.O. Box 317, Oxford OX2 9RU, UK

British Library Cataloguing in Publication Information Available

Library of Congress Cataloging-in-Publication Data

Tétreault, Mary Ann, 1942–
    Global politics as if people mattered / Mary Ann Tétreault and Ronnie D. Lipschutz.
        p.   cm. — (New millennium books in international studies)
    Includes bibliographical references and index.
    ISBN 0-7425-1089-1 (cloth : alk. paper) — ISBN 0-7425-1090-5 (pbk. : alk. paper)
    1. International relations—Social aspects.   I. Lipschutz, Ronnie D.   II. Title.
III. Series.
JZ1251.T468   2005
327—dc22   2004023463

Printed in the United States of America

♾ ™ The paper used in this publication meets the minimum requirements of American National Standard for Information Sciences—Permanence of Paper for Printed Library Materials, ANSI/NISO Z39.48-1992.

Contents

1

Global Politics Because People Matter

"The time has come," the Walrus said, "To talk of many things: Of shoes—and ships—and sealing wax—Of cabbages—and kings."

—Lewis Carroll

This book is about how people behave as actors in world politics. In most international relations (IR) textbooks, nearly all the people you are likely to read about are political leaders. Leaders populate this book too, but so do people living normal lives in what are ordinary settings by the standards of their time and place. Our focus here is on what we call the "social individual." We chose this term to emphasize two things: the free will and agency of the individual and the social structures that set limits to human thought and action.

The Western tradition emphasizes individual free will over social constraints, but it does so in peculiar ways. For example, in his seventeenth-century work *Leviathan*, Thomas Hobbes imagines that people living before the invention of society existed in what he calls the "State of Nature."[1] But his image of human beings in that State of Nature is a good reminder of how much all of us, in reality, are social products. Hobbes writes as though people never were born; never had families, friends, or neighbors; never went to school; and never worked together. As Christine Di Stefano observes, Hobbes's human beings "spring up like mushrooms."[2] They appear as fully adult and autonomous, able to speak, reason, and perform complex tasks like hunting, gathering, and even agriculture, in total isolation and without any education or history. Hobbes's people also have emotions—simple ones like fear, and complicated

1

ones such as "diffidence" and a desire for glory—emotions that in themselves presume both knowledge of others and a desire to impress them.

How do people learn to fear others? How do they learn ways to make others fear them? This is where the "system" comes in. In Hobbes's world and ours people are hemmed in by structures, not only physical constraints but also social conventions, rules, and common practices.[3] Although it is presented as ruleless, Hobbes's world has very strict rules. Every player is required to play alone in a "game" the objective of which is to survive. To eat, find shelter, and live for another day, she must find what she needs and defend it from others ready to take it from her. Everyone is forced to behave in exactly the same way, because the rules of the game demand it. Any player who trusts another is likely to find herself dead or at least robbed of whatever she has managed to wrest from her harsh world. In Hobbes's own words, life in the State of Nature is "solitary, poor, nasty, brutish, and short."

Hobbes invented the State of Nature in part to persuade us to accept the necessity of a strong central government. His solution to end the terrors of the State-of-Nature game is for every individual player to surrender her autonomy in return for protection. The frontispiece to Hobbes's book included a picture, a kind of political cartoon, illustrating this message. It shows the "Leviathan" as a king holding a sword and a mace (instruments symbolizing the coercive power of the state). His body is packed with tiny little persons, all of whom presumably have agreed to a "social contract," surrendering their individual rights to him in return for his protection. Note that there are no little people in the king's head. Unlike that of his subjects, the king's will is fully autonomous. He is the only player in the Leviathan game, the one who makes all the moves for the "body" of the nation.[4]

This sketch of a philosopher's imaginings would be amusing if the hidden assumption in them, the belief that people are inherently uncooperative and in need of strict regimentation, were not contradicted by logic and by what we see around us every day. Yet it is a powerful image, and, in spite of what is around us, it is widely held. This odd article of faith explains why so many texts about world politics ignore persons. If, as Hobbes says, people are fundamentally alike in their capabilities and desires—and if states are just "heads" that reason and behave like people—then you don't have to think about any of them as individuals or examine the rules of the games they are playing. Instead, you can talk about units filling various roles: parental units, student units, professor units, farmer units, consumer units, and, in the case of the state, national [leader] units. All are playing one or another version of the State-of-Nature game, in which "choice" is nonexistent because the system forces each unit to do the same thing in any given situation.

Decisions and Actions: The Agent-Structure Puzzle

Our perspective in this book is neither that people (or states) are identical units, nor that personality or "character" is the only determinant of human action.[5]

We conceive of the social individual as capable of acting on her own volition, but with the proviso that no one acts in a vacuum. Each person has a history (upbringing, family-supplied resources such as emotional security, nutrition, and education), individual capacities (intelligence, health, energy, and attractiveness), interests (social and economic locations), and temperament (optimism/pessimism, initiative/passivity). We think that, even though similarly situated persons face the same range of choices, they bring different *human* as well as other resources to the act of choosing: different ambitions, ethics, likes, and dislikes; more or less zest for life, different amounts of money, ideas, support from friends and family, and good or bad luck. A few of these qualities are inborn. Most depend on social position and socialization—everything from how much food and love each kid gets to her parents' wealth and income and the value systems in which she is reared. Throughout, we emphasize the interplay between the structure of situations and the intentions a person forms and the efforts that she makes to achieve her goals.

We start with the premise that every person is a potential agent, someone "able to make a difference to the world . . . [someone who has] power (where power means transformative capacity) . . . [and] the ability to carve out spheres of autonomy of [her] own."[6] We also believe that the human capacity for autonomy is highly constrained by structures. Structures are such things as systems of rules and values, resource endowments, and what sociologist Anthony Giddens calls the "'containment' of resources," by which he means the capacity to control the settings in which groups of people use those resources for collective ends.[7] Some of this capacity is innate, but much of it is the product of social position and prior learning. A child whose caregivers show her that she is entitled to claim resources and teach her how to use them to achieve her goals will have more power as an adult than another whose experience is of deprivation and abuse.[8]

What about States?

Even if people have individual talents and unique abilities to use them—a proposition that most of us can accept on the basis of personal observation—why should we expect collective actors like states to be similar? One reason is that states are governed by persons, and the behavior that is attributed to states is the result of leaders' choices and actions. This is a common perspective of historians but rarely of IR theorists, most of whom do think of states as functionally similar units along the lines that Hobbes describes.[9] Even so, some imagine states as having individual qualities too, a perspective that has its own history. Until the last fifty or so years, it was common in popular culture and in academic writings to treat states as though they had personalities, a "national character" based on history, climate, economic activities, and even cultural artifacts like cuisine, music, and writing. The state's personality was imagined as shared by its citizens. So Germans were thought of as regimented, tidy, and precise; the French as logical, romantic (we didn't say that these characteristics were consistent!), and lovers of good food; Italians as religious, excitable, and talking with their hands; and so on. Much of the national-character literature was based on geographic determinism. People who lived in cold climates were said to be hardworking and unemotional (English, Germans, and Swedes). Those living in warm climates were said to be hot tempered and sexy (Italians, Spaniards), although the climate could be entirely too warm, leading to laziness (Africans, Arabs, and South Asians).[10]

Whole theories were built around ethnocentric views of how geography shapes people and their states. One of the most prominent is the hydraulic culture model. Analysts from Karl Marx on the left to Max Weber and Karl Wittfogel on the right were convinced that nations whose agriculture depended on large-scale irrigation were bound to have despotic governments.[11] They argued that such states would develop leviathan-style governments to force people to work on the irrigation infrastructure on the assumption that no one would work voluntarily on something owned by everybody. Contemporary anthropologists like Clifford Geertz have found real-world examples of participatory politics in states with large irrigation networks,[12] but some writers continue to believe that the societies that grew up around large systems of irrigated agriculture are naturally biased toward authoritarianism, while societies supported by rain-fed agriculture are naturally biased toward democracy.[13] Geographers like J. M. Blaut call this perspective plain and simple prejudice, identifying it as part of the widespread "Euro-centrism" that dominates most theories of world politics.[14] These theories present the states and populations of northern Europe and its former settler colonies (like the United States and New Zealand) as inherently better than others. (It should not surprise you to learn that most of these theories were invented by people from northern Europe and the United States.)

A new type of theory of national character takes a somewhat different tack. Instead of identifying "good" states by their geography and weather, such theories evaluate the moral qualities of states according to the type of political regime they have. One currently popular example holds that democracies are less aggressive than other regimes. People who share this point of view suggest that important characteristics of democratic states, such as regular elections, keep leaders from declaring war without clear provocation. This "democratic-peace" thesis became popular during the Clinton administration, under a president who believed that "democracies rarely wage war on one another."[15]

Upon investigation, however, there seem to be holes in this theory, too. Joanne Gowa finds evidence supporting the democratic-peace thesis only during an anomalous period in world politics, the cold war, when democratic states banded together in formal and informal alliances to oppose Soviet expansion. She argues that it was not democracy but rather their shared interests that kept these states from declaring war on one another during that time.[16] Ido Oren comes to a similar conclusion based on a careful analysis of the writings of prominent U.S. political scientists prior to and following the start of World War I. He shows that democracy was defined differently during these two periods. Before the war, qualities such as constitutionalism and electoral participation, in which Germany scored higher than Britain, France, and the United States, were regarded as the most important indicators of democracy. After the United States found itself allied with France and Britain in a war against Germany, what made a country democratic or not changed in Americans' minds to reflect the political characteristics shared by the United States and its major allies.[17]

Who's Really in Charge?

Why is so much effort expended to explain the behavior of states—the decisions of their leaders—as though the states and not the leaders are in charge? We believe that there are several reasons. One is that leaders can thereby avoid responsibility for their thoughtless, stupid, or dangerous decisions and actions. A classical example of someone taking this "Pontius Pilate" approach to political responsibility is that of Sir Edward Grey, Britain's foreign minister on the eve of World War I. In a controversial book on that war, historian Niall Ferguson presents Grey as a man with a private political agenda vastly different from the position of his party and prime minister.[18] Grey disdained the official position of the Liberal Party, which was to take a neutral stance toward France and Germany. Grey, who disliked Germans and Germany, instead engaged in secret negotiations with French leaders, hinting that Britain would come to the support of France in the event of a continental war.

Did the resulting uncertainty about what Britain actually would do encourage the Germans to "consider a pre-emptive strike," thereby making "a continental war more rather than less likely," as some historians believe?[19] It's a plausible assumption. Yet to whatever extent Grey's confusing actions contributed to making the conflict between Germany and France into a world war, he refused to associate himself with the results. In his memoirs, he presents himself as a tragic figure caught up in events he could not control. In fact, he is remembered as the man who greeted the coming of war with the observation that the lights were going out all over the world and would not come on again during his lifetime. Of course he never mentioned that his own hand was on one of the light switches.

A second reason for presenting state actions as automatic is linked to the first. It lets observers avoid confronting the effects of past policies and practices whose outcomes, whether consciously intended or not, turn out to be bad for the national interests of the state whose leaders chose them. One example is the nurturing and arming by U.S. policy makers of the Taliban and persons who later became the nucleus of the al Qaeda network. Mujahideen (holy warrior) groups who, as revolutionaries in Iran, were regarded as dangerous to U.S. interests were embraced as U.S. proxies in the war that raged throughout most of the 1980s between Afghanistan and the Soviet Union. The U.S. government sent support to these groups directly and via intermediaries such as Pakistan, and it also gave them military training. At the behest of then CIA director William Casey, high-tech armaments such as Stinger missiles were provided by the U.S. Congress to the mujahideen. Casey also committed the CIA to support Pakistan's intelligence agency, Inter-Services Intelligence (ISI), in its efforts to recruit Muslims to fight with the Afghan mujahideen. Among the ISI's recruits were the Saudi Osama bin Laden and other young Arabs from places as far away as Algeria and the United States.[20]

When the Soviet Union withdrew from Afghanistan, the United States turned its back on the devastation that a decade of war had inflicted there. The CIA did offer to buy back the leftover Stinger missiles, but it was oblivious to the situation of the human beings trained to operate them. The young fighters who had been mobilized from across the Arab and Islamic worlds suddenly lost their mission, their proxy role, and the material and status rewards that role had brought them. They did hold on to their weapons, however, along with their training and their desire to be powerful figures in their respective countries and in the world. Within a few years, one group of mujahideen, the Taliban, took over most of the Afghan state. Meanwhile, al Qaeda had turned into a terrorist organization; its members mounted attacks in their home countries and elsewhere in the world, including the United States. The most spectacular of these attacks took place on September 11, 2001, in New York and Washington. But when participants in Republican administrations reminisce fondly about the "Reagan legacy," they never mention the Reagan administration's support of the mujahideen.

A third reason why the fingerprints of specific actors on the policies they make are so frequently overlooked is because many people see bad outcomes as inevitable, a product of economic and other conditions outside anyone's control. Yet political economies are not accidents or forces of nature. They are structures produced by rules and practices established and enforced by powerful governments and their agents. Even so, policies such as the conditions imposed by the International Monetary Fund (IMF) on developing countries experiencing trade deficits are discussed as though the actions of powerful countries had nothing to do with the falling prices of developing country exports—or the policies of IMF. But as Herman Schwartz notes about declining terms of trade for developing nations, these balance of payment problems are directly connected to economic specialization and trade dependence, and to protectionist policies imposed by powerful potential importers designed to support their own domestic industries.[21] Peter Uvin traces the impact of IMF demands for "structural adjustment" requiring deep cuts in employment and social services on the government and society of Rwanda. He argues that these policies contributed directly to the massive genocide that Rwanda's Hutu government inflicted against the Tutsi minority during one hundred horribly bloody days in the spring of 1994.[22]

Agents *in* Structures

In spite of our belief that structures are important causes of undesirable outcomes, we acknowledge that accounting separately for the contributions of agents and structures is hard to do. Structures help to shape agents, who, in turn, alter structures if they can to give themselves a greater scope of power and more choices in the future. Sir Edward Grey, who was able to undermine the stated policy of his party and the government it led, started out with structural advantages that enhanced his agency. He was from a wealthy family whose prominence increased the likelihood that he would get a university degree, even though he had been "rusticated" (suspended) by two Oxford colleges for laziness. Social connections also smoothed his path into politics in spite of what one contemporary, Lloyd George, called his lack of vision. The political environment also worked for Grey. While he was foreign minister, his Liberal Party was divided. Leaders worried more about keeping the party together than about what Grey might be up to. Meanwhile, the Conservative Party agreed with Grey's pro-France policy and had no reason to encourage anyone to look too closely at what he was doing. As a result, "the detail of Grey's policy (and the devil lay there) was not subjected to close enough parliamentary scrutiny."[23] What Jane Mansbridge calls "adversary democracy"[24] depends on public scrutiny—today we call it "transparency"—and open debate. In this case, neither party was following accepted practices for exercising checks and balances.

Adolf Hitler is another agent who used favorable structural conditions to pursue destructive policies. After World War II, what amounts to a scholarly industry grew up to explain how a lower-middle-class, indifferently educated, and undistinguished Austrian rose to become the leader of the German state, initiated a global conflict, and masterminded the extermination of a majority of the Jews of Europe. Daniel Goldhagen does make Hitler responsible for mobilizing what he calls Germany's "willing executioners" of the Jews. But he also argues that Germans followed Hitler and supported the Holocaust because they grew up in an anti-Semitic culture that defined Jews as evil and deserving to be killed.[25] This is a structural thesis that removes responsibility from individual Germans—after all, if they had been socialized in a virulently anti-Semitic culture, how could they help but be anti-Semitic? Some scholars who emphasize Hitler's agency also point to structures that might account for his behavior: an abusive father, the horrific death of his mother, his alleged drug addition, his sexual problems, and an evil soul are suggested as causes of his anti-Semitism and his lethal policies.[26] The tacit message in these studies is that anyone with such problems couldn't avoid growing up to be a mass murderer and therefore is not fully responsible for his actions.

How would we navigate through these various explanations that focus on culture and personality, two factors that we do believe supply partial explanations for action? Let's start with culture. Anthropologist Eric Wolf also explains the rise of the Nazis in terms of German culture, but he draws the connection between culture and behavior differently than Goldhagen. Wolf argues that the German middle class, unlike the middle classes of France and England, developed without a tradition of citizenship. Indeed, Germany took shape as fragments, each with a middle class cut off both from the autocratic "petty princelets" who ruled the many little German states prior to unification at the end of the nineteenth century, and from the masses of illiterate peasants and workers. During the founding period of the modern German state, all that unified German social groups was a common language and a common "high culture" of music and literature. There was no common experience among Germans allowing them to think that they shared a unique history that defined them as members of a community in which they had earned rights and owed obligations. German autocracy left intellectuals without an opportunity to engage in politics and therefore without practical experience in governance. Wolf tells us that German revolutionaries in Europe's year of revolution, 1848, couldn't even agree on how the state they were fighting for should be organized. As a result, it was relatively easy for Prussian and Austrian troops to close down their assemblies, parliaments, and "security committees" and reinstate autocratic rule.[27]

Although German activists failed to democratize their politics in 1848, they did succeed in making their fellow Germans see themselves as a united people. Germans did not feel united because they were fellow citizens, however, but because they belonged to the same ethnic group or tribe—in German, a *Volk* (folk). A political community is imagined as a social construction based on values and goals that people choose together and alter when they wish—like Hobbes's picture of a social contract. A *Volk* is "natural" and therefore permanent. It is shaped by "vital forces driving physiological and psychological life, binding individuals to the *Volk*, people to the landscape, landscape to nature, nature to cosmos."[28] As a *Volk*, Germans were unified by their Germanness rather than because they were a responsible political community. Even after Germany was formed in 1870 from a collection of smaller states, continued autocratic rule retarded the development of institutions in and through which citizenship and political responsibility could develop as normal social practice.

The strongest institution in the new Germany's narrowly based state was its large professional army. The army's needs took priority over everything else. Before Germany was united, people used to joke that Prussia, the statelet that became Germany's nucleus, was little more than an army with a state. United Germany was Prussia writ large, and the now-German army began its existence with a spectacular early success. Its defeat of France in 1871 made Germany a world power, and the army took full credit for the new state's achievement.

But as U.S. president John Kennedy observed after his first major foreign policy act, an invasion of Cuba, had crashed and burned, success has many fathers, but failure is an orphan. After Germany was defeated in World War I, army leaders refused to take responsibility for the loss, arguing that the military had been "stabbed in the back." They looked for scapegoats, and Jews and socialists, categories with substantial overlap, became the favored targets for the army's defenders. Ian Kershaw traces how ruthlessly the army put down postwar movements attempting to create a socialist democracy in Germany.[29] As part of its campaign, the German army funneled arms to right-wing paramilitary groups that shared its views on the desirability of a militarized Germany and the undesirability of a social revolution. These groups also opposed the disarmament provisions of the Versailles Treaty, which laid out the postwar settlement, arguing that the authority of military leaders should be preserved.

The Nazi Party was among the groups that received arms and ammunition from the army. Like other *volkisch* parties, the Nazis capitalized on Germany's postwar economic collapse and growing popular discontent with the postwar government that had replaced the kaiser after his sudden abdication at the end of the war. The government of Bavaria, the state where these right-wing parties were strong, rarely arrested party members for their violent behavior. In 1923, one of the Nazi Party leaders, Hitler, was arrested for a failed attempt to lead an armed, right-wing, populist rebellion (the "Beer Hall Putsch"). Sentenced to a year in prison, he was treated like a king by prison authorities. After he was released, he was even more popular and more powerful than he had been before.

The Nazi Party was good at manipulating structures. It used the electoral system to run candidates for the national parliament but avoided criminal penalties from the justice system when it used terrorist tactics against its opponents. Ron Rosenbaum describes how Nazis terrorized and even killed some of their "enemies," not only candidates who ran against them (on the right and on the left) but also newspaper reporters and publishers who dared to criticize them and expose their activities.[30] Protected by their connections in the army and by a Bavarian state that looked the other way when their brand of politics led to violence, Hitler and other Nazis were elected to the German parliament. However, they were not effective legislators and soon lost some of their appeal. The proportion of the German vote that went to the Nazi Party was already declining when, in 1933, a government crisis prompted the country's president, former general Paul von Hindenberg, to tap Hitler to become chancellor. Von Hindenberg thought that Hitler was so insignificant that he would be easy to control. This is how a politician who might have ended his career as a curiosity found himself in charge of the levers of the German state.

Hitler came to power in Germany in part because German culture ensured that racist appeals were acceptable in a "mainstream" political platform. But Nazi successes were due at least as much to the kind and amount of support the party received from the army and from the Bavarian government. Guns, money, and impunity allowed the Nazis to swagger in front of unemployed young male voters and buy them drinks at party meetings (which usually were held in beer halls). Meanwhile, Nazi thugs could eliminate critics and opponents by beating them up or killing them. Hitler himself was an energetic agent and used his position to manipulate and transform structures in his favor. A talented speaker, he used his year in jail to make an end run around his rivals for Nazi Party leadership. He held court from prison and also wrote a book—*Mein Kampf*, "my struggle." The book impressed his followers, whether they read it or not, and chilled his opponents, who read it very carefully. When Hitler was offered the position of chancellor, he surprised his backers by taking control of the state, changing the laws, and altering the constitution to carve out for himself a unique and unchecked position as the *führer* (leader) of the German people.

Even though the Nazi Party was in decline by the time that Hitler was invited to head the government, it still allowed him to be in the right place at the right time when powerful, behind-the-scenes manipulators were looking for a front man. But that Hitler could take control of the entire state so quickly and easily was due as much to the lack of democratic institutions in Germany as to his personal qualities. Hitler's anti-Semitism was very much a part of his personality and shaped what he did with the German state when he was put in charge of it. Even so, neither culture nor personality can explain as much about the rise of Hitler and the Nazis as the actions of the army coupled with the lack of democracy and of a tradition based on the rule of law in Germany and in its constituent states.

The Creation of the Social Individual

The stories of Edward Grey and Adolf Hitler illustrate the importance of institutions in creating what sociologists call "opportunity structures," situations through, against, or within which individuals have room to exercise their agency. The household is one of several powerful institutions that shape opportunity structures for social individuals. Households are where people are produced: children are reared (socialized), educated, and prepared for adult life by the people who live with them. Although every child has her own temperament, what she can do—and what she can get away with—is first learned at home.

A household also is an economic unit. Children receive money, goods, and services from the adults in their households (in many parts of the world, they also contribute money and services to their households). The home, its inhabitants, their collective resources, and the rules they use for sharing such resources are part of the legacy of every human being. There is an African saying that "it takes a village to rear a child." This reflects an understanding that the road from the infant's dependency to the adult's autonomy is necessarily populated by caregivers in and outside of the household. Each potential caregiver provides or withholds resources from those persons and institutions that depend on them, including the household itself as a productive and reproductive unit. As a result of how and in what quantity resources are provided or withheld, children learn who they are and what kind of claims they can make on their world.

Some caregivers teach children by hitting them or humiliating them in front of others. Their philosophy of education is to punish children so that children will avoid what is forbidden. If punishment is made into a spectacle, even children who are not punished directly might be terrified enough to refrain from the activities that caused suffering to their siblings or peers. The technical term for this strategy is "deterrence." Similar tactics, applied to adults, are concrete manifestations of the philosophy behind state terrorism. They include the torture and murder of citizens by their governments[31] and capital punishment: advocates believe that killing criminals can deter others from becoming criminals.

Michel Foucault, a twentieth-century analyst of knowledge and power, argues that the standardization of punishment by legal means, along with the development of institutions that rely on regimentation, surveillance, and isolation, increased states' capacity for social control. When he speaks of "institutions" Foucault refers not only to prisons but also to schools and workplaces, and the beliefs and practices they embody. Here individuals are taught to control themselves through subjection to routines presented as the results of "laws" or universal systems, and through punishment when they fail to conform. Forced conformity and the loss of individuality shape the mind to submit to the will of others, a will that is disguised in the presentation of its demands as objective laws (such as supply and demand in the market) or even as divine commands ("Spare the rod and spoil the child").[32] Philip Greven offers the example of Susanna Wesley, who, centuries earlier, applied her own version of Foucault's model to the rearing of her children.

> Susanna Wesley recalled that her infants had been "put into a regular method of living" from the outset, in their patterns of sleeping, eating, and dressing. . . . [She] was insistent upon harsh physical punishment from a very early age: "When turned a year old (and some before) they were taught to fear the rod and to cry softly, by which means they escaped abundance of correction which they might otherwise have had: and that most odious noise of the crying of children was rarely heard in the house."[33]

The similarity between the regime imposed by Susanna Wesley, an eighteenth-century parent, and Foucault's discussion of disciplinary institutions illustrates how much the technique if not the technology of discipline and punishment predates "modernity," generally understood as a worldview in which human reason and rationality are regarded as superior to religion and custom as sources of guidance for life decisions. But as Anthony Giddens emphasizes, it is the application of surveillance in a complex system defined by industrialization and militarization, and its coordination by the nation-state, that gives modernity its unique qualities.[34]

The modern state is most commonly defined as an institution that monopolizes the legitimate use of violence, but, as with the violence inflicted by Susanna Wesley on her children, we should question how legitimate this violence is and what the source of that legitimacy might be. By defining states' or parents' use of violence as legitimate from the outset, we deny ourselves the right to withhold or withdraw our consent to their actions, and the right to hold those in charge responsible for any atrocities they might commit.[35] We substitute "the law" for the truth. Elaine Scarry makes this point in her examination of torture and how it is justified by being paired with interrogation.

Pain and interrogation inevitably occur together in part because the torturer and the prisoner each experience them as opposites. The very question that, within the political pretense, matters so much to the torturer that it occasions his grotesque brutality will matter so little to the prisoner experiencing the brutality that he will give the answer. For the torturers, the sheer and simple fact of human agony is made invisible, and the moral fact of inflicting that agony is made neutral by the feigned urgency and significance of the question.[36]

That there is a question, even though "everyone knows" that a person being tortured will say anything to stop the infliction of pain, removes moral responsibility from the torturer and those in whose name he works. As we have seen with U.S. and British torture of prisoners in Afghanistan, Iraq, and Guantanamo Bay, torturers deny what they are doing by recasting it as necessary for "reasons of state." Similarly, parents who beat their children justify that as necessary to make them obey, for "until a child will obey his parents, he can never be brought to obey God."[37]

Stanley Cohen argues that denial is what allows adults to observe and even participate in the abuse of children, and allows persons in authority to order, observe, and participate in the abuse of their fellow citizens as well as aliens.[38] Denial requires knowing and not knowing at the same time.[39] Persons in denial know what is happening and what they are doing, but they distance themselves from responsibility. Some do this through "normalization," a claim that the violence being inflicted on others is deserved, either because of the actions of the victim or because that is the routine way that things are done. Others "turn a blind eye," not really failing to see but being indifferent to the harm inflicted on others as long as there is no danger that similar harm will come to themselves. Some select particular atrocities as blameworthy and shut others out completely.

Why . . . was the My Lai massacre—the deliberate killing, one by one, of unresisting women and children—viewed as more repugnant than achieving the same results by the standard mechanical means of smart bombs dropped invisibly from a distance? Perhaps because knowledge of impersonal mass killing is much like the background knowledge that children are starving while you eat.[40]

Thus we use boundaries to close off the world we "see" from the worlds we turn a blind eye to.

Much of the creation of the social individual is concerned with defining boundaries. Boundaries, which we discuss in more detail in chapter 6, allow us to feel safe and protected by marking places where we can feel secure enough to "be ourselves." Boundaries mark off those whom we can trust from those who are not obligated to be especially kind to us or sympathetic to our interests. They also indicate our communities of obligation, those persons who are obligated to assist us and whom we are obligated to assist, and in what ways that assistance is to occur. "Those X-group members always stick together," some grumble, and yet one of the most important benefits of group membership is being able to call on someone else in your group—your mom, the person who sits across from you in class, a helpful neighbor, or your nation's embassy in a foreign country—to do something that you need to have done.

There is no magic formula for deciding how to navigate the distance between "us" and "them." One way to look at the problem comes from Immanuel Kant. In his essay "Perpetual Peace," Kant talks about obligations to "the stranger," the person who is not a member of our community. Kant says we should show "hospitality" to strangers by being polite and offering what they need to be safe and comfortable while they are with us. But Kant also says that we should not treat strangers as though they were members of our community. He wants both to preserve diversity, which includes the right of strangers to be different and to make claims and confer benefits on other strangers, and also to preserve the integrity of each group, which privileges those qualities that all members share along with their right to make claims and their capacity to confer benefits on others like themselves. Mutual obligations are the key to Kant's distinction between the stranger and the community of obligation. Neither the stranger nor the community is obligated to the other except with regard to being courteous, and neither should be punished for being who or what she or it is.

The problem in today's world is that the stranger lives in constant peril if she cannot mobilize others to come to her aid if she is victimized by her family, her employer, or her state. It is the denial of personhood to "the other," by the parent to the child, by the firm to the worker, by the torturer to the victim, by the state to the citizen, that gives the agent-structure problem its moral urgency. Those who make the rules must take responsibility for them and for their effects, and for this to happen, the rules must apply equally. As Stanley Cohen writes,

> There is only one way to include the distant stranger: to define the threshold of the intolerable as *exactly the same for everybody*. The starting point is not pseudo-universalism or touchy-feely empathy, but a recognition of the radical and irreducible differences that do matter. These differences derive not from my ethnicity, culture, income, world-view, age, sexuality or gender, but from the primeval facts that *my children have not and will not die from hunger* and that *I have not or will not be forced from my home after watching my wife be hacked to death with a machete.*[41]

The Social Individual and World Politics

The fact that multiple forms of political and other communities exist indicates that people are not alike. There is neither a single way to be human nor a single way to organize human communities. This is a liberating thought. It means that we as human beings build our own institutions and can build them to suit a wide variety of needs and desires. At the same time, we shouldn't feel too liberated. Structures of power insulate institutions that support the powerful and make them resistant to agents who would challenge their legitimacy. Talented young socialists like Rosa Luxembourg had little opportunity to take charge of Germany after World War I given the large, demobilized army dispersed among the population. With plenty of weapons and a desire to deny its responsibility for having lost a long and terrible war, this army lavished structural supports on those who wished to crush leftist dissidents and created structural impediments to those who wished to control rightist dissidents. Although these structures did not guarantee that Hitler would come to power in Germany, they made it far more likely that social movements would push Germany's postwar government toward an authoritarian state because they created conditions under which right-wing groups were favored. Unusually gifted leaders might have been able to navigate around those biased structures but, sadly, Germany's postwar leaders were mediocre at best and had little experience at governing democratically. There was no German George Washington or Mohandas Gandhi to champion the democratic institution building that could have made a paper constitution into a reality of democratic practice, and no German Alexander Hamilton to ensure that the life savings of middle-class Germans would be protected against hyperinflation, and their spirits thereby protected against impoverishment and bitterness.

Social fragmentation also discouraged the kind of unified popular uprising in post–World War I Germany that Iranians from across the social and political spectrum successfully mounted against the shah in 1978–1979.[42] We "remember" Iran's struggle as a religious revolution, but the clergy took over only after bitter battles among these many and highly varied groups. In reality, Iran's revolution was a model "united front" against a despotic regime, one so idealistic that many participants couldn't even imagine that their revolution might be hijacked until it actually happened. But as in Germany with respect to the army, in Iran there were few institutions other than religion that had permanent structures, and there were almost no experienced leaders other than among the clergy. A different situation operated in the postrevolutionary United States, where long-standing local governing bodies, along with revolutionary institutions like the committees of correspondence and the Continental Congress, generated scores of leaders across social and geographic divisions, and served as foundations for new representative institutions after the British were defeated. Few other former colonies or dependencies were left such an institutional legacy, because colonial powers learned from the British experience in the United States that competent local governments could undermine their power. As a result, many subsequent postcolonial states foundered after liberation because the imperial powers had destroyed or so deformed local governing structures that they no longer were able to generate leaders and check their power.

We emphasize the simultaneous need for good leadership and effective social organization. Outcomes that are democratic and fair depend on both. A gifted leader can overcome poor institutionalization by creating better institutions, just as effective social organizations can compensate for poor leaders by training better leaders. But either pattern is rare. It is more common for talented leaders to use their positions as opportunities to do whatever they think is best. (After all, aren't they their nation's best and brightest and entitled to do as they like?) Some might use their talents to devise autocratic structures to make that possible. Too, social organizations with poor leaders are ineffective. Poor leaders avoid making tough decisions and lose the respect that would enable them to coordinate and mobilize members to achieve the organization's goals. In consequence, the organization either finds itself unable to attract necessary resources and gradually becomes even less capable, or it is captured by opportunists to serve ends likely to be very different from the ones it started out with.

Opportunities come to those who are prepared. Following the democratization of the French army under Napoleon, there was a saying to the effect that every soldier carried a marshal's baton in his backpack. Although it was almost as unlikely then as before that a common soldier from a peasant or working-class background could become a field marshal, this saying encapsulates the concerns that brought us to write this book. People prepare for lives of action by learning how to evaluate situations and mobilize others to help them work for what they desire. The image of the common soldier is useful because it carries with it the image of an army and thus the importance of coordinated collective action. It also reminds us that action can be dangerous. The young soldier promoted on the battlefield stands among the dead and dying and risks the same fate if she fails to use her opportunities wisely to achieve her objectives and preserve her life.

The capacity for human agency is itself the product of prior choices, chance events, and the ability of human beings to see and understand how they can be effective. Embedded in webs of relationships and structures, some that enable and others that constrain, each social individual is part of many different groups that intersect and overlap at every human point. This is how social individuals create and occupy the various opportunity structures from which they act. In these chapters, we hope to show you how such social individuals participate, whether they realize it or not, in decisions that affect their own lives and the lives of others in the world.

What Is in the Rest of This Book?

Our intention in this book is to offer a different perspective on and analysis of what we call "global" politics. One way we do this is to consider global politics from a perspective far broader than the state and relations among states, or economies and relations among states, corporations, and other "economic" bodies. Indeed, in chapter 2, we begin with people and households.

2

People, Households, and the World

"Who are you?"
"I'm fine, thanks, who are you?"

—Chico Marx to interlocutor

How do we know who we are? And what does such knowledge have to do with global politics? Especially in the United States, we tend to think of ourselves in individual terms, as individuals different from every other individual, with fates different from every other person, but this is largely a myth. It is a myth because every human being is born into a social setting, into a network of social relations. Conception is a biological process, of course, as is birth, but both result from relations between human beings, and both are fraught with social and symbolic significance. And, even before birth, even before conception, the new person is already enmeshed in these social and economic webs. We call this person—and every other person—the *social individual*.

This chapter is about the social individual and what makes her who she is. It is also about the role of the social individual in the household—and the family—and the place of the family and household in global politics and global political economy. We don't ordinarily think of these two institutions as playing a significant role in global politics, but, as we shall see, they are foundational in ways that are very important yet rendered almost invisible.

We begin by defining what it is that we mean by the terms "liberal individual" and "social individual." We then turn to a discussion of the household and family, and the ways in which they are constituted by society and economy, on the one hand, and the ways in which they contribute to the constitution of society and economy, on the other. In the third part of the chapter, we address the relationship between the social individual and global politics.

Defining the Liberal Individual

In mainstream liberal political theory,[1] there are two primary agents: the individual and the state. Classically and historically, the first theorists of liberalism as we understand it today could not explain how the state came into being. As we saw in chapter 1, applying logical reasoning to the problem, Hobbes proposed a solution. He argued that men (never women) came together out of mutual fear, selected a ruler (sovereign), and gave that man the authority to govern and maintain a social order in which every man could enjoy his possessions without fear that he might lose them to another. It's a nice story, but badly flawed and wholly fictional. Nevertheless, it has influenced many generations of political theorists and scholars of international politics and provides the basis for what is usually called "Realism." Why has Hobbes been so influential?

To provide a fully developed explanation would require several books and an intimate knowledge of seventeenth-century English history. More briefly, Hobbes was writing at a critical juncture in European political and economic development. Feudalism had largely disappeared from England, and capitalism was in its early stages of development. The English Civil War between the Puritans and Royalists had ended with the victory of Oliver Cromwell over King Charles I, but Hobbes feared a reignition of the passions and hatreds that had killed one king and torn the country apart. He was concerned, moreover, to root the sources of the sovereign's authority in some kind of natural law in order to limit future political conflict over the form of England's government. He also wished to illustrate what could happen if men did not willingly yield up their freedom to a sovereign and remained in a "warre of all against all." Whether Hobbes actually believed that men had ever lived in a true State of Nature is less than clear; what is clear is that his notion later came to be applied to relations among states, which were said to exist as isolated individuals in an environment without a world sovereign.

It is curious to note, therefore, that Hobbes had very little to say about international relations. In fact, his analysis hardly applied to the European world of his time, which was largely constituted through alliances concluded on the basis of royal marriages, and whose territories were, for all practical purposes, the property of kings, queens, princes, and various other nobles. Not until the beginning of the nineteenth century, after the American and French Revolutions, the Napoleonic Wars, and the first stirrings of nationalism, did interstate relations begin to resemble Hobbes's State of Nature. The field of international relations came into its own as an area of study separate from international law only in the twentieth century. But, whereas international law conceives of states as existing within a society of states, however underdeveloped, international relations in its more vulgar forms denies the existence of any sort of interstate society.[2]

International relations theories and, to some degree, its practices, were thus constituted around the idea of the state as an isolated agent in a condition of constant danger from other, similar agents, each of which constantly threatened war and death. Within states, it is only by virtue of a "social contract"[3] between men and the sovereign that a similar condition of danger and fear is avoided, according to this line of reasoning (whether correct or not). Therefore, continues this argument, any polity or community is constituted by isolated individuals who willingly contract with the state and one another to live peacefully in society. The law—both as it is written and as it is personified in the police—ensures that the contract is kept, and it deals harshly with those who violate it. Because there is no social contract among states, and no sovereign to force them to behave in a civil manner, states are like Hobbes's uncivilized men. They must always be on guard against other states.

A little reflection on the story of the State of Nature forces us to ask some difficult questions. After all, how do we know that men [*sic!*] were ever in a State of Nature? And when did this state exist? How could men have reproduced? Who would have taken care of babies or provided food? How could language have developed, and why would it, especially if men had nothing to do with one another? For Hobbes, such questions were neither germane nor especially interesting; he was concerned with providing a naturalized narrative that would prevent internecine warfare. Liberal theorists, however, saw individual consciousness and self-interest as evident characteristics of every person and, consequently, thought they must be the starting point of any theory of politics. Further, to ensure the continuity of this material form of individual, a disciplinary structure of legal documentation was necessary.

Indeed, the legal construction of the individual is one result of the exercise of the policing power of the state. Western legal and political systems are organized around the notion of the *liberal individual* (historically a male citizen) to whom obligations, rights, duties, and liabilities are made manifest through legal documents whose material existence testifies to the constitution of each particular individual. John Locke argued that a man could not truly be a reasoning, political being unless he owned land. In the modern world, the ownership of property is confirmed through legal title. Hence, according to Locke's reasoning, title constitutes the citizen. Or consider the matter of work. In the United States as in many other countries, to work one must possess and present on demand legal documents that show property rights in the self that we call "citizenship." Without such documents, one is not legally permitted to sell one's labor for wages. It is also understood that without such authorization one cannot collect entitlements from the state, such as unemployment benefits. Indeed, without such documents, one does not even *exist* in the eyes of the state.

In order to acquire representation as a "real" person, the liberal individual must generate the documents that testify to her legal and material existence. To travel outside U.S. territorial borders (an abstract right), a citizen must obtain a passport (material documentation) granting that right. To obtain the passport, the prospective traveler must produce a birth certificate (or comparable document) "proving" the occurrence of a specific historical and material event (that she was born within the United States). But any single individual's birth certificate exists only by virtue of the duty of parents to register her birth legally as the issue of two liberal individuals—spaces on the birth certificate identify both mother and father, and the child without a documented father is regarded as somehow less than fully legitimate. The parents' registration of the child generates the material document proving the future adult's existence. (A failure to register a birth might result in the paradox that one does not exist legally and has no objectified identity.) Moreover, *this very act of registration by two liberal individuals, an act required by law, produces in the eyes of the law the object whose material existence is undeniably (but not legally) demonstrated by virtue of her having been born.* The puzzling questions become: How is it that such documentation has come not only to signify but also to substitute for the individual's physical existence? And what has been lost or ignored in this construction of a liberal individual?

Defining the Social Individual

What if, contra the theorists, there is no such thing as the "individual" of liberal theory? What if a human being born alone and left in isolation never develops into a person? What if the "individual" is constituted by society rather than society being no more than the aggregate of the actions of many individuals? What if we can't have one without the other?

That is the premise of this chapter. By using the term "social individual," we recognize people as *social beings* born with and socialized into relationships that grow over a lifetime, who create and rely on mutual relations with others and responsibilities to them, who develop through their own histories, and who act historically, materially, and collectively. What does this mean? The material reality of the social individual is almost never in doubt; the very event of birth is an occasion of pain and joy, to be shared, and often witnessed, by those close to the parents. Hearing parents recount the event, even decades later, who can question its reality? And birth is only the first step in a lifetime of such social experiences. People are born into their social situations, and, for the most part, every social individual develops as a result of interactions with other social individuals, especially those who are older, more authoritative, more powerful, and—usually, but not always—parents (indeed, those who are largely isolated during the first formative months don't develop in this way and often never recover).[4] One's initial concept of self is microsituational, generated by the practices and structures of everyday life. Ultimately, we are who we are not because of our beliefs, actions, and self-ascribed "identities," but by virtue of our being embedded in webs of social relations that constitute that sense of self and those identities. The fully autonomous and atomized individual, however well documented on paper, is not a human being except in the legal sense; we become and remain human by virtue of our sociality. Whereas the liberal individual is an object produced through rational law—a law that is so deeply naturalized as to be regarded as inviolate and unremarkable—the social individual is constituted by emotional relations among people as subjects rather than by contractual relations among people as objects.

The Household and the Family

Evidently, then, social individuals do not live isolated lives, and very few are ever able to live in anything approaching Hobbes's mythical State of Nature. Even the hermit who has rejected society can be committed to her mission only by virtue of her relationships to the others from whom she separates herself. The social individual is both a political and an economic actor, engaged in production and reproduction. Thus, the fundamental unit of social organization is not the social individual; it is the *household*. As Immanuel Wallerstein and Joan Smith point out, "most individuals live on a daily basis within a 'household' which is what we term the entity responsible for our basic and continuing reproduction needs (food, shelter, clothing)."[5] They make a clear distinction between the household and the family: "The former refers to that grouping that assures some level of pooling income and sharing resources over time so as to reproduce the unit," the latter to a group of individuals, generally related by biology, law, norms, or custom.[6] A family may constitute a household, but it is not necessary that a household be constituted by a family. Indeed, a household may include one person or many.

Although the biological family appears to be a "natural" formation functionally organized to enable survival and nurture children, it is actually a very political institution. Historically, which is to say for as long as we have evidence of what happened in the past, human beings were organized into kin groups, that is, extended families of persons related by blood and others whom they treated as blood relations.[7] Within these groups, there were normally hierarchies of authority and power based on age, lineage, and gender. The survival of the kin group depended on members fulfilling their roles within that hierarchy. While "nuclear" families of parents and children existed in some societies, they were not in themselves political units. That is, the *social* organization of the kin group did not dictate the *political* organization of the family.[8]

This changed radically with the coming of the modern state. Recall Hobbes's vision of the state as described in chapter 1: the sovereign's body filled with his people. In fact, the sovereign occupied a position in relation to his people exactly like that of the husband and father, or patriarch, to his wife, children, and servants. People were the "property" of the sovereign; wife, children, and servants were the property of the husband.[9] ("A man's home is his castle" is not just a saying.) The rule of law exercised by the patriarch over his family was precisely like that exercised by the sovereign over his "family."

The famed nuclear family of 1950s America served to exaggerate this parallel, for its isolation from extended kinship groups meant that power was concentrated in the male head, and all of the subordinate roles—servant *and* wife—were loaded onto the wife. The iconic representation of this family form was *Leave It to Beaver* (*LITB*), a sitcom featuring Ward Cleaver, the wise father who worked outside the family domain, June Cleaver, the servant-wife who wore pearls while she vacuumed the carpets, and Wally and Theodore (aka the Beaver), the two male children whom June served and for whom she acted as an intermediary with their father. The family's isolation from the extended kinship group made it difficult for the woman in the family to challenge Ward's authority. June was contained.

The nuclear family also served a broader political purpose in the post–World War II (WW II) United States. There is a parallel between the patriarchal organization of the family, with its internal relations of power and property, and the organization of the American state: pay close attention to the importance of family relations in political campaigns, especially the family of the president, which is held up as the desired model.[10] Moreover, just as the father was deemed to be the primary authority when political opinions and decisions were involved, so is the president the primary authority on behalf of the country. The father's authority relationship was stabilized by its parallelism to the source of political stability—at least, in theory—allowing family members to be socialized into the essential "rightness" of patriarchal authority structures. The structure of authority was materially reinforced by a system of entitlements that were of particular benefit to nuclear families, such as the home mortgage tax deduction.

Thus, while the terms "family" and "household" are often used interchangeably, they are identical only under very specific conditions. More generally, the internal organization of a household is contingent and depends on the relationships among the household's members. The American concept of the "normal" household constituted by the nuclear family is very much a product of post–WW II politics and political economy and is not a God-given or natural institution. A household of four men or six women is likely to be organized very differently, as is one consisting of an extended, multigenerational group of related individuals.

The key point is that each of these households should be seen as a unit of *reproduction*. Its members are engaged in *production* to generate the resources necessary for the household to maintain itself. This is how the members of the household supply their basic material needs, as noted above, and how they reproduce various kinds of social relations. These social relations don't always involve the rearing of children. Some households form and remain in existence for decades. Others form and dissolve after weeks or months. The stability and longevity of any household depends on both its internal and its external relations, which shape the continuing ability and willingness of its members—who, in some instances, are coerced and compelled—to engage in the productive activities necessary to ensure reproduction. In every society, there are social customs, norms, and laws that encourage the establishment and maintenance of some kinds of households and discourage other kinds. As we saw above, the reasons have less to do with the ability of the household to reproduce itself than with the maintenance of social discipline and structure in the larger society. Again, there are both political and economic processes behind this favoritism, although changes in modes of production can make some forms of household quite dysfunctional and thereby drive changes in the dominant form of organization at other levels.

To illustrate these propositions, let us consider some examples from the United States. The *LITB* nuclear family became the idealized form of household in the mid-twentieth century, a result of U.S. economic expansion following WW II and elite concern that consumer demand continue to support the growth of businesses and the economy.[11] Earlier, household *reproduction* relied largely on *production* within and by the household, supplemented by weak market relations to producers in the larger economy. Farmers, like peasants, usually controlled the means of production (land), and provided for their own subsistence (food, shelter, water), while depression and war had encouraged families living in towns and cities to cultivate gardens to supplement food supplies. People in similar circumstances living in developing countries practice the same sort of subsistence agriculture—if they can. One consequence of the spread of cash-crop (capitalist) agriculture has been to limit the land available for families to produce food for their own use.

After WW II, Americans found themselves with disposable incomes, some for the first time in their lives. Enforced savings thanks to high employment and rationing during the war, coupled with benefits to returning veterans, gave American families money to spend at the same time that U.S. industry had to switch from producing war matériel to producing consumer products. Single-family houses in newly constructed suburbs were filled with labor-saving appliances, along with the cars needed to carry men to their jobs in the cities. Smaller households tend to consume more per capita relative to large ones, and, not surprisingly, as appliances, automobiles, and other consumer products became cheaper and more widely available, more households acquired them. As suburbanization took hold and spread, the single-family dwelling that could be filled with all kinds of goods came to be seen as the norm. The nuclear family became the economic ideal and, therefore, the social ideal.[12]

Not that it was ever a stable structure. As is the case with most social institutions, the *LITB*-style nuclear family was the product of the social relations and economic organization contingent on and unique to a particular era. That nuclear family depended on parents fulfilling specified roles—one high-wage earner, one home worker—and children who were educated and trained for eventual employment in the industrial economy of the time. There were working mothers even then, but it was possible for most "average" families to live on a single income.[13]

The stability of the nuclear family as an institution also relied on a U.S. foreign policy that ensured a continual flow of cheap raw materials, while U.S. foreign policy was buttressed by the American nuclear family as an exemplar for the rest of the world. Stories of collectivized life in China and images of families crammed into crowded communal apartments in the Soviet Union loomed in the public mind as part of the narrative of communist rule. Fear that the broadly based material prosperity of that time might be lost made family support of containment seem all the more critical. Inevitably, however, the emerging contradictions of national and international politics and economics also affected the fate of the nuclear family.

As we can see in films from the 1950s, such as *Rebel without a Cause*, the *LITB*-style nuclear family was (and remains) a structure of discipline and power. Both were exercised not in direct fashion, but through obedience to implicit rules and fear of the chaos that might follow from breaking those rules. Complete discipline is difficult to accomplish under any circumstances. Marriage is not a conflict-free institution, and children are only too sensitive to power struggles between parents. Social and economic pressures also undermine this fragile regime. What if a father lost his job and the mother had to seek outside employment? The need for income produced contradictions that engendered resistance, and adaptations that failed to conform to social ideals.

These effects reverberated from home life to international affairs. During the 1950s, resistance to nuclear-family discipline appeared as the "Beat Generation," while rock and roll challenged race relations.[14] Such explicit rejection of America's internal social relations was almost as threatening to those in power as the external threat posed by communism. During the 1960s, the Beatles mounted a further challenge, questioning gender relations with their long hair and social assumptions with their subversive lyrics. Politically, the failure of the U.S. war in Vietnam undermined the authority structure of the American state and eroded the broader disciplinary arrangements that fostered obedience. That decade became a time of social experimentation and opposition to authority. Paradoxically, perhaps, the relative prosperity of the time also made the nuclear family seem less necessary. The 1960s supported all kinds of innovations in household organization, sexual practices, and gender relations. Divorce became more common, and some couples didn't bother to get married at all.

Not until the 1970s, however, was the economic base of the nuclear family really destroyed. Spikes in the price of fuels, virulent inflation, and the rising costs of running a household and owning a house pushed and pulled more mothers into the job market. Despite the Civil Rights Act of 1964, employers still found they could pay women less for comparable work (a phenomenon hardly unique to the United States). Nuclear families increasingly found that they could not maintain a middle-class lifestyle, with children, on the income of only one wage earner. As a result, households became more complex, and new forms of familial relations began to acquire social legitimacy.

Ultimately, the impact of globalization made the "traditional" nuclear family almost impossible to maintain. Today, not only is the two-income family virtually the norm, but the constant restructuring of modes and relations of production also means that wage earners must change jobs often and may have to relocate several times during their working lives. This phenomenon is not unique to developed countries, either. For example, the vast increase in wealth as a result of the oil boom of the 1970s generated floods of migration in the Middle East and other parts of the world, as wage earners in poor countries left their homes for employment opportunities in the booming economies of oil-exporting countries.[15] None of this is conducive to stability of the nuclear family.

The decline of the *LITB*-style nuclear family was not regarded as a positive development by those with a vested interest in maintaining power relations of benefit to them, such as men in working-class families.[16] Their response was fierce, and it continues today. After all, if the maintenance of social discipline and authority relations throughout society is dependent on their reproduction within the household, and if a particular family form, such as the *LITB* model, helps to maintain a broad acceptance of elite dominance, then the collapse of the nuclear family threatens elite power and its ability to accomplish its political and economic objectives. During the 1970s, the emergence of the Religious Right, in coalition with right-wing neoconservatives, was motivated in no small part by this perceived threat. These forces worked hard to establish a link in the popular mind between discipline in the family and broader social stability and American power. Their appeal to working-class men, who otherwise might have been tempted to get involved in progressive labor politics, was based on working-class men's fears of losing power in the family.[17] The irony in this strategy was, perhaps, that it is the very economic institution to which the neoconservatives are most loyal—the laissez-faire market—that is most erosive of the nuclear family they profess to revere. But note carefully: the household continues to be essential to the global economy. Indeed, work within the household—especially work by women—constitutes a major subsidy to that economy. It is said that working women hold two jobs (often called "the double burden") because, even in households with two or more wage earners, important tasks that *someone* must do, such as child care, cooking, and cleaning, are mostly performed by women. Except where servants are involved, no wages are paid for this work, and no records are kept of its value. Nonetheless, by some estimates, the unrecorded value of "housework" is between one-third and one-half ($10–15 trillion) of the world's estimated economic output ($30 trillion).[18] This unpaid labor is a subsidy to capitalism, a form of "articulation" made possible because capitalism is a mode of production uniquely able to extract the surplus value generated by other modes. For example, commodities such as wheat or rice can be bought for low prices from peasants who have little market power. These goods can then be sold in cities at much higher prices, especially if a few individuals or firms have dominant positions in processing and marketing them. In a similar fashion, if the holders of capital had to pay the costs of housework, many now-profitable industries would lose money.

Recognition of the role of this now-unrecognized labor in industrial and postindustrial economies also brings into question the bias in capitalist systems that favors capital over labor through such practices as taxing capital gains at lower rates than wages and salaries. It is hardly surprising, therefore, that proposals to pay women for housework are usually dismissed as ridiculous, impractical—and far too expensive.

Despite all attempts to hide this fact, the household is integral to the global economy. It subsidizes capitalism. It educates and socializes children. It is a locus of consumption, and it produces the next generation of consumers and producers. It is the most important institution responsible for the reproduction of social, political, and economic relations. As such, it ensures that the global political economy will continue.

The Social Individual and Global Politics

We all are members of a household, whether it consists of one person or one hundred. But how do we, as social individuals, fit into global politics and the world economy? Or, rather, what is our unmediated relationship to both? Few of us are directly involved in the business of running countries, attending international conferences, managing transnational corporations, or fighting foreign wars. Even fewer hold positions in which they can actively influence the course of present-day politics and economics. Geographer John Agnew has noted, "[People] are *located* according to the demands of a spatially extensive division of labour, the global system of material production and distribution, and variable patterns of political authority and control,"[19] a claim that suggests we don't have a great deal of choice in the matter. Nonetheless, without the active involvement of billions of people, our political and economic systems could not function. So, how much autonomy (or agency) *do* we have?

Considering the liberal individual conventionally conceived, we don't have much. Inasmuch as the global economy is organized according to certain rules and practices that must be followed if one is to have any hope of success, economic autonomy extends only as far as being able to choose a field of specialization (with the hope that it will not become obsolete), a job (with the hope that some are available), and a place to live (assuming that housing is affordable somewhere close enough to that job). The so-called private sphere—household, family, religion, civic associations, personal consumption—is generally treated as though it were untouched by such external constraints. This is a heroic assumption that relies on the belief that the individual is fully autonomous in the private sphere. But because activities in the private sphere are essential to social reproduction, which, in turn, is necessary to system stability, autonomy begins to look pretty limited here, as well.

To put this point another way, the much-vaunted freedom granted to the individual in a liberal society is a highly structured freedom. It is not that people do things because they are directly threatened or coerced (although this does sometimes happen). Rather, it is that available choices are limited in particular ways, such that in many realms, alternatives are virtually nonexistent. This can be illustrated by a story from Harvard economist Amartya Sen. In *Development as Freedom*, he tells about the Muslim man who continued to work in a Hindu neighborhood even during the worst of the intercommunal violence accompanying the partition of India in 1948.[20] One day, the violence was particularly intense, but he went to work as usual because it was the only way to earn money to feed his family. As a result, he was killed in the fighting. We could say that he should have stayed at home, but it is easy to see why he did not include this among his choices. If he had stayed away, his family would have gone hungry. For most readers of this book, options are neither so stark nor so extreme, but consider carefully the kinds of freedoms you possess and how they might limit or discipline the choices you do make.

The social individual does not necessarily possess greater autonomy—after all, to paraphrase Marx, we live in the world as it is given to us. Much of that world today is a liberal one—but the social individual lives in a somewhat different epistemic context. ("Epistemic" refers to particular ways of knowing and groups who share them.) By this, we mean that an awareness of the social and emotional relations that constitute the social individual can also help us to understand her relationship to global politics and the world economy. This awareness also opens up new possibilities for action and autonomy. Autonomy and freedom should not be understood merely as choices to be exercised in the private sphere but rather as the kinds of politics that become possible through social power exercised by tightly knit groups. The suppression of such social bonds and alternative social relations, and their relegation to the "private sphere," are constitutive of the liberal individual, global politics, and capitalism. Just as the household is central to the global order, so too is the social individual, albeit one who is "liberally educated" about the necessity of separating the realm of emotion from the realm of interests.

What, exactly, do we mean by this jargon? As we saw earlier, no one is born into the world as an isolated individual; yet, in a society marked by capitalism and markets, the newborn is almost immediately inducted into a matrix of commodity relations (think about how relentlessly maternity and baby stuff are advertised and sold). In the ideology of capitalism, the baby's primal desire for self-satisfaction at the mother's breast is transformed into the psychological basis for liberal self-interest. *I want!* But a child's basic wants and needs conflict with the demands of the modern political economy. Because it costs money to maintain a household, parents must work, making time a scarce resource. Things are offered to replace the absent parent, but, because things cannot supply a child's emotional needs, ever new and ever more things are demanded. Those parents who do not, or cannot, fulfill their child's desires through the accumulation of things (while they are bombarded with constant messages to buy more stuff) feel they are shortchanging their child. They feel like inadequate parents.

Paradoxically, as the child matures, the deferral of satisfaction encountered as denied time with beloved adults is treated as a critical moral lesson, while, at the same time, a constant barrage of advertising encourages the immediate fulfillment of desires for commodity goods and services. The message is that property relations to things that can be accumulated only through exchange in the market are an adequate substitute for emotional relations among people. Even emotional relations within the private sphere can be commodified and sold; there is much money to be made from love, hate, envy, desire, and passion, and the consumer is led to believe that she can and should experience and fulfill these emotions via the market: "Diamonds are forever"; nannies are a necessity; trophy wives are evidence of a man's power.[21]

Marx wrote about the alienation of the worker from the products of her work; today, we face alienation of emotion through the endless consumption of goods. Is such alienation a necessary and inevitable corollary to the global expansion of capitalism and democracy? Perhaps not, although it is difficult to imagine how alternative arrangements might appear. In a subsistence society, with very limited exchange, production and reproduction are closely tied to trust and mutual obligation. Survival is paramount and self-interest is equivalent to the collective interest: if one does not fulfill one's obligation, the group cannot survive. Yet, the member of such a group rarely thinks in terms of "interests," Rousseau notwithstanding: one does what one does because that is what one is supposed to do. In a society with more extensive exchange (say, early capitalism), markets foster a division of labor and provide things not easily produced within the household.[22] Nonetheless, trust and obligation within the household remain important. As capitalism developed in Europe during the eighteenth and nineteenth centuries, much of this emotion was displaced into nationalism and patriotism. The individual was still obligated to family, but his [*sic!*] love was for his country. Both production and consumption were directed, in part, toward national ends.

Only in very rich societies like ours, which are motivated by consumption rather than production as traditionally understood, do such emotions and bonds of trust and obligation become a drag on the economy.[23] National(ist) capitalism is limited by the size of a country's domestic markets,[24] and even a consumption-driven society cannot accommodate an infinite number of refrigerators and cars. But manufactured emotional need that seeks satiation through the market is virtually a bottomless pit, especially if one's sense of self-worth comes to depend on one's level of accumulation and consumption rather than on the strength of one's relations with others. Under these conditions, human attachment is relegated to the private sphere and becomes an appendage of, and even an obstacle to, the main business of life: consumption.

Consider one example already alluded to above: diamonds. Diamonds—jewels, more generally—have long been associated with wealth and royalty, and their relative scarcity made them very costly. Moreover, they had no practical use. They were signifiers of "conspicuous consumption" associated with high status.[25] The demand for them *as jewelry* was limited, too, although diamonds were sometimes acquired as an easily portable store of wealth. It was not until diamond mining became a large-scale endeavor, with enormously prolific discoveries in southern Africa, that the supply of diamonds began to exceed the demand for them by a significant margin. As we are told repeatedly, in an oversupplied market the price of a commodity will fall, perhaps even below the cost of production. Some sellers will go bust, supplies will decrease, and a new equilibrium will be found.

But there is an alternative. Sellers can restrict supply. Fearful of a diamond glut, those corporations involved in the diamond trade set up an international cartel—the Central Selling Organization (CSO), based in London and often associated with the DeBeers family—to limit supply and keep prices high. Every year the CSO would decide how many diamonds would be put on the market and at what price. But cartels are difficult to maintain. When the market price of a commodity is maintained by restricting supply, an incentive develops for others outside the cartel to search for new sources of that commodity and to sell it at a slightly lower price. This is what happened with diamonds. The CSO managed to bring some, but not all, producers into the association, and the uncontrolled product put downward pressure on prices.[26]

But there is, of course, another way to keep prices high: stimulate demand. This can be done by advertising diamond jewelry not only as beautiful and status oriented (and a store of wealth) but also as a signifier of *heterosexual* love.[27] No matter that diamonds are simply lumps of carbon, possessing no intrinsic value or utility; artificially maintained scarcity and high retail prices are transformed by a constant and relentless campaign into an emotion portrayed as unique to a particular relationship. Indeed, women are all but warned by these advertisements that only through diamonds can love be truly consummated, implying that their absence from a relationship indicates an absence of "real" love. In this way, an emotion that is social, if not instinctual, and found in every human society is commodified, sold, and even controlled.

The reader should not think that she is the victim of conspiratorial forces beyond her control. These forces can be resisted, although peer pressure to conform and the potentially high costs of nonconformity are powerful incentives to go with the flow. Moreover, trying to resist as a liberal individual by limiting one's own consumption while everyone else does not makes the individual's effort even more difficult, as well as unlikely to be effective. For the social individual, the task is somewhat easier, because emotions such as love and respect for others can become the basis for group resistance to commercial entreaties.

We are all familiar with, and may even belong to, groups motivated by a sense of shared emotion (gangs, punks, Goths, bird watchers, bikers, drag racers). Such groups are often regarded as threats to the society around them, not because they have the power to destroy that society but because their members do not seem to be motivated by the interests and desires of the larger society in which they live (even bird watchers, who are seen as entirely too concerned with environmental protection). Consequently, they cannot be controlled (or normalized) by society's disciplinary apparatus. It is ironic to note that many of these alienated groups are nevertheless deeply engaged in consumption, and that their affectations often become commodified and quite profitable—think of tattoos, big pants, and gangsta rap (and, for those bird watchers, fancy binoculars and ecotourism trips to Costa Rica).

Social groups organized into activist modalities or "social movements," motivated by political objectives and bound together by emotional commitments, are the primary locus of resistance in the world today.[28] Social movements should be distinguished from interest groups whose members are bound primarily by class or other group characteristics; such groups confer or withhold privilege and lack emotional commonality, and their members are motivated primarily by what they can gain individually from membership in the group.[29] Social movements vary greatly in terms of size, formality, focus, spatial reach, and influence, but they all share one characteristic: their basis is the *social* individual, who has decided to make her commitments on the basis of affection rather than reason or self-interest (the latter two are not excluded, but they are not primary). And while emotions are easy to manipulate, they are difficult to control and order. For those in positions of power and authority who wish to maintain control and order, the social individual presents a constant challenge.

Conclusion

In this chapter, we have attempted to situate people, households, and families in a global context. Most mainstream writers on global politics and economics focus primarily on the impacts of structures and processes on individuals, leaving them "free to choose" within the narrow confines of liberal democracy and markets.[30] Many critical observers point out that the disciplinary structures of globalized capitalism leave very little wiggle room for autonomous action, and, short of a major crisis, it is not very clear how opposition can ever become general and motivate social change (see chapter 10). We acknowledge the limits to freedom implicit in contemporary liberal societies and the low probability of a mass breakout from this "iron cage." But we are very far from thinking that all is lost.

We observed that one key element in the creation of the liberal individual is replacing emotional ties with reason, self-interest, and commodified relationships among people. This move is essential to liberal democracy in that it makes political organization more difficult and costly, since people must seek out others who share their particular interests. It also is essential to capitalism, because it allows everything to be measured in terms of its monetary value rather than its meaning or a person's commitments or obligations. In this scheme of things, the household—idealized in the form of the *LITB* nuclear family—becomes an economic unit responsible for reproduction and for subsidizing capital, and the social mechanism for modeling an external order characterized by atomization and hierarchy. Households need not be nuclear families, however. Indeed, changes in familial and household organization required by globalization seem to pose a threat to the preferred social order of traditional elites.

We also argued that emotional relations can be commodified, as in the equation of love with diamonds, but that this is another move that is neither necessary nor inevitable. It arises from systemic pressures for growth and accumulation, which encourage putting a monetary value on *everything*. Moreover, by cultivating consumption without constraints, capitalism fosters the development of interest-based associations and discourages collective action by social movements acting according to ideas or affections. There are strong disincentives to the creation of solidary groups based on affective bonds and commitments; Mancur Olsen argues that they do not serve individual self-interest and, therefore, ought not to exist.[31] Solidary groups nevertheless remain a powerful basis for a politics of resistance and social change. What this means is that we must bring emotions into the open and treat them not as dangers to the political order but as essential to political freedom.

In the next chapter, we examine the role of power in contemporary global politics and political economy. Power plays a central role in structuring the patterns discussed above, while it also offers extensive and creative means for resisting and changing them. Most international relations texts look at power in terms of force and influence, but here we take a much more nuanced view. Power serves to structure institutions, but it is not a substance. Rather, it is a relational concept. Emotion is as much a form of power as suppression of emotion in the pursuit of rationality and self-interest. As a form of power, emotion can be abused and manipulated, leading to fascism, but the same is true of interest-based forms of power. The task is not to fall into that trap—easier said, perhaps, than done.

3

People and Power

One dark night, a passer-by offered to help an obviously inebriated man who was searching for something under a lamp post. "What are we looking for?" asked the volunteer helper. "My keys," answered the drunk. "Did you lose them right here?" asked the helper. "No," answered the drunk. "I lost them down the street." "Then why are we looking here?" asked the bewildered helper. "Because the light is better," the drunk replied.

—Anonymous

Defining Power

Political scientists frequently look for power under the intellectual equivalent of lampposts. What they see is stuff: territory, populations, soldiers, guns, bombs, tanks, money, food supplies, oil—all of which are visible and, more importantly, can be measured and counted. Soldiers, weapons, and the money to buy more of them match up with what political scientists like Kenneth Waltz and Robert Dahl define as power: "the ability of A to make B do what A wants when B would prefer to do something else."[1] Those who look at power more comprehensively see this as only one of its aspects, calling it "power-over," or power based on the threat or use of force.[2] This is the image of power in war: power is what A can bring to bear to destroy B. It equates power with violence.

Others disagree. Philosopher Hannah Arendt argues that violence erases power.[3] If you have to maim or kill people to make them do what you want, they probably won't be able to do it very well after the dust settles. We remember an American soldier during the Vietnam War who explained why his

33

company had obliterated a village by saying, "We had to destroy the village in order to save it." But what was saved? Violence eliminated the village and its people. Nothing material survived. Arendt would take that a step further to point out that power itself wasn't saved: the destruction of the village revealed that the Americans, despite all their bombs, guns, and chemical weapons, could not change the perceptions and choices of large numbers of Vietnamese people.

Arendt's definition of power is very different from the power-over model. She thought of power as what political scientists like Robin Teske call "power-with," the ability to join forces to achieve a common goal.[4] Arendt imagined power as generated by people acting together in what she called "spaces of appearance," public forums in which "I appear to others as others appear to me, where men exist not merely like other living or inanimate things but make their appearance explicitly."[5] In such spaces—examples include legislatures, boardrooms, clubhouses, and family councils held around the dining room table—power is not an attribute of individuals. As we suggested in chapter 2, power grows out of an ensemble of persons who empower one another when they decide to act.

Theoretically, people are more or less equal in spaces of appearance, but some are more capable than others of shaping the final outcome of deliberations. So stuff is important in this understanding of power, too. Everyone knows who has land, money, networks, servants, and clients, and they probably have pretty good estimates of how much. But stuff is not everything. The space of appearance and the power it generates also depend on the personal qualities of the participants. How tall are they? (Powerful leaders from King David to George Washington were admired for their imposing size as well as for their military reputations.) How smart are they? (Alcibiades and Bill Clinton impressed their friends with their intelligence, even though they also irritated them by their sexual behavior.) How well do they speak in public? (Hitler and Franklin Roosevelt could mesmerize multitudes.) How well did their earlier ideas turn out? (This is how James Madison got to be president despite being short and a terrible speaker.) Do they have friends who stick up for them to create a "bandwagon" in favor of their proposals, or do they have enemies who make their ideas look ridiculous, reducing confidence in them and drawing their followers away? This is how a lot of people did or did not get to be leaders.

It's clear that power is not merely how much stuff anyone has but what happens when people with different collections of stuff get together and decide what to do with it all—the quintessential image of collective decision making, from town meetings to caucuses to international organizations. This image describes both how citizens agree to levy taxes on themselves or choose candidates to run for office, and how groups like the Concert of Europe decided to intervene anywhere that revolution threatened early nineteenth-century Europe, or how the late twentieth-century United Nations decided to eradicate smallpox or liberate Kuwait. It also explains why, although all participants have equal access, their voices do not carry equal weight.

Formal and Informal Rules

Our discussion of the social individual as an agent embedded in structures leads to another way to think of power: as the ability of agents to create and enforce rules. Following the Italian political theorist Antonio Gramsci, we call this kind of power "hegemony." Rules alone are frail supports for desired action: laws against stealing and murder have not made these crimes obsolete. But this doesn't mean that *enforcement* is nothing more than *force*. Think of the rules that define property rights or appropriate behavior in a household or a classroom. Theoretically, parents and teachers can hit kids (or one another) to force them to obey the rules, but, as Arendt observed, such behavior is a better indicator of power failure than of power. Most of the time, most people obey rules voluntarily. They believe in them; they believe in the people and institutions that made them; and they care what other people think. It's only when law givers and rule enforcers demonstrate that they are not worthy of respect and trust that they have to resort to force to get people to do what they want (and even then, often fail).

We don't want such "consent of the governed" to seem too benign, however. Consent rests on a large measure of invisible—structural—coercion. Think of the Fourteenth Amendment to the U.S. Constitution. It was ratified after the Civil War to give former male slaves the same protections, privileges, and immunities that white male citizens enjoyed (the Fourteenth Amendment is the first place in the Constitution where the sex of citizens is mentioned). But in exchange for resolving the disputed 1876 election in their favor, the mostly northern Republicans agreed to end Reconstruction, along with federal enforcement of the post–Civil War amendments and the laws to implement them, if the mostly southern Democrats would support the loser of the popular vote, Republican Rutherford B. Hayes, for president. The special commission set up to decide the election agreed to this "compromise of 1877," after which Reconstruction began to be dismantled.[6]

The Supreme Court was an important tool for liquidating Reconstruction. Its representative on the election commission, associate justice Joseph Bradley, was also chair of the commission. Bradley wrote a series of opinions that at first asserted and then drew back from an energetic interpretation of the three Civil War amendments setting out the rights of former slaves. Among these were the "due process" and "equal protection" rights embedded in the Fourteenth Amendment. The court redefined these rights in steps that withdrew them from former slaves and applied them to corporations.[7] Soon corporations were defined as "persons" under the law and were accorded the same rights as white men. Not incidentally, both were treated equally under the law, even though corporations are larger, richer, and more powerful than persons. Americans' respect for the Supreme Court and the law still supports this rule change. Today, despite massive corporate scandals that lost thousands of workers their jobs and pensions, and millions of stockholders billions of dollars of their investments, most Americans continue to think it would be unfair to deny corporations "their" constitutional rights. A corporation can claim all the rights accorded to persons under the Fourteenth Amendment, including privacy rights. This let tobacco companies argue that "proprietary" information, such as evidence that nicotine is addictive, should be protected from disclosure.[8] Corporate rights are enforced by the U.S. government unless a plaintiff can "show cause" why they should not be. Even when we get down to life-or-death issues, corporations almost always have the advantage over people.[9]

Sovereign Rights and Wrongs

A similar attachment to rules made it hard for nations to come together to stop genocide in Bosnia in 1991 and in Rwanda in 1994. As we discuss in chapter 5, the usual understanding of the rules governing behavior among states emphasizes sovereignty over human rights. Sovereignty is defined in part as a government's right to do as it likes on its home territory. The United Nations, whose members all are states, thought it would be unfair, even illegal, to intervene against the governments of Yugoslavia[10] and Rwanda—even to save the hundreds of thousands of citizens they could see agents of these governments displacing, imprisoning, raping, and murdering every night on their TV screens. After these horrible crimes were halted, war-crimes tribunals were set up to punish the ethnic cleansers and *genocidaires*, but critics called these tribunals "victors' courts" and claimed that they violated state sovereignty. Ironically, the United States used similar arguments in 2001 to take back its signature on the 1998 Rome Treaty setting up a permanent International Criminal Court (ICC), even though the United States led those demanding that war-crimes tribunals be established after the genocides in Bosnia and Rwanda—and also in Germany and Japan after World War II.[11]

As these inconsistencies demonstrate, views of sovereignty often depend on whether the critic is among potential interveners or those likely to be intervened against. Many who accused the United Nations of callousness for ignoring the genocides in Bosnia and Rwanda, while Security Council members demanded that the sovereignty of these states be upheld, had earlier accused the Security Council of interfering where it wasn't wanted when it voted to intervene after Kuwait had been invaded by Iraq. To great human rights activists like Václav Havel, a new era appeared to have dawned with the 1999 NATO intervention in Kosovo. Havel believes that Kosovo signaled that the value of human rights had begun to supersede the values protecting nation-states.[12] U.S. policy since then makes this assessment appear optimistic. Halfhearted peacekeeping in Afghanistan following the 2001 defeat of the Taliban, a preemptive war against Iraq grounded in a controversial new strategic doctrine that contradicts provisions of the United Nations Charter, and U.S. efforts to create obstacles to the successful implementation of the ICC put hopes for the rapid evolution of an international rule of law very much in doubt.

Yet the fact that there are plenty of advocates opposing negative sovereignty from a variety of perspectives shows that hegemonic ideologies and their associated institutions are not invincible. This judgment is confirmed by the twentieth-century restoration of civil rights to the descendants of former U.S. slaves in spite of the nineteenth-century reconstruction of the Fourteenth Amendment to award these rights to corporations instead of citizens. Ongoing war-crimes tribunals in Arusha and the Hague, along with recent trials of old Ku Klux Klanners in Birmingham, Alabama, also reflect a shift in acceptance of the rule of law. Both kinds of courts convicted murderers who long had believed that they would suffer no adverse consequences for their actions. Because their governments did not stop them at the time—indeed, some of the killers were acting under the direction of government officials—they had come to believe that no one would ever be able to bring them to justice. But minds change and, with them, the consensus on rules and how they should be enforced.

Powerful Ideas

Making counterhegemonic ideas concrete is how people fight what Gramsci calls a "war of position." Alternative ideas and different ways of doing things were used by dissidents in Eastern Europe to oppose oppressive communist regimes during the cold war. One such strategy was "the parallel polis." *Polis* is the Greek word for a political community. Anticommunists in Eastern Europe wanted to change their political communities, but they were barred even from talking or writing about reform. Step by step, dissidents created shadow political communities, parallel universes/*poleis* that embodied their desires for democratic life.[13] They wrote, read, talked about, and did things by their own rules, just as if their actions were legal even when they were not. At first the dissidents faced constant danger, and their parallel universes had to be kept secret. In Czechoslovakia, scores of dissident women used manual typewriters and carbon paper to type essays, poetry, and stories and distribute this forbidden samizdat literature through underground networks. Mothers put whole typed "books" in their babies' carriages when they went out for walks, and delivered them to the next person in the "chain" by switching grocery bags in food markets. "I left my place in the line apparently with the same bag, but the contents were different," reports Czech dissident Jiřina Šiklová about her life at that time. "Instead of cauliflower there were correspondence texts—and once a carrot which I did not intend to buy."[14] When their activities were revealed, dissidents were arrested and tried. Many were imprisoned under conditions that shortened or ended their lives. But their persistence and the justice of their cause attracted new adherents from among their fellow citizens in the other—the "real"—polis, and hollowed out those authoritarian regimes.

Dissident movements also had help from abroad. Samizdat writings left Czechoslovakia via a courier service manned by foreign embassy personnel, and were taken where they could be published. Dissidents used special signals to let couriers know when a package of writings was ready to go. One was a small piece of a postage stamp pasted on the window of a Prague bar called the Blue Duck. When he saw the stamp fragment on the window, a young Swedish diplomat knew to walk by a certain apartment house and pick up an envelope of samizdat that would be sent abroad by diplomatic pouch. Other external assistance came from new nongovernmental organizations (NGOs) like Amnesty International and Human Rights Watch, which shone an international spotlight on the brutal actions of "real" governments. These actions kept the imprisonment of dissidents on the political agenda of Western states and prevented these men and women from being "disappeared." In Czechoslovakia, prominent dissidents eventually signed a manifesto, Charta 77, that declared openly the existence of their parallel polis. The government gradually crumbled under all these pressures, giving us a new concept, "velvet revolution"—the nonviolent collapse of an old regime when the people withdraw their belief in the authority of the state and stop complying with its strictures.

Remaking Reality

A differently oppressive, postcommunist regime in Poland is currently the target of a war of position by Polish feminists. Political scientist Diane Duffy calls their strategy "power-as-if," the creation of "facts on the ground" that the state finds it difficult to ignore—or destroy.[15] In Poland, women's human rights, along with social services for families, have been severely curtailed by the postcommunist regime. In response, a handful of Polish women's organizations are creating structural power for themselves by providing social services such as family planning, job training, and health-care education, which the government no longer offers. Members of these feminist NGOs also participate in meetings of international organizations with their counterparts from other countries, reporting on domestic conditions facing women and families and suggesting ways in which poorly performing countries could improve.

　　The Polish government would like to eliminate these feminist groups, both to avoid their demands and to be spared the embarrassment they cause by reporting accurately how badly the government is treating Poland's most vulnerable citizens. Yet too many families and local governments depend on the services the women's groups provide, and too many potential investors and foreign aid donors would be angry to see them suppressed. A similar situation constrains the ability of the government of Egypt or the Palestine National Authority to close down Islamist organizations, groups that provide schools, feeding programs, jobs, and disaster relief to populations the governments cannot serve because of their own limited resources. By acting as if they have power, well-organized and dedicated groups can acquire power.

　　Facts on the ground aren't always used to promote democratization and human rights, however. After Israel almost accidentally captured territory populated by Palestinian Arabs during the Six-Day War in 1967,[16] its leaders decided that, in spite of UN resolutions demanding an end to the occupation, Israel would try to keep the territory. "Settlements" of Jews were planted throughout the Occupied Territories, creating armed enclaves of Israeli-held

Palestinian land. The settlements had two major structural effects. First, they dispersed Israelis throughout Palestinian territory, justifying military intervention by the state to protect them, and preventing Palestinians from moving freely from place to place within the Occupied Territories. The Gaza Strip and especially the West Bank were carved up into islands of Palestinians separated by highways connecting the settlements to one another and to Israel proper. Palestinians could travel from one island to another only by passing through checkpoints where they were stopped and searched before being allowed to cross Israeli-held roads and lands. Second, the settlements gave more than four hundred thousand Israeli settlers a vested interest in keeping "their" land part of Israel rather than returning it as part of a peace settlement, while the settlement program convinced many Palestinians that they could never have their own state without destroying Israel first.[17] This is a clear example of how structures constrain agency and influence thinking.

Structures of Power in the International System

Each definition of power we've discussed is built on a set of ideas about the world and how it works. Each definition also is partial: the world is a complicated place, and power exists and operates differently in different parts and at different times. Power-over operates where force is the primary authority. Some political scientists see the whole nation-states "system" as that kind of world. If all states have negative sovereignty—if there is no external authority to make them "behave"—then they exist in a state of "anarchy" or "no government," a "self-help" universe where might makes right. Stuff is integral to this vision of power because it is what you need to crush your opponents as you try to make them do what you want. From this description, we can classify systemic theories/ideologies like "Realism" as power-over models.

Balancing Acts

Anarchy is the image of the world that people have in mind when they talk about "the balance of power." It reflects the assumption that because no one is in charge of the world, every state must defend itself from attacks by other states. Some versions of this model assume that the most powerful states are self-conscious actors, interested not only in preserving themselves but also in upholding "the system," the current division of power and rules of the game, which put them in charge. This view adds to power-over an element of power-with, and is reflected in the proposition that, for most states, the primary objective of international relations is to avoid war. In this variation of the balance-of-power model, states use diplomacy, alliances, payoffs, persuasion, and appeasement to keep the peace. In contrast, the standard version of balance-of-power theory assumes that no state is committed to the system; each is committed only to itself. Here, it is war, the ultimate power-over strategy, that keeps the balance among the major powers.[18]

Why does a power system become unbalanced? Political scientist Robert Gilpin offers a simple and elegant answer: because things change, and, when they do, they don't change evenly.[19] Powerful states inevitably become weaker—maybe their militaries get self-satisfied and fat, and their governments so complacent that they allow their clients to loot the state and steal its capacity to act. Perhaps their citizens refuse to pay taxes or rebel against how the state spends the money it takes from them. But even if a powerful state maintains huge armies and weapons stockpiles, other states still can beat it. They can invent better weapons systems; their economies can expand because they innovate more successfully than their rivals in commercial markets; they can acquire colonies that produce valuable materials and offer strategic bases. Any state that convinces its people that it is under threat can devote a disproportionately large share of national production and wealth to increase its power as an international competitor, making the military a tool of the government, not just the only way to protect populations when all else fails.

If a balance of power becomes unbalanced, the next question is how balance can be restored. When we look at real cases, however, it becomes clear why balance-of-power theory by itself is not a useful predictor of the future. Perhaps the best example of this is the mental image analysts have when they think of "classical" balance-of-power theory, the states system envisioned as operating from about 1820 to the start of World War I (WW I) in 1914. Prior to WW I, Britain, formerly the dominant world power in a multipolar international system (one with more than two major powers), suffered a relative decline in its economy. New competitors, especially the United States and Germany, had developed more efficient industries that undermined British products worldwide, including in its home markets. Although the British navy remained the most powerful in the world, Britain had not fielded a large army, even during wartime, since the seventeenth century. Meanwhile, the armies of Germany, France, and Russia were large and growing, while Japan surprised the European powers by demonstrating excellent war-fighting ability against Russia in 1905 (Japan won the conflict).

This brings us to another problem with applying balance-of-power theory: depending on which version you use, you get different answers. Historian Niall Ferguson, basing his analysis on the self-conscious "balancer" model (power-over plus power-with), argues that Britain should have allied with Germany, which became the continent's weaker power/coalition following the alliance between France and Russia. Had Britain done so, Ferguson suggests, there would not have been a world war. There might not have been a war at all if Germany had not seen itself as being in a "now or never" position, fearing it would have to face all three of the strongest powers in Europe on the battlefield in the not-too-distant future. Even if Germany had continued to feel "surrounded" by what former U.S. diplomat George Kennan called the "fateful alliance" between France and Russia, Ferguson asserts, a war between the alliance and Germany (with or without its allies, Austria and the Ottoman Empire) would have been limited. Whether Britain had joined Germany or not, Germany was strong enough to defeat the French rapidly, as it had in 1871 in the Franco-Prussian War, and then it could have decided whether to fight Russia or seek a diplomatic end to the conflict on its eastern front. Instead, Ferguson argues, Britain acted as though it were following the unconscious (power-over only) balance-of-power model. It allied itself with what looked like the stronger side with the expectation that war would come and its side would win.[20]

In response to difficulties in applying standard balance-of-power models to real situations, some theorists have built models based on "mitigations" of anarchy, or how anarchy can be modified to give agents more scope. These models add more dimensions to balance-of-power theory. They also offer better explanations of events and, analysts hope, better predictions of what might happen in the future. Most still focus on the nation-state, but many include nonstates as agents in their descriptions of the international system and how it works.

Political scientist Hedley Bull looks at what he calls "international society," mostly heads of state and their relationships with one another.[21] If U.S. president George Bush really thinks that Russian president Vladimir Putin has a beautiful soul, Bush is more likely to rely on face-to-face diplomacy than on war, cold or hot, to get what he wants from Putin. Cynics might say that Bush finds beautiful souls in the bodies of leaders of countries that could fight back effectively if the United States were to attack them, just as Britain decided to evade the balance-of-power game in favor of joining the stronger side before WW I. But personal relationships do influence foreign policy, sometimes drastically, as we recall from Niall Ferguson's story about Sir Edward Grey. Even though Edward Asquith, the prime minister Grey served, wished to pursue a neutral policy vis-à-vis a Europe that seemed to be moving toward war, Grey made informal, secret agreements with representatives of France and behaved rudely to German representatives, rejecting their overtures toward closer relations with Britain. Grey's behavior built up expectations in France that Britain would come to its aid in the event of war. At the same time, Grey projected enough ambiguity to make other major powers, including Germany, uncertain of exactly what Britain would do, all this at the precise time when each was making decisions about whether or not to go to war.

"Market Power"

Other theories describing the mitigation of anarchy focus on economic actors. Prior to WW I, British writer Norman Angell wrote a popular book suggesting that British investments throughout Europe might inhibit a major war, because British policy makers would not want these investments to go up in smoke. A counterpoint to that book was published by another Englishman, Edward Hallett Carr, shortly before WW II. Angell's analysis was ambiguous regarding whether he thought foreign investments actually could keep the peace. But

Carr's book, *The Twenty Years' Crisis*, was openly critical, even scornful, of the idea that economic interdependence was a deterrent to war. It dripped with sarcasm at what the author described as the utopian notion that markets promote a harmony of interests either among nations or among social classes within a nation.[22]

Carr identifies fundamental contradictions in the widely held assumption that markets keep the peace. Looking closely at market theory and basic balance-of-power theory, we can see that they are based on similar assumptions about motivations and behavior. Each assumes the existence of a universe of unitary competitive actors all trying to maximize their individual power and wealth. If basic (power-over) balance-of-power theory predicts that war, as the regulator of the balance, will be frequent, why should we assume that market competition, especially nationally based market competition, won't also regulate the balance through war?

This, after all, is the message of most standard theories of industrial organization. Like nations seeking hegemony, firms seek monopoly. In a competitive market, big firms lower prices below costs, hoping to drive out the weak firms, which they can either take over or simply allow to die. Economist Joseph Schumpeter called this "creative gales of destruction," but the targets of hostile takeovers are less cheery about this process; they call it "cut-throat competition."[23]

The "harmony of interests" theory thus has the same flaw as balance-of-power theory. Both rely on events and behaviors coming from outside the model. Will firms avoid cut-throat competition by sharing markets? According to the theory, we shouldn't count on it. Will policy makers avoid balance-of-power wars through accommodation—a strategy that was called "appeasement" before it failed so spectacularly with Hitler in 1938?[24] As we noted above, these are "empirical" questions that can be answered only by looking at actual cases and figuring out why things happened as they did.

Complex Models

Other theories incorporate elements of hegemony and power-as-if. As we noted earlier, a hegemonic system is directed by a single major-power authority that makes the rules for the world as a whole. Gilpin devotes substantial attention in his analysis of the role of power in war and change to just that kind of authority. He calls it "prestige" and defines it as a reputation for being powerful that a state earns through winning the last big war. The winner gets to make the rules for the postwar international system and thereby alters international structures to reinforce its own dominance. The winner can persuade other states to go along because it has so much prestige that it rarely has to use direct force to get its own way.

The coalition that won WW I consisted of Britain, the United States, and France.[25] The Versailles Treaty ending the war established a new international system based on German disarmament, arms limitations for all the major powers, a revived gold standard, and a relatively open trade regime. It also imposed severe reparations on Germany for having started the war, requiring the country to pay damages. However, these arrangements could not be successfully enforced. The United States refused to ratify the treaty, and the other winners were too weak to make it stick on their own. Meanwhile, Germany's rule-imposed disadvantages allowed its government to justify avoiding, evading, and actually defying those rules, even to non-Germans. German policy makers were able to persuade a prominent British economist, John Maynard Keynes, that the reparations were unjust, and he became one of the most influential advocates of reducing them.[26] Just as the perception that a system of rules is legitimate makes enforcement easier, Germany's successful campaign to make the post–WW I rules look unfair undermined the victors' ability to extract reparations, enforce free-trade relations in Eastern Europe (where Germany had an advantage that free trade would have eliminated), and stop Germany from rearming openly after the world economy had collapsed into depression.

But individual countries were not solely responsible for the management of the post–WW I system. At the urging of U.S. president Woodrow Wilson, the major powers set up the League of Nations, which they hoped would prevent another disruption of the balance of power like the one they thought had led to what they called "the Great War." The League of Nations was charged with applying a special understanding of balance-of-power theory, "collective security," to future occasions of conflict. Under collective security, if any country or alliance were to attack another, all the rest are supposed to band together against the aggressive power(s) and defend the one that was attacked. In practice, the League of Nations did not work any better than the anti-Germany measures (disarmament and reparations). Having spurned the Versailles Treaty, the United States also refused to join the League of Nations. The powers that did join refused to defend nations and territories that were attacked by another European state. The pattern was set when Italy invaded Ethiopia in 1935. The League of Nations expressed disapproval but did not unite against Italy and force it to withdraw, as the U.S.-led "coalition" governments united against Iraq after it invaded Kuwait in 1990.

Indeed, with the exception of Germany and Italy, throughout the 1930s the nations of Europe were reluctant to go to war for any reason. Having sustained huge losses in the trench warfare of 1914 to 1918, they had little stomach for another exhausting conflict. When a general war in Europe became unavoidable in 1939, the countries opposing the European "Axis powers" (Germany and Italy—Japan was the third member of that axis) were unprepared to fight, and nearly all were rapidly defeated and occupied. Only two major European powers escaped German conquest. The Soviet Union, which started out as a signatory to a treaty with Germany that theoretically bound each partner to nonaggression toward the other, survived Hitler's unexpected 1941 invasion, just as Russia had survived Napoleon's invasion more than a hundred years earlier. The Soviet Union was so huge that the Germans were forced to extend their logistical lines too far to fight effectively, although they did manage to kill more than twenty million Soviet citizens during nearly four years of fighting. Britain survived the bitter air battles of 1940 and after with the help of massive arms transfers from the United States through a program called Lend-Lease. But even after Germany declared war on the United States following Japan's attack on Pearl Harbor in December 1941, the prospects for an Allied victory were far from assured; this changed only with the successful June 1944 invasion of occupied France.

The colossal failure of both parts of the post–WW I settlement forced the victors to think more broadly as they organized the postwar international system. Once again, a relatively open trading regime was a prime objective. Another was a "League of Nations II," the United Nations, based on new rules governing intervention against aggression. These rules provided that, if all of the victors agreed and were able to persuade a few additional countries to support them, they could intervene legally, even with military force, against another sovereign state. This is the UN Security Council system, in which all five major-power "winners" of WW II—the United States, Britain, the Soviet Union (now once again Russia), China, and France—are "permanent" members. There are ten rotating members of the Security Council, but only the "big five" have veto power. If just one of them disagrees with a measure, it is defeated.

How that post–WW II system worked in practice was altered abruptly as relations between the two biggest winners, the United States and the Soviet Union, deteriorated after 1945. Each gathered allies in Europe and elsewhere. Each "superpower" created and sustained its own "international" economy, one capitalist and one centrally planned, and knitted its alliance together by forging strategic and economic dependencies with its allies. Each "bloc" operated as if the other were totally evil in every way and, in the process, each superpower exacted a high price from its allies and its own population in lives, money, and environmental degradation (most of the nuclear waste that infects the world today came not from power plants but from U.S. and Soviet weapons production and deployment). Pieces of nuclear and other so-called weapons of mass destruction that the superpowers developed for use against each other are now traded and deployed in the murky world of thieves, defectors, and terrorist organizations. Current concerns about chemical weapons, "dirty bombs," anthrax, smallpox, and other deadly infectious diseases arise directly from the detritus of those cold war arms races, while continued production of nuclear weapons has created a huge stockpile of "depleted uranium" now used by the United States and Britain to make "conventional" bombs. Scientists and legal specialists are only now beginning to understand the devastating impact the use of these weapons has had on the health of populations and soldiers.[27]

The end of the cold war between the United States and the Soviet Union, and the subsequent collapse of the Soviet Union itself, left the United States as the only major world power. It has the world's largest military, deadliest weapons, and largest economy. The more than $400 billion (and still rising) the United States spends each year on "defense" is equal to what the entire rest of the world spends for the same purpose. The United States presides over a system of international rules that tilt the playing field in its favor, including revamped post–WW II economic rules that operate through institutions like the International Monetary Fund (IMF) and the World Bank to give the United States disproportionate influence over international finance.[28] The United States is a global hegemon.

Before Americans celebrate, however, we should recall that hegemony has three parts, not only lots of military stuff and economic rules that favor the dominant actor but also the agreement of others that the dominant actor has the right to rule. Hegemonic theory and practice include elements of power-with, making hegemony depend on consent. With regard to the current U.S. hegemony, this consent is under stress. Consent has been damaged by U.S. decisions to act unilaterally, without first persuading others that its decisions were being taken in pursuit of good for all. Many disapprove of the U.S. refusal to honor the Kyoto Agreement to fight global warming; its "unsigning" of the Rome Treaty, which established a permanent international criminal court to try persons charged with war crimes and genocide; and its rejection of treaties designed to organize and implement inspection systems for biological weapons, limit international trade in small arms, and ban land mines. The U.S. decision to put weapons into space required it to abrogate (back out of) another treaty, the Anti-Ballistic Missile Treaty with the old Soviet Union; this is perhaps the most potentially damaging of the U.S. decisions listed here, for both the global environment and world peace. Meanwhile, the war in Iraq, undertaken in spite of UN objections, alienated most allies and provided a platform in the heart of the Middle East for anti-U.S. terrorists. Such decisions parallel how previous hegemonic powers undermined their authority by estranging allies and degrading significant parts of the physical, economic, and political environment in which they and everyone else must live.

Who Has International Power?

From under the lamppost, power seems to be concentrated in the hands of large states, firms, and other corporate bodies such as churches and international organizations that control vast physical and monetary resources. How this power can be wielded in quiet ways was revealed during the Soviet war in Afghanistan, in which U.S. economic sanctions were critical to the withdrawal of Soviet forces, over the objections of the nation's military leaders, by a new general secretary whose program for reforming his country depended on a strong economy.[29] Yet, as Anthony Giddens points out, no one is without power. Even the weakest person can resist a tyrant, if only by refusing to obey. Other examples of "weapons of the weak" are described by journalist James William Gibson in a book about the American war in Vietnam. Gibson writes of the ingenuity of impoverished Vietnamese who mounted ambushes against U.S. troops, threw stones into the rotors of helicopters to make them crash, and tunneled under military installations to spy on, steal from, and destroy U.S. forces.[30] In the Vietnam War, the country that looked the most powerful under the lamppost was defeated by a smaller and militarily weaker adversary. Yet there is never a guarantee that agents will be able to alter structures in the ways they envision. The defeat of the United States in Vietnam did not change overall U.S. power and prestige or diminish bipolarity in the international system. But the defeat of the Soviet Union in Afghanistan did hasten the Soviet collapse, changing the structure of the international system from bipolarity to hegemony.

States are not alone in their ability to exercise political power. Individuals also can check tyrants. Mohandas Gandhi led hundreds of thousands of Indians in nonviolent protests against British colonialism and mobilized them to refuse to buy British products. Similar movements, such as the civil rights movement in the United States and the anti-apartheid movement in South Africa, also used nonviolent protest successfully against armed and dangerous adversaries. When opponents used violence against these movements, such as by assassinating Martin Luther King Jr. and Malcolm X in the United States, and murdering Steven Biko in a South African prison, it focused popular opinion domestically and internationally against these racist governments and their policies, and hastened the pace of progressive social change.

A single individual who acts successfully against a powerful adversary seldom acts alone. The example that proves the rule is the young man who stood in front of the tanks rolling into Tiananmen Square in June 1989. The tanks all stopped. Not one ran him down. But this was not a single-handed victory. This very brave man stood in front of cameras as well as tanks; whatever happened to him would have been witnessed by millions worldwide, and the officers directing the tanks knew this. Similarly, Gandhi was effective not only because he persuaded Indians to give money to the nationalist cause, boycott British textiles in his famous buy-Indian campaigns, and engage in selective marches and strikes but also because he took his stand in front of the world press at a time when the British government was reluctant to be seen treating a tiny, elderly, unarmed man with brutality. Still, the main requirement for success in a long campaign is effective organization. Although Martin Luther King Jr. stood at the head of the civil rights parade, Rosa Parks, Ralph Abernathy, Fred Shuttlesworth, Jesse Jackson, Ella Baker, Andrew Young, and many others marched alongside him. Tens of thousands of others followed. Luckily for some of them, cameras often were there too.[31]

Such examples show that effective power lies in the capacity of the social individual to mobilize and participate in a social network, appeal to "public opinion"—an even larger social network—and ensure transparency, public visibility, for her work. An individual can resist on her own, but individual resistance (and the resister) can be ignored, ridiculed, marginalized, and even eliminated. The Soviet gulag (prison camp system), like the dungeons of the emperor of China and the doge of Venice, made corpses out of rebels and dissidents. Publicity is a crucial tool of effective action. It was not until the domestic political hegemony established by Stalin had been eroded, first by Nikita Khrushchev's 1956 revelations of his myriad abuses and then by the success of Mikhail Gorbachev in opening the entire Soviet system to public scrutiny and criticism, that the government of the Soviet Union could be brought down. When people stopped believing in the Soviet Union, it disappeared.

Collective action also is crucial to protect individual dissidents. The limits of small-scale action are evident in Nazi Germany. Resistance to the Nazis was minimal and dispersed throughout a population that either feared retaliation or actually agreed with the Nazi program.[32] Small dissident groups like the White Rose, a student movement, were discovered and liquidated. Dissent within the Nazi Party was not tolerated. The "Night of the Long Knives" in 1934 saw the murder of as many as four hundred followers of Ernst Roehm, himself a Nazi but one who seemed too independent and too popular for Hitler's taste. Stalin also was a ruthless pursuer of dissidents, arresting some twenty million Russians he feared had or might turn against him during his long reign of terror in the Soviet Union. Some were executed, but most were taken to prison camps in remote areas of the country. Evgenia Ginzberg's memoirs recount not merely the loss of her freedom but also the loss of her family and her health after more than twenty years in the gulag.[33] Internationally known writer-dissidents like Anna Akhmatova, Boris Pasternak, and Andrei Sakharov were variously imprisoned, denied work, and, in Akhmatova's case, hounded to death by the Soviet secret police.

Totalitarian systems are built on force, on structural power—jobs, schools, and housing are all controlled by the state so that dissenters risk not only themselves but also their children and parents if they continue their activities. They also depend on a hegemonic ideology that puts the state and its leader at the pinnacle of power. Ginzberg relates an experience at a movie theater several months after her release from prison. The film included a sequence showing part of a Roman Catholic mass. Two women were sitting behind her. "Fancy that," said one. "[T]hey used to worship God! Just as if he were Stalin!"[34]

Power and Democracy

The collapse of the Soviet Union shows the difficulty of maintaining a power-over system in the modern world. As Charles Tilly notes, the evolution of Europe during the modern period is a story about the gradual imposition of accountability on governments. Kings became "constitutional monarchs," encouraged by various means to share power with parliaments, courts, and voters.[35] As we shall see in chapter 5, even the most powerful kings had to accommodate at least some of the demands and needs of the economic actors who produced the wealth on which their kingdoms depended. Towns and cities within their territories, along with firms and banks whose activities transcended boundaries between town and country and between realms, negotiated concessions from kings in return for gains from trade and loans to support the kings' military adventures.

The power of moral authority and its capacity to mobilize public opinion was foreshadowed in the challenges by popes, bishops, and priests to the authority of "temporal" rulers. Even after the Protestant Reformation had erased the empire of the Catholic Church from vast swaths of Europe, clergy and "holy" persons still managed to criticize kings and mobilize people to oppose them. Indeed, scholars like Michael Walzer see the Reformation not only as initiating structural changes in relations among European states but also as the primary generator of social movements the long-term effects of which included the democratization of much of Protestant and Catholic Europe.[36]

The democratic-peace thesis we discussed in the introduction makes a special claim for democracy as a structural deterrent to war, but, despite its attractiveness in theory, it doesn't hold up in practice. Democracy is a political system that incorporates the wishes of masses of people in decisions affecting the whole community and has many positive (and some negative) effects on conditions other than war and peace among states. Democracy is empowering. Going back to Hannah Arendt's vision of power as something that happens when people get together to accomplish a common goal, democracy enables groups, communities, and states to mobilize active participation in the formation of and consent to a chosen policy. As Jane Mansbridge observes in the case of town meetings in Vermont, however, this does not mean that everyone is treated equally or that every alternative is debated—democracy is a process, not an outcome.[37]

Democracy also supports entitlements to a nation's collectively produced goods and services. All states take money from people to finance the government. Democracies force governments to haggle with citizens over how much will be taken and what will be given back: good governance, social services, protection from harm (this is the theory, at any rate). Above all, democracies entitle their populations to demand a high standard of conduct and performance, whether they actually do so or not. This entitlement is guaranteed by regular and peaceful opportunities to dismiss leaders and replace them with others who might do a better job.

Like most of the other terms we use in this book, "democracy" means different things to different people. In the United States today, we believe that we live in a democracy, but the Greek citizens of fifth-century Athens would disagree. They (like Rousseau) would see our representative institutions as making us "democrats for a day" every few years when elections are held and, the rest of the time mere subjects of the state. Eighteenth-century supporters of the U.S. Articles of Confederation (which preceded the Constitution) would agree with the Athenians. They saw the consolidated state outlined in the Constitution as the end of democracy, which they understood as empowering citizens to govern their own communities.

Kevin Phillips, the man who designed the "southern strategy" used by

Richard Nixon's successful 1968 presidential campaign, also has serious doubts about the nature of democracy in the United States, where, he argues, the very rich and their busy interest groups crowd the rest of us out of politics.[38] There is much truth in all of these critiques. But let us end this section with an acknowledgment of the power of citizens in a democracy as compared to the lack of power among subjects of an autocratic regime—even one that holds regular elections. This affirmation comes from Hamid Zageneh, an Iranian who now lives in the United States:

> [U]nelected American Lobbies (hired guns) who try and do influence American policies [are] quite different from the unelected political organs of Iran who . . . control and make policies without much accountability. If the American citizenry do find a policy, regardless of how it became law, repugnant and repulsive enough, they have a choice. They [can] go to the polls and remove the politicians who were responsible. In Iran, there is no such mechanism, with real enforcement. No one could seriously suggest that the unelected organs of the political system in Iran are accountable to the people [or that they] are in any "peaceful" danger. As a matter of fact, the paralysis of the Iranian political system at this time is due to this very fact, that there is no accountability other than through violence.[39]

Zangeneh argues that power remains with the people as long as they can act politically without violence. When this freedom is taken away, and the only support for popular political action is the Kalashnikov, democracy disappears and power with it, both destroyed by force and violence.

International Power Today

Today most observers believe we are living in an age of "globalization," when nations and cultures experience increasing contact with one another and are transformed by it. As we describe in chapter 9, globalization also causes power to shift from states and their agents to individuals and their agents. Nonstate agents include NGOs, religious organizations, social movements, labor unions and professional organizations, firms and banks, and the myriad other organizations and methods used by social individuals to create "societies" that transcend differences between people and borders between states. Some believe that globalization is creating a new international "civil society," while others believe that civil society always has been international. Among the latter, Alex Colás argues that the international system itself is a product of civil society, however much twentieth-century IR theorists chose to ignore civil society to concentrate on states.[40]

The civil society debate, which we examine more closely in chapter 5, is part of the struggle to assert international power, whether as power-over by those trying to limit civil society and bring it under control or through power-with by activists pursuing strategies to achieve human rights and a better life for themselves and others. In this struggle, we should not assume that states are negative forces in civil society any more than we should assume that nonstate organizations and institutions are good.[41] All actors embody positive and negative qualities. Churches send missionaries overseas to overturn the values, beliefs, and practices of other cultures, however generous the motives of individual missionaries might or might not be. International firms bring new investment and job opportunities, and they also bring pollution, corruption, and ways of changing values, beliefs, and practices different from the missionaries' but no less destructive. At the most extreme, activist organizations like the Red Army Faction, al Qaeda, and the Irish Republican Army all are or were parts of international civil society—and at the same time they are terrorist groups. As Colás makes clear, states also are part of international society. Hannah Arendt's observations about the incompatibility of violence and power offer a better way to distinguish between mostly constructive and mostly destructive international actors and organizations: death and empowerment are mutually exclusive states of being, and an organization that is powerful is the one that can accomplish its goals without force.

International civil society offers an even better model for examining power than one that includes only nation-states, but it is far more complicated to specify and use. As we discussed in the introduction, states are imagined as functionally similar and juridically equal even though they have widely different resource endowments, capacities, and internal organizations. The nation-state system is conceived as fundamentally egalitarian, in part because of the theoretical homogeneity of the states that are its constituent parts. In contrast, international civil society has many different parts that no one even pretends are homogeneous. Its units are not only different but also overlap in a way that nation-states, imagined as territorially distinct agents, cannot. Consequently, imagining power in civil society is a lot more complicated than imagining it in an "international system." But it is not impossible.

4

People and Economy

Since the turn of this century, three million American manufacturing jobs have disappeared. Some economists and politicians attribute this loss to global trade deals. Others credit improvements in production efficiency. But, however the responsibility is apportioned, most people agree on one point: the need to retrain displaced workers. . . . After she lost her job, Lupita had tried to reinvent herself in accordance with market imperatives. First, she earned a G.E.D. and a certificate at the local branch of the University of Texas, as a "Microsoft Office Specialist." When she discovered that this certificate provided her little entrée into actual offices, she took out a $3,500 loan and trained to be a certified medical assistant—taking vital signs, scheduling appointments, and drawing blood (a task at which, given her dexterity with a needle, she excelled). . . . Lupita's friends who did make the necessary financial sacrifices to educate themselves were increasingly worried that their investments might fail to pay out. Alicia, one of Lupita's former co-workers, completed computer training and went to work as a grocery-store cashier—part time, no benefits. Aracely, a medical-assistant classmate, took a restaurant job. Becky, from Levi's, worked at a hospital, cleaning floors; Roberto, also from Levi's, went back to Mexico to fix up and sell junk cars. Another former co-worker sold picture frames door-to-door. And Lupita was loading two ice chests' worth of food into the family's Dodge Intrepid, to sell to other low-paid laborers who wanted a cheap, home-cooked lunch.

—Katherine Boo[1]

In chapter 2, we examined how people form households, and how households constitute both economy and politics. Chapter 3 discussed the relationship between people, power, and global politics, and how particular forms of power locate people in the global political economy. This chapter addresses how the global economy—that is, globalized capitalism—functions to produce human needs and desires, and reproduces individuals and societies. The framework we present here strongly emphasizes two points. First, in a market-based or "marketized" society—a capitalist one—the individual is "free to choose" among a great variety of goods and services that are for sale, which creates the illusion that a similar freedom extends to all aspects of life. Second, the very real limits to choice in a capitalist society are highly obscured, but they serve to maintain a high degree of political and social order. The paradox is that "freedom" has the effect observed by John Agnew (cited on this point in chapter 2), that "[people] are *located* according to the demands of a spatially extensive division of labour, the global system of material production and distribution, and variable patterns of political authority and control."[2] We suggest that the "freedom to decide" is more important than the "freedom to choose," but, if we are to decide, we'd better understand choice. That is one of the central goals of this chapter.

We begin the chapter with a review of the dual roles of the individual in production and reproduction. Recall that *production* refers to making goods and providing services essential to individual and social survival. *Reproduction* refers not only to producing the next generation but also to activities and institutional practices that give meaning to action, reinforce belief systems, and maintain the social order. The line between the two is not as clear as it might seem. Many people make their living through cultural activities that reproduce meanings, beliefs, and social order, while the funding of cultural activities by wealthy individuals, organizations, and the state enables people to engage in cultural projects as their livelihoods rather than doing other things to survive.

Next, we examine the concept and reality of *modes of production* and all that entails. The term is usually associated with Marxist analysis, and it is a useful way to conceptualize contrasting forms of economic organization and their social impacts. In brief, a mode of production entails three things: (1) the *material base* that is dominant in an economy, including technology and the ways in which things are produced or manufactured (the *means of production*); (2) *relations of production*, which involve the authority relationships between those who decide what and how much will be produced and those who do the actual work of production; and (3) *social relations*, which are the forms and patterns of relations among the members of a society dominated by a particular mode of production. According to classical Marxism, the mode of production determines the social relations of a society; our understanding is less deterministic.

In the third part of this chapter, we turn to a discussion of the contemporary global economy and its capitalist organization, leading to the phenomenon of *globalization*. While we have already used the last term in earlier chapters (and will return to it in chapter 9), here we define it more carefully, all the while recognizing that it is a highly contested concept, and examine the relationship between the individual and the global economy. This section elaborates the distinction and relationship between the two "freedoms"—to decide and to choose—in particular, the ways in which the reified "freedom to choose" within market economies tends to abstract away the politics implicit in the "freedom to decide." In effect, and drawing on the conceptions of power discussed in chapter 3, we argue that highly liberalized capitalist markets—in a system that is commonly called "neoliberalism"—eliminate politics from much of everyday life, replacing it with consumer choice.

The third and final part of chapter 4 asks whether there are different—better—ways to understand and act in terms of "people and economy." To put this in terms of contemporary events and movements, does putting people back into economics require that globalization be stopped in its tracks, as protesters in Seattle, Washington, Geneva, Goteborg, and Genoa have demanded? Are there other ways of humanizing capitalism to make it more just, fairer, and more transparent? Can we facilitate the freedom to decide rather than merely providing growing supplies of goods and services to some, while leaving shelves empty for others? Our answers will probably satisfy no one. We do not believe that a return to a mythic Golden Age of caring states and domestic justice is possible, because such an age never existed. We do believe that an unregulated system of global, neoliberal capitalism cannot be sustained in the long term. We argue, however, that the key to social change lies in politics, not economics.

People, Production, and Reproduction

Production is at the heart of every social system and of the institutions and political arrangements that enable that system to "operate" in a particular way. The term literally means the making of things, but it is also useful to recall a second meaning: the creation and display of an intentionally designed arrangement of people, objects, and actions, as in plays, exhibits, or even theme parks. For our initial purposes, the first meaning is most relevant: the manufacture and delivery of basic necessities such as food, water, and clothing. While we tend to take for granted the ready availability of these things (for a price), several *billion* of the world's people struggle every day, and not always successfully, to meet these needs.[3]

Without the ability to produce or acquire basic necessities, the individual and household can neither survive nor reproduce, in either biological or social terms. What might be less obvious is that the bare minimum of necessities can support only the bare minimum of social development. When all of a household's time and energy must be devoted to procuring food, water, and shelter, reproduction means little more than maintaining the labor supply through giving birth to children and socializing them to the arrangements that allocate responsibilities among household members. Many people in many parts of the world still live at this very basic level.

Explaining the origins of society and state, Thomas Hobbes was not troubled by this dilemma. Even though people in the State of Nature did not live in the Garden of Eden, food and shelter were available, and no one had much more than anyone else. It was only when someone did manage to accumulate an excess of goods that she had reason to worry that others might become jealous and resort to theft—even murder—to take what they had. Theft is not, of course, a legitimate means of acquiring necessities. In this light, Hobbes suggested that the state can be seen not only as the provider of security and law to men but also the guarantor and protector of property rights.

Anthropologists speculate that it was the ability to accumulate food and goods beyond subsistence levels, accompanied by a "division of labor" that divided tasks across members of a social order, that supported increasingly complex social arrangements. The emergence of professional classes (kings, priests, managers) not engaged directly in production became possible only when excess production could be expropriated for the needs of these ruling classes. Although such expropriation might be done with force, it could not be done willy-nilly—that would be theft. It had to be justified on the basis of the centrality of the professional classes to household security and societal survival. This could be expressed as religious doctrine, but it was always couched in legal terms.[4]

In addition to explaining the sources of life, death, and natural phenomena, and resolving conflicts without violence, religion legitimated the hierarchies that organized the production of social necessities and the reproduction of social arrangements.[5] The ruler was associated by blood with one or more gods; the gods ensured the provision of those natural elements (land, water, seeds) that gave and sustained life; it followed, therefore, that the ruler bore major responsibility for seeing that those elements continued to be provided.[6] Peasants worked the land, raised the crops, and relied on the good will of the ruler and the gods to maintain the cycle of life that allowed them to survive. Rulers and priests could not raise their own food because their work was to connect the material world to the cosmos. Therefore, peasants provided the food so that the professional classes could eat and perform the rituals necessary to continuing the cycle of life and the reproduction of the hierarchy, rules, and practices that maintained the social order. Thus the circle was closed.

Capitalism, although a materialist rather than a spiritual ideology, is similar in that production of goods is central to system maintenance. What is different is how little of what is produced is required for subsistence and survival. Consequently, because basic needs can be so readily supplied, capitalism requires the continuous transformation of products into "necessities." For example, in Los Angeles, a car is a basic requirement for finding and keeping a job that enables you to buy food, find shelter, and pay the bills. Perhaps. But two cars? Each costing $40,000? Why these particular cars? And how do they maintain the legitimacy and hierarchy of the social system within which the individual and household are embedded? Are there other, less costly and less frustrating ways of living? These are good questions (we made 'em up ourselves!).

There are a few important points to note here. First, within capitalism, the distinction between production and reproduction is difficult to make. Many things that seem to be part of reproduction—such as art, foods prepared in customary ways, or even music—are produced and sold like food and shelter. Clearly, large and growing numbers of people "produce" goods and services that individuals do not produce for themselves—Happy Meals, houses, clean laundry, air travel, and so on. This frees up time for those being served to engage in other occupations. Some produce "intellectual goods,"[7] such as books, music, films, laws, research papers, video games, newspapers, and so on, that support the cultural infrastructure so necessary to social reproduction. Second, as we noted above, consumption of nonsubsistence goods is integral to sustaining the production from which people earn their livings (we return to this point later in this chapter). Third, higher rates of consumption of nonsubsistence goods are required for the *reproduction* of capitalism. Capitalism must either grow or stagnate, and, if it stagnates, not only will profits decline but people will find it more difficult to acquire both necessities and luxuries. Finally, the smooth operation of all these arrangements plays an important role in maintaining political legitimacy and social stability. As in the religious system outlined above, the circle must be closed to avoid social and political crises.[8]

Modes of Production: Which Way Do the Arrows Point?

As we noted earlier, a mode of production constitutes the basic organization of a society through which the material requirements necessary for social reproduction are produced. Marx argued that a society's mode of production determines the authority relations within it. A factory in a capitalist economy requires an appropriately skilled group of workers who will obey the orders of the owner or manager. These relationships mirror others outside the factory wall. A capitalist society depends on people who must sell their labor power for wages as well as those who, owning the means of production (in this case, factories) must pay wages to workers. Owners (capitalists) and workers (labor) constitute distinct *classes*, groups of people whose similar economic situations give them common interests. Marx thought that conflict between classes would ultimately lead to the replacement of capitalism by communism, a system characterized by a different mode of production and different social relations. Unlike Marx, we believe that the mode of production is only one of many determinants of social relations, although it is a very important one. We return to this point below.

Anthropologist Eric Wolf starts from the Marxian viewpoint that modes of production are critical to understanding social relations. Unlike Marx, however, he works from a theoretical model of each distinctive mode rather than an analysis of individual societies whose modes of production may be only superficially distinct. Thus, rather than five or eight or thirty-seven different modes of production, Wolf categorizes all complex societies (beyond hunters and gatherers) into three ideal types. These types highlight, in addition to the societies' authority and social relations, how the various parts connect up with one another—how they *articulate*—and direct change in actual ecological settings. We discuss each of these three modes—capitalist, tributary, and kin-ordered—below.

The Capitalist Mode of Production

Capitalism is an arrangement based on several key concepts and practices. First, goods are produced through a *division of labor*, whereby individual parties, usually unknown to one another, specialize in making what they produce most efficiently. This leads to a reduction in the amount of time needed to make a single item and therefore to an increase in the number of items that can be made in a given time. Second, everything must have a *price* so that it can be bought and sold. Price is generally understood to be established by the interplay of supply and demand, although this is not a hard and fast rule. Anything that has no price is considered to be without value in the market. Third, things to be sold (alienated) in a market must be *private property*. A seller must possess title free and clear to an item in order to transfer it to someone else through exchange; otherwise, there is no assurance that the item has not been stolen or is not counterfeit or inauthentic in some other way.

Prices and markets are, in themselves, not unique. What Wolf calls ''merchant trade'' involves a similar exchange of goods and services for money. What is different about capitalism is a third element: it depends on *profit and accumulation*. That is, exchange involves not only the consumer paying the cost of producing a good or service but also an additional amount representing a premium—the profit—beyond the cost of providing the good or service. This profit can then be reinvested to generate further returns through additional production or through speculation. Profit arises because the means of production are under the control of capitalists, who own what is produced by the laborers whose wages they pay. The difference between the cost of labor (and other necessary inputs, including wear and tear on tools) and the price at which what is produced is sold is called the *surplus value of labor* (neoclassical economists deny that such a thing exists).[9] It is transferred from the worker to the capitalist by virtue of the latter's ownership of the means of production (i.e., the tools and the factory). Finally, capitalism is able to *articulate* with other modes of production and extract *surplus value* from them, too. As we saw in chapter 2, the unrecorded value of housework provides a massive unrequited transfer that subsidizes profits.

Profit makes possible the growth and expansion of capitalism as a system, and not merely a mechanism for the exchange of goods and services. Profit can be seen as a reward for the risks that suppliers take in offering goods and services to the consumer; after all, there is no guarantee that there will be buyers, and it is quite easy to take a loss or even fail in business (in the United States, most small businesses never make it beyond their first year). Profits also are an incentive to growth if they are reinvested, making it possible to offer more goods and services to larger numbers of consumers, generating further profits. Of course, making money is not simply contingent on a decision to become rich; one needs to find eager buyers of goods and services as well as a way to provide goods and services at a lower cost than these buyers are willing to pay. In a perfectly competitive market, where there are many sellers of identical goods, it becomes increasingly difficult to realize profits. Each seller is motivated to underprice her competitor. If she is desperate for cash to pay her workers (or her taxes), she might even cut prices below her break-even point. Indeed, it is quite possible—and common—to sell out one's stock in trade and lose money on the deal. An example of this might be helpful.

Some years ago, the International Studies Association held its annual conference in Acapulco, Mexico. Most of the time, visitors fly into the local airport, which is located down the coast from the tourist section of the city. Ronnie Lipschutz, however, took a bus from another city and entered Acapulco via the road traversing its barrios. These impoverished neighborhoods are the homes of the very cheap labor supply that supports the tourist sector. Along the way, the bus passed a row of some twenty or thirty identical stands selling coconuts. There was no evident difference between the goods on offer and no difference in the price. The question that came to mind was: How does a shopper wishing to purchase a coconut decide from whom to buy? In this instance, it would seem logical that she would prefer to buy from family or friends, although that question is irrelevant according to standard market theory. If there is no reason other than price to choose one seller over others, however, each has to charge an identical price or go out of business. If even one were tempted to sell her coconuts at a lower price—even at a loss—all the others would have to do the same or risk being left with unsold coconuts. In the effort to move their stock, the stand owners might well sell *all* their coconuts and still lose money.[10]

Similarly, in order to sell all their stock in a competitive market, the owners of factories must offer attractive prices to buyers. Price-cutting reduces their profit margin, as do increases in wages and other production costs. This is described as the tendency in capitalism toward a "declining rate of profit." If the factory owner tries to keep his profits up by raising prices, customers will buy from other companies. He could try to reduce wages, but this is difficult to do, especially if he is competing against companies whose production is located in low-wage countries. Indeed, if goods of comparable quality and lower cost are imported from other countries (e.g., automobiles from Korea), he might have to automate, relocate production overseas, or go out of business. The now-jobless domestic workers will no longer be able to afford to buy goods, domestic or imported.

In contemporary capitalist markets, therefore, it is important to develop consumer desire *and* find a way to differentiate one's product from other, similar ones in order to limit competition and its pressure on prices and profits.

This is not a recent insight, of course. It was developed in the United States, during the last few decades of the nineteenth and first few decades of the twentieth centuries, with the growth of public literacy and print journalism.[11] Advertising became the linchpin of American capitalism by telling consumers what they lacked, what they needed, and most of all, what they wanted, whether they needed it or not. But even stimulated needs are not infinite. The average refrigerator will last for fifteen years or more. Capitalism cannot depend for growth on the demand for replacement refrigerators (and in the absence of sufficient income and reliable electricity in developing countries, demand is too sporadic there). How, then, to get the well-off to buy new appliances more frequently?

One way is to produce more elaborate versions (designer colors, ice and water dispensers in the refrigerator door); a second is to offer variants on the basic idea (wine refrigerators, freezers); a third is to develop entirely new appliances (microwave ovens, dishwashers). Another approach is to offer goods that become obsolete (go out of style or out of date) quickly. In the 1950s, this niche was filled by automobiles; today personal computers do the job. Each successive computer generation is faster, with more memory, more hard-drive space, and fancier CD players, cameras, scanners, and other capabilities. Each generation requires new software that is usually incompatible with older hardware or too large to fit on the old hard drive. Computers are typically replaced every three years. Finally, all kinds of new gadgets—cellular phones, personal digital assistants, MP3 players—are linked to new systems of communication, new ways of keeping records, and new ways of consuming cultural products (all of which also must be purchased) that promise a happier, more fulfilling life. Spiritual fulfillment comes to depend on material satiation. Both make people happy with their situation and status, which legitimates the political and economic system that makes such happiness possible.

The Tributary Mode of Production

Under the tributary mode of production, the means of production (usually land) also is owned by a specific class (landlords), and production is undertaken by a different class (peasants). Goods can be sold in markets for profits, but the process here differs from capitalism in that accumulation takes place through conquest (stealing from outsiders), and reinvestment rarely takes place at all. Finally, whereas in capitalism social relations are expressions of the economic system, in the tributary mode they also depend on such things as religion and tradition. Although there have been, historically, a variety of tributary forms—and some would argue they still exist today, even in the United States, in practices such as tenant farming—here we will consider European feudalism because of its role as the ancestor of capitalism.[12]

Feudalism as a system existed only for a limited period in Europe, developing during what is often called the "Dark Ages," between the fall of (western) Rome in 410 c.e. and about 1000 c.e., and declining, but not disappearing, after about 1400 C.E. Under feudalism, the hierarchy of social relations was overseen by the Catholic Church, with the pope in Rome at the apex and serfs or captive labor at the base (a differently organized feudal structure existed in Japan until the mid-nineteenth century). The rule of sovereigns and nobles over particular territories was legitimated by the church, which demanded, in return, their loyalty to the pope and priests. These rulers were the owners of the agricultural lands they governed as well as the people who lived on them and, by extension, of whatever the people and land produced. Serfs and peasants held rights to cultivate and graze their livestock on specific lands, but they were obligated to give some part of their annual production to the lord of the land (landlord) as a form of rent. They also were required to work on the landlord's property or to do particular jobs for him without pay. This was called *corvée* labor. If the landlord didn't need the goods produced by his serfs, he could sell them in the market for money. Military service was one form of corvée labor, and some landlords rented out their peasants as mercenary soldiers to fight other landlords' wars.

Under this tributary system, towns and cities occupied a different and often anomalous role. They usually emerged around market sites at which peasants might sell some of their produce and buy goods that could not be manufactured on the landlord's estate. Markets were located outside of the walls of a noble's castle, usually along a road or waterway. Port cities and long-distance trade had been destroyed through most of northern Europe during the seventh and eighth centuries. What trade remained took place at markets located in large towns and cities, and at fairs. Over time, local skilled workers were attracted to these places to produce for their markets. During the high Middle Ages, much of the production of skilled workers was overseen by guilds, producer organizations that regulated the supply and prices of goods by limiting the reproduction of skilled craftsmen. Some towns specialized in producing particular goods (like fine woolens or glass), and merchants transported and sold them in other towns and special markets, such as the Champagne fairs (discussed further in chapter 5), which convened for weeks at a time every year. Out of this system developed continent-wide networks of merchants and traders, such as the twelfth-century Hanseatic League, and independent cities such as Venice.

Capitalism emerged out of this tributary system, but scholars disagree about when it emerged and why. Markets had existed for thousands of years before capitalism, but until land, labor, and, especially, money were commodified, accumulation was limited. This commodification happened concurrently with the development of the autonomous, sovereign nation-state ruled by a prince or king—in Thomas Hobbes's words, by "a mortal God." Two other important movements—which also inspired Hobbes—were the rise of science and rationalism as a way of understanding how things worked, and Protestantism along with the individualism it inspired. We discuss this aspect of development in chapter 5.

Whereas wealth had once been acquired and accumulated largely through war or forcible expropriation by a powerful few, capitalism made it possible for more people to accumulate wealth. The Jews of Europe and other transnational ethnic minorities, such as Armenians, played a central role in this process. Transnational minorities often dominated activities such as trade and finance. Jews specialized in banking. They had been a privileged population in northern Europe during the Dark Ages, when the power of the church prevented Christians from engaging in banking and trade. As the power of the church declined, Jews became targets of envious Christians. Laws were passed forbidding them to own property. As the bourgeoisie or middle classes grew and began to encompass members of noble families as well as skilled craftsmen, merchants, and minorities, they demanded protection by and recognition from the sovereign. At the same time, the sovereign had an interest in fostering the growth of the bourgeoisie as both a counterweight to still-powerful nobles and as a source of status goods and loans to support military activities. The power of the nobility lay in the land they owned and controlled, and their feudal relationship to those who lived within those territories. The sovereign also was an owner of land, and he was expected to use his income, which included taxes such as tolls, to finance his own living and court expenses. But financing wars was another matter. The rulers of consolidating nation-states needed huge sums to establish sovereign autonomy and maintain their position vis-à-vis the nobility. Taxes provided some of this money, but loans also were necessary. The financial systems that were devised to facilitate trade turned out to be equally useful for raising money for wars. Thus, there was a confluence of interests between the new bourgeoisie and the sovereign state in fostering and facilitating economic growth through capitalism. Their interdependence had the added attraction of reducing the ruler's fiscal dependence on the nobility, allowing a greater concentration of authority and control in the person of the king or queen.

Ellen Meiksins Wood argues that it was the specific organization of English agriculture during the transition from feudalism that led to capitalism.[13] Wood's account is not entirely satisfactory, but it does explain why capitalism first appeared in England. According to Wood, property relations between landlord and tenant farmer in sixteenth- and seventeenth-century England were no longer of the pure feudal type. Landlords wanted to get their rents in money, not goods, in order to accumulate wealth for investment, at the same time that better-off farmers wanted to rent more land on the basis of their individual needs and capacities, and their estimation of the land's productivity. Money rents were bid up by competition among farmers. To meet the rent, the farmer had to make the land as productive as possible by "improving" it so as to increase crop yields. The farmer's profit then could be used to acquire other plots of land, concentrating land holdings among the most productive. Poor or unsuccessful farmers were outbid by wealthier ones and forced either to work for wages or migrate to the cities. Ultimately, there were limits to how high rents could rise, set by limits to productivity and the availability of land and transportation to markets. Rich farmers and landlords sought other ways to invest their profits, and the newly developing factories were an obvious place. The rest is history.

The Kin-Ordered Mode of Production

Kin-ordered (or kinship-based) societies are based on both biological (parents-children) and social (husband-wife) linkages within and among specific groups of people. Within such societies, both the production of goods and the reproduction of the social order are governed by familial relations. A kin-ordered society is often organized hierarchically, with leadership limited to specific descent lines even though all members might be related either biologically or socially. Eric Wolf provides a useful description of kin relations in "the context of political economy":

> Kinship can . . . be understood as a way of committing social labor to the transformation of nature through appeals to filiation [parent-child relations] and marriage, and to consanguinity [lineage] and affinity [descent groups]. Put simply, through kinship social labor is "locked up," or "embedded" in particular relations among people. This labor can be mobilized only through access to people, such access being defined symbolically. What is done unlocks social labor; how it is done involves symbolic definitions of kinsmen and affines.[14]

Generally speaking, kin-ordered societies are characterized by a social division of labor in which specific tasks are assigned to men, women, and children, and by a lineal division of labor in which other (often cultural-symbolic) tasks are limited to specific descent lines. Such kin-ordered societies can be pastoral (nomadic) or settled (farmers). In their smallest forms they rarely produce much surplus, but as groups practicing settled agriculture grew and produced surpluses that could be appropriated by elite lineages, tributary-based societies and cities began to develop.

Such societies are often regarded as "tribal" or "primitive," but kin-ordered relations are both complex and essential to capitalism. Consider, once again, the modern household constituted by a nuclear or an extended family. In either, certain members, often related by blood or marriage, engage in wage labor outside of the household, while others perform housework and child rearing. The wages become the "property" of all members of the household, making reproduction possible. (Contrast this to households in which each unrelated member works for wages and contributes only to those costs, such as rent and utilities, that cannot be individualized.) Kin-ordered relations can extend beyond the household, such as when nonresident biological and social relations provide child care at no cost or offer financial support to college students or elderly parents. Urban societies appear to be more atomized and less dependent on kin relations for support, but even in cities, families pool housing, labor, and resources to maintain their households.

Kin-type relations are reflected in what economists and political scientists call "social capital."[15] As Robert Putnam defines it, "social capital refers to connections among individuals—social networks and the norms of reciprocity and trustworthiness that arise from them."[16] As we noted in chapter 1, people routinely do things for one another, not for money but as a result of family ties, social bonds (churches, clubs, schools), occupational and informational networks, and other linkages. A person in need can call on the assistance of others who may (but generally are not obligated to) provide assistance. Indeed, the old cliché "It's not what you know, it's who you know" describes perfectly the concept of social capital. Anyone who has worked in a large organization, be it government, corporation, or university, knows that things would never get done without such relations, even though they don't show up in organizational charts. As such, social capital provides another large, albeit invisible, articulation of the kinship mode of production to capitalism.

The Origins of the Global Economic System

How did capitalism become what it is today? To answer this question we need to look back to the early part of the twentieth century and the production process that later came to be called "Fordism." Henry Ford took the model of the mass production assembly line from other industries, mechanized and electrified it, employed unskilled and semiskilled workers to assemble autos, and paid them $5 a day, twice the going wage at the time, for their labor. Workers could produce enough cars each day to lower the cars' unit cost, while the high wages the workers received allowed many to buy their own Model Ts. During the early years of the company, Ford also provided housing and other social amenities to his workers, and even kept an eye on their moral behavior. "Company towns" were the norm in industry, in part because they made it possible for owners to exercise greater control over workers than they could if the workers lived independently.[17]

Fordism was adopted throughout American industry and elsewhere. During the 1920s, the United States and much of the world prospered. But, as you might have guessed, demand for the items produced through Fordism was not insatiable, and, by the end of that decade, many industries in many countries were producing more than could be sold domestically or in world markets. Demand declined, unemployment rose, stock markets crashed, countries put up barriers to international trade, and economies contracted. This horrible state of affairs was called the Great Depression, and it persisted until WW II was well under way.

The lessons of depression and war were many, but the economic ones were not lost on the leaders of the United States and the United Kingdom. Their plan for the postwar global economic system—the Bretton Woods agreements—sought, in effect, to internationalize the American form of capitalism through Keynesian demand management (government deficit spending during recessions and tax increases during booms) and encouragements for consumer spending.[18] The cold war played a significant role in entrenching these arrangements throughout the "Free World."[19] Fordism made possible the high standard of living that characterized prosperity in the United States, Europe, and Japan, as the growing desire for household goods was met through mass production in factories employing workers whose wages were high enough to enable them to buy houses and fill them with the things they produced on the assembly line.[20]

But Fordism could not be sustained indefinitely. As we noted earlier, capitalism is characterized by rising production, competition, and market saturation. This is what happened to Fordism toward the end of the 1960s.[21] The system entered an economic crisis as growth stagnated and a political legitimation crisis as people began to question the system itself.[22] One "normal" response to such crises is what economist Joseph Schumpeter calls "creative destruction."[23] In order to revive itself, capitalism must encourage the destruction of already existing goods and infrastructure so they can be replaced by new ones. Wars are one way for capitalism to do this. The emergence of new means of production is another.[24] A third is to reorganize relations of production and relocate production from high-wage, high-cost regions to low-wage, low-cost areas. The planned obsolescence described earlier is another important strategy, as is differential accumulation.

All of these and more were applied during the 1980s and 1990s. First, beginning in the late 1970s, the United States relaunched the cold war against the Soviet Union. The military buildup of the 1980s, begun by President Jimmy Carter, reached full flood under Ronald Reagan. This "imaginary war," as Mary Kaldor put it,[25] was never fought to the full, but vast resources were injected into the defense sector and its subsidiaries.[26]

Second, the full development of the "information revolution," with its proliferation of electronic devices and infrastructure, required new skills, new equipment, and new social relations of production, all helping to destroy Fordist practices and institutions. Companies "outsourced" and "downsized" to reduce labor costs. Older workers whose skills were no longer needed found themselves in what Marx called the "reserve army of the unemployed," competing for low-wage, low-skill jobs.

Third, factory owners began to move production "offshore" in the 1960s to jump foreign tariff barriers. Beginning in the 1980s such outsourcing became a flood. Capitalists located production in countries with much lower wages and lax labor laws, and exported goods back into the United States, Europe, and Japan. As a result, in industrialized countries the numbers of workers in agriculture and manufacturing has been declining steadily despite rising demand for their products.[27] Today a growing fraction of production takes place in relatively poor countries—the developing countries, or the Global South—from which goods are exported to relatively rich countries—the developed countries, or the Global North.[28] The many job seekers in the Global South constitute another reserve army of unemployed, ensuring that the wages paid to those who do have jobs never rise too high. While those who work in factories, call centers, and outsourcing consulting firms[29] are, at least, receiving a wage, and often can save enough of their earnings to buy nonsubsistence items, they do not (as yet) constitute a primary market for these goods and services. The remaining billions of truly poor are of little or no interest to global capitalism.

This does not mean, however, that those poor do not participate in capitalist markets. In economies where jobs and money are scarce, there are always niches in which small volumes of high-demand items can be sold, such as individual cigarettes. An enterprising individual who has a little money saved up can buy a few packs and sell individual smokes to those too poor to aspire to even this level of investing. The "profit" from a day's sales can support a family and finance the purchase of a few more packs of cigarettes to sell the next day. Such "gray markets" are widespread and appear to constitute a significant fraction of economic activity in many developing countries. As long as the cost of doing business is relatively high compared to the rate of profit, large capitalists ignore these petty opportunities, allowing the very poor to survive.

One definition of "differential accumulation" describes the limited production of high-priced, high-status goods for sale to elite consumers rather than the production of standard goods for mass markets (e.g., Lexus vs. Camry).[30] By making fewer units of the high-status model and charging a price two or three times that of the low-status model, the manufacturer can make higher profits even if, as is true in the case of these two Toyotas, the insides of the products are pretty much the same.

The most important response to the crisis of the 1970s was a reorganization of capitalism into what is now called "neoliberalism."[31] Neoliberalism encapsulates a set of fiscal and monetary practices and principles designed to restore profit rates for capital investment. It has been followed by many nation-states, often under duress. We can summarize neoliberalism's practices and principles as follows:

- Investment should be based on a country's comparative advantages in the context of an international division of labor. Such advantages include low labor costs and taxation, limited social and environmental regulation, domestic political and economic stability, and well-developed infrastructure.
- Governments must not impose undue restrictions on investment or forbid investors to send profits abroad.
- Government spending must be constrained to maintain the value of the currency. This means reductions in expenditures on health, education, and welfare and increases in spending that facilitate investment and production.
- Governments can impose only those restrictions on imports and exports permitted by international agreements, so as to maximize trade.

While these principles and practices might not seem onerous or unreasonable, especially if they are intended to contribute to national and global growth, there are a number of distributional consequences to consider. The logic behind the principles and practices listed above is that overall economic growth in a society will generate jobs, higher tax revenues, resources, and consumption, which will "trickle down" to the poor and unemployed in the form of demand and payment for their services. This often does not happen, for a number of reasons.

First, the principle of specialization according to comparative advantage in an international division of labor puts a premium on minimizing the cost of inputs, including labor, into the production process. The cost of labor in developing countries (and among recent immigrants, both legal and illegal, in industrialized ones) is quite low—even relative to the cost of living. This is a strong incentive for capital to move operations to developing countries and explains why production moves continually from low-wage to lower-wage countries. A very large low-wage workforce might keep industries from migrating, but ultimately it is the overall cost of operations that determines production location. Thus, the People's Republic of China, with its larger well-educated workforce, remains competitive as compared to India, where the highly skilled workforce is smaller.

Second, even the trickle of wealth downward may be blocked by the state. Governments, international financial institutions, and foreign investors often demand that their loans be matched by local capital. To generate these funds, the state forces workers to save a portion of their wages by law or by suppressing consumption (which means workers have to save in order to buy nonsubsistence goods). This strategy was pursued by both Japan and Korea after WW II, and it persists in many countries that put heavy taxes on "luxury" items. The state may also actively repress labor, forbidding the organization of unions and collective bargaining to keep wages from rising and to assure investors that the labor force is under control.

Third, the requirement that governments give maximum freedom to investment and production sets up a "race to the bottom" among countries. Corporations threaten to relocate when workers unionize or minimum wage levels are increased and leave promptly when lower-cost opportunities open up. Attempts by authorities to enforce environmental and other social regulations are met with similar responses. Indeed, in the effort to make a particular location as attractive as possible to investors, some governments lower fair labor standards and environmental protection regulations, and actively suppress movements to improve social conditions.[32] The race to the bottom is visible within countries, too, as in the United States, where states compete against one another to attract industry, and the European Union (EU), where member countries do the same even though the EU has adopted rules to limit competition of this kind.[33]

Fourth, governments are enjoined by international financial institutions and private banks to avoid "excessive" expenditures and deficit spending, especially for social services. Many developing countries hold substantial foreign debt, and funds expended on domestic needs cannot be used to repay loans. Moreover, deficit spending is usually inflationary, lowering the value of the currency and raising the prices of inputs and products. The taxation of industry, especially foreign-owned firms, might be an attractive source of revenue, but this would provide another big incentive for such firms to relocate (in fact, many investors demand tax rebates or holidays in return for their investments).

Finally, under the rules of the World Trade Organization (WTO), entry and exit taxes on imported and exported goods are restricted in the name of free trade. These are the easiest taxes for developing countries to collect; in the past, they were the revenue mainstays of countries that are developed today. Even where state capacity allows the collection of income taxes, however, free trade increases international competitiveness and puts downward pressure on wages in all countries, thereby limiting tax revenues from this source.

The picture presented here is complicated by the transnational distribution of capital and labor. Both workers, regardless of where they live, and developing countries find themselves in disadvantaged positions relative to capital and rich countries. In a global economy, the division of labor applies not only to countries but also to people. Again, there is nothing new about this state of affairs; differential wages to skilled and unskilled workers has a long history. What is new is the rapidity of change in demands for particular types of specialized labor and the ability of firms to select the lowest-cost labor force from a global menu. Fifty years ago, a person living in an industrialized country could learn a trade or skill and be relatively certain of full employment until retirement. Today, there are no such skills or jobs. People must expect to change jobs, and even fields, five or more times during their lifetimes. Even individual capabilities or skills that earn high incomes today may be outsourced, unwanted, or obsolete in five years.[34] Life trajectories are dictated not by choice but by necessity.

Also, what work is available is shorter term and "flexible." People are hired on the basis of capital's immediate requirements, often on contract rather than as full-time employees entitled to benefits and training. Companies pay only the wages necessary to get a job done and, where benefits are not provided by the state, engage employees on terms that avoid the additional costs of health, unemployment, or retirement insurance. Anyone unwilling to work under these conditions will, quite simply, not work, at least not for wages.

This is not a pretty picture, but it is already visible in many sectors of the economy, including higher education, where fully qualified teachers with degrees from prestigious institutions are unable to find full-time, tenure-track positions. To make ends meet, they commute from one institution to another, teaching one or two courses at each, at a small fraction of a full-time salary and without benefits. Growing numbers of undergraduate students—the "echo of the baby boom"—were expected to require colleges and universities to add positions, but this has not been the case. Instead, both permanent and temporary faculty are pressed by their employers to increase "productivity" by teaching more classes, each with more students, while their salaries stagnate or fall behind increases in the cost of living. Graduate programs provide prestige and cheap labor to universities, and also produce growing numbers of advanced-degree holders, most of whom join yet another reserve army of unemployed.

All these changes are intended to increase the "efficiency" with which capital can be deployed and profits maximized. Again, there is nothing new or innovative about these goals; the difference is that neoliberalism, globalization, and what some call the "contraction of space and time"[35] make it easier and faster to hire and fire, to invest and withdraw capital, and to do this worldwide. Under these conditions, capitalists make choices without much consideration of the impacts of their decisions on people. Labor is hired where it is cheapest and for only as long as it is required. The desire for work and uncertainty about employment motivates workers to take whatever is offered. They are paid wages far less than the price for which what they produce is sold, and capital expropriates that additional surplus as part of its profit. This arrangement puts downward pressure on incomes from wages, and workers find themselves falling behind those outside of the flexible workplace and those whose income comes from capital.

Another example illustrates this last argument. American and European clothing companies have closed down many domestic operations and subcontracted with apparel manufacturers overseas, where labor costs are a fraction of those paid at home ($5 or less per day compared to $15 per hour, an amount that includes taxes and benefits). The labor cost of making a T-shirt destined for an American company might be on the order of $1 in the overseas subcontractor's plant as compared to $5 in a domestic factory. Even after transportation and other costs are included, the imported shirt might cost $3 as compared to $10 for the domestic shirt. The American company wholesales the shirt to retailers for $15, who sell it for $30 (this is a designer T-shirt, of course). Thus, the company makes three times the profit on the import as on the domestic product, a premium that is the direct result of wage differentials. The same logic extends to other goods and services. To the extent that lower wages abroad put pressure on workers in the United States and other high-cost labor markets to accept lower pay, the "efficiency" of capital deployment will be increased, resulting in higher profits for companies and higher returns to shareholders. Relatively speaking, however, domestic workers will be worse off.

This could be a political hot potato. After all, people who work for wages in industrialized countries are also voters. If they were to become fully aware of this state of affairs, they might express their displeasure in the polling booth. But things are not so simple. Restoring the domestic production of goods and services would make them more expensive to buy. The lower cost of imported versus domestic goods not only is a boon to profits but also an implicit subsidy to consumers. Manufacturers lower their prices to big retailers—like Wal-Mart—in return for a higher sales volume, and retailers pass on some (but far from all) of their savings to consumers. Consequently, the consumer dollar "stretches farther," and the relative decline in wages is not felt so strongly.

Furthermore, with a few notable exceptions, it is a violation of WTO rules to impose trade barriers on imported items (and it is virtually impossible to block trade in services that can be provided through international communications networks). The treaties and agreements establishing the WTO and other international trade regimes severely limit the freedom of governments to restrict trade. Free trade does benefit developing countries. It permits producers to sell into rich, high-demand markets abroad as well as into domestic markets. In practice, however, capitalist markets are subject only to those kinds of rules and regulations that facilitate the flows of goods, services, and capital, while the domestic social and environmental costs of free trade and globalization are, for the most part, hardly addressed. Most countries do have laws and mechanisms addressing these costs, but they may be weakly enforced or even superceded by international rules. We look at this issue in greater detail when we discuss Chapter 11 of the North American Free Trade Agreement (see chapter 9).

Just as problematic for poor countries is the tendency of wealthy and powerful states to ignore free-trade rules when they are inconvenient. For example, several years ago the United States and the European Union became involved in a "banana war." The U.S.-based Chiquita Brands International (formerly United Fruit) grows bananas at very low cost on large plantations in Central and South America. During the early 1990s, anticipating growth and new markets in the EU, Eastern Europe, and the Soviet Union, the company bought large tracts of land to increase production. These "dollar" bananas are sold in the EU, but it is difficult for them to compete against bananas from small farms in former Caribbean colonies imported under preferential trade rules that were negotiated after decolonization. The EU defended these rules successfully, and, as a result, Chiquita and other U.S. companies suffered a "banana glut" that depressed prices. Chiquita pressured the Clinton administration to demand that the WTO declare the trade preferences illegal. The result would have been greater profits to Chiquita but a loss of livelihood for the small banana farmers in former European colonies. A settlement was reached in 2001, but it appears that a second banana war is in the offing, launched once again by big Central American producers.[36]

This problem extends beyond bananas. Both the United States and Europe restrict imports of agricultural goods from developing countries and offer domestic producers production and export subsidies that depress prices in international markets. These actions undermine small (and often lower-cost) operations. Developing countries lose once again.

Can such predation by big corporations and industrialized countries be stopped or prevented? Amartya Sen and others have proposed the notion of "fair trade."[37] As Sen puts it, "There needs to be a watchdog institution which is concerned with inequality and fair trade, [that] asks why the USA and Europe are so restrictive to products from the third world."[38] Fair trade should not only redress the legal and institutional barriers put up by the rich but also see that more of the profits generated in industrialized countries be repatriated to primary producers. While the prospects for such a watchdog institution seem dim at the present time, there are increasing numbers of organizations engaged in the direct importation of goods from producers in developing countries. Groups like Equal Exchange for coffee and Marketplace for textiles bypass the intermediary chains along which potential returns to producers are dissipated. Still, fair trade focuses on changing the distribution of income along the commodity chain, not on the particular organization of global capitalism that gives so much power to the rich and so little to the poor.

Where Are the People?

Where are the *people* in capitalism? Are they condemned to be passive consumers free to choose cereals, ties, and automobiles but compelled to accept low wages and poor working conditions, and to have no say in the kind of society they'd like to live in? Are there any strategies for restoring politics to market societies? Answering these questions requires a detour to consider the relationship of power to markets and politics and to discuss the role of people in those relationships.

The individual plays a dual role in capitalism—as a worker-producer and as a consumer. As we noted earlier, freedom in the market is limited to the freedom to choose from what is on offer with regard to where to work and what to buy. There are few opportunities available for a say in the organization of markets. To put the point another way, the individual might have a say in which bits of the pie she would like, and could even lobby to have her share of the pie increased, but she has little or no power to demand a different kind of pie or even some other dessert. The rules of the market were fixed long before we, as workers and consumers, came to it.

It is common to hear policy makers and economists bemoan political meddling in markets. If things were left to the free market to decide, they often chant, everything would turn out for the better. Politics makes markets inefficient; governments don't know how to invest; markets are natural because of the human propensity to truck and barter (in the words of Adam Smith). Such claims disregard the fact that today's markets are historically novel institutions and not at all "free."[39] They operate on the basis of rules and regulations that structure and organize exchange, specify what is permitted and what is forbidden, enforce contracts and guarantee a particular regime of property rights, and provide the stability and trust required for people unknown to each other to exchange goods and money.[40] Without politics, there might be exchange but probably not capitalism. What this means is that markets and capitalism are constructed institutions. They can be changed. The nation-state changed localized medieval economies to integrated national economies. Globalization changed the organization and structure of national and international markets over the past several decades, and it is possible to change them again, in other ways. But such change requires an assertion of the power to *decide*, and that, in turn, requires more politics, not less. It also depends on becoming politically aware of how power maintains the fiction that capitalist markets are natural. The claim that markets must remain outside of the sphere of politics rests on both discourse and practice, and these are part of the *reproduction* of social life. They are not fixed.

It is helpful to keep a few points in mind while thinking about such changes. Stopping globalization and global capitalism in their tracks is neither practical nor wise, but allowing globalization and global capitalism to continue along their current path is not a smart move either. Focused, collective action through politically aware social movements and organizations is essential. But the first step is political awareness. Where do things come from? How are they made? What is the history of their production—not only how they came to be produced, but how certain places are situated in the international division of labor? Who decides what is to be produced? How much—or how little—power do workers have? How are things and services sold? Why do people buy them? Why are so many people poor and lacking in basic necessities? What can be done about this state of affairs? Where do we begin? We return to these questions in the chapters that follow.

5

People and States

L'État, c'est moi!

—Louis XIV

"International relations" refers to how nation-states get along with one another. "World politics" reflects a more complicated perspective. Nation-states are still in the picture, but so are other corporate actors, such as firms and banks, labor unions and religious organizations, choral groups and theater companies, sports teams and terrorist cells, along with individual persons from the Dixie Chicks to the pope, all engaged in purposeful activities that constitute and shape our world. We'll begin this chapter by looking at states, the "big guns," and then we'll enlarge our viewpoint to consider "civil society." The objective is to examine some of the variety of actors and activities that constitute world politics.

States before Nation-States

Most people agree that all of the earth (with the exception—and maybe not for much longer—of Antarctica) is now divided into nation-states. The subject of states is complicated. The verdict is not in yet about what is and is not a "real" state, and exactly how nation-states are different from other kinds of states. Scholars continue to disagree over when nation-states first came about, how that happened, and what other kinds of agents are important enough to include when we talk about international relations.

Most contemporary notions of the state are taken from the history of modern Europe, that is, Europe since 1500. A defining characteristic of all states is territory. In addition to where a state is located on the planet, territory includes what that land contains in material, strategic, cultural, and psychological assets and, of course, people. But when we look at politics and organization, the nation-state seems to be something new. Although in reality national boundaries continue to shift, especially as the result of war, we imagine nation-states as being relatively more fixed as compared to premodern states and empires, and also more exclusive. When Mary Ann Tétreault was little, she and her sister liked to stand in the middle of the Peace Bridge with one foot in the United States and the other in Canada, a rare opportunity to be in two places at one time. Less than one hundred years ago, the U.S.-Canadian border was not so clearly marked physically or in people's minds. During the 1920s, some houses built in Derby Line, Vermont, were constructed to straddle the border, a great convenience to householders and their guests, who could find at least one room where they could drink alcohol legally despite Prohibition.

Our genealogy of the modern states-system is one story of how it took shape.[1] Imagine the international system today and compare it to Europe after the fall of Rome in 410 C.E. Then the emperor continued to reside in Constantinople, but political organization in Western Europe had fragmented into kingdoms ruled by victorious "barbarians," Germanic kings. Even so, the basic organization of European society and economy did not become Germanic but remained Roman. The kings were absolute rulers who enforced Roman law; the society was secular; the economy was organized around international trade based on the *dinarius* and other gold coins acceptable everywhere in the Mediterranean (and beyond).

The Muslim conquests that began in the mid-seventh century took Western Europe and Constantinople by surprise. Muslim forces were halted at Constantinople in the East and on the border between what now are France and Spain in the West. But wars and resistance took a terrible toll on the Roman Empire, dividing much of it into two distinctive political economies. The East remained cosmopolitan and wealthy, ruled by the emperor in Constantinople and protected by his powerful navy. Muslim Spain also retained its cosmopolitan character, although now it looked culturally to the Fertile Crescent rather than to Rome.[2] In Western Europe, beyond the reach of the emperor's naval power, the fight to keep Islam from spreading east of Spain was spearheaded by palace officials who parlayed their military conquests into claims to rule. These Carolingians and their Muslim foes looted and destroyed port cities, schools, and church properties. Without a protecting navy and the necessary shipping and banking infrastructure in port cities, trade ground to a halt in northern Europe. Literacy, which had been widespread, virtually disappeared, and Latin as a living language disappeared along with it. During these "Dark Ages," artifacts of Roman culture were preserved by Irish monks and also by clerics in Britain.

Political fragmentation in the West, along with the growing divergence between Rome and Constantinople, offered political opportunities to the Carolingians and to the pope, who, until this time, had been a mere bishop of a large city in an empire the ruler of which lived in an even larger and richer city very far away. Popes disagreed with emperors over dogma but found themselves liberated by the inability of the emperors to protect Rome militarily. The effective head of a church that remained the only unifying institution in the disintegrating West, the pope found allies in the Carolingian rulers, who struggled to create a new governing order. Each needed the other. The pope needed the military power of the kings, especially of Charlemagne, who united, however briefly, most of the West under his rule. The Carolingians needed the pope, who offered them the legitimacy they lacked as upstart overthrowers of the old order. The Carolingian Empire, or rather, the Empire of Charlemagne, was the scaffolding of the Middle Ages. The state on which it was founded was extremely weak and would presently crumble. But the empire would survive as the higher unity of Western Christendom.[3] Eventually, the position of Holy Roman Emperor became elective, but the pope remained an independent power in Western Europe.

When the Roman "state" crumbled, governance became highly local. The states were in effect the "estates" of various ruling landlords who also were warlords. Through conquest, they enslaved and enserfed the local population, while the vanished international economy gave them enormous power as the holders of the primary means of production, which was land. The sacking of port cities left inland towns with varying degrees of autonomy and different kinds of relations with the lords as sites of a highly localized commerce. In the absence of empire, effective political organization became localized, too, and the boundaries of these fragmented polities were highly fluid. During the Middle Ages, "states" were in effect the "estates" of the lords. Their boundaries were fluid. Estates could be divided up after the death of a ruler, as when the sons of Charlemagne's heir, Louis the Pious, struggled to resolve their sometimes violent conflict over who would get which parts of their father's realm. Medieval states also changed shape when their owners married or divorced. Eleanor of Aquitaine held title to a large territory in what is now France, which she brought as a dowry to her husband, King Louis VII of France. His concern about losing her property made him hesitate before divorcing her—rightfully so, because Eleanor married Henry II of England mere weeks after her marriage to Louis had been dissolved, transferring Aquitaine to the English king's control.[4] Occasionally kingdoms were reorganized when the king of one country was invited to rule another. James VI of Scotland became James I of England *and* Scotland after the English queen Elizabeth I died without leaving a child or sibling to take her place. Emperors sold off properties for ready cash well into the nineteenth century. Not only did Thomas Jefferson buy "Louisiana" from Napoleon in 1803, but U.S. secretary of state William Seward bought Alaska ("Seward's Ice-Box") from Czar Alexander II of Russia in 1868, during the presidency of Andrew Johnson.

Medieval and early-modern European rulers dreamed of recreating a European empire to rival empires in Asia, and each strove to preserve and extend his own wealth and power.[5] They engaged in almost constant warfare to seize more territory and defend what they had. European wars were frequent, ugly, and long. During the Hundred Years' War between England and France, thousands died in battle. Thousands more died as the result of the "normal" rape and pillage fighters felt entitled to indulge in. Armies lived off the countryside, supporting and amusing themselves with whatever they could find. "Free lances," knights for whom war was an opportunity to get rich and become famous, took captives and held them for ransom, sacked cities, and looted homes.[6] Population movements in war, as in trade, spread disease. Writing about the Hundred Years' War, part of which coincided with an epidemic of bubonic plague, Barbara Tuchman says that it defined the "calamitous fourteenth century" for all that it consolidated the power of French and English kings among their peers.[7]

Very much like President Hamid Karzai in post-Taliban Afghanistan, European rulers struggled to subordinate locally entrenched warlords to their authority. In Europe, it took centuries to bring large (and often remote) baronies under control. Aspiring centralizers had to fight rivals and resisters among their peers and offer superior services to win and hold the allegiance of the wider population. One of the most valuable services supplied by kings was "justice," or regularized procedures and institutions for resolving disputes and punishing criminals. Historian Joseph Strayer believes that the main magnet attracting loyal supporters to the developing English and French states was the development of formal legal institutions and the involvement of citizens in making them work.[8] Unlike China, where by that time courts were centralized and judges went out from the imperial capital to hear cases, medieval and early modern states in Europe had very little judicial—or any other kind of—capacity. Kings had to rely on local officials and assemblies to assess and collect taxes to support their wars.[9] Justices of the peace were local officials; they and juries helped to legitimate the decisions of the king's courts. Local residents could gauge the truthfulness of testimony against their own local knowledge, information that an outsider simply wouldn't have. The lack of medieval state capacity had positive value. As with jury verdicts, extensive local collaboration ensured that "state" policy would be seen as legitimate; having to accommodate local interests also acted as a check on kings.

Towns and cities were key elements of the later medieval order. Church and state officials tended to be located in reconstituted port cities, trading centers, and major towns, where industry, commerce, and the production of culture were primary activities of local populations. This is where artisan-crafted trade goods were produced and sold, along with domestic and imported luxuries like furs, jewels, and tapestries. Luxuries showed everyone, especially rivals and peers, how rich and important the buyers were. Medieval authority rested on performance and demeanor; obvious wealth, reflected in the ownership of impressive works of art, was a mark of power.[10] Historian Janet Abu-Lughod tells us that even the Mongol warrior Tamerlane "assembled artisans and craftsmen who . . . produced goods for a luxurious court life" in his capital city, Samarkand.[11]

Rulers could make life easy or difficult for merchants and artisans. Traders traveling to the medieval Champagne fairs were protected by the counts of Champagne and Brie. The counts guaranteed safe conduct for merchants on their way to and from the fair and sponsored a local system of dispute resolution and contract enforcement that "created a nonnatural monopoly for the fairs, which assured that they would be preferred to those held elsewhere under less attractive conditions."[12] After the French kings had succeeded in subordinating Champagne and Brie, the fair towns lost their ability to offer these services. French rulers harassed Flemish merchants and restricted access to the fairs by Italian merchants. This raised the cost of overland transport compared to water-borne commerce. The latter also benefited from new technology that expanded shipping from Genoa and Venice to North Sea ports in what are now Belgium and Holland. The Champagne fairs disappeared.

The Imperial Church

Before the Protestant Reformation, every European king also had to contend with another powerful rival to his authority. This was the Roman Catholic Church, a virtual empire that included all of "Christendom," the places throughout Europe where Roman Catholics lived. The symbiosis between the institutional church and kings forced kings to share power and authority with the clergy. Unlike relations between church and state in the Byzantine East, the relations between these two authorities in the west were soon marked by conflict.[13] The church was an "amphibious" actor, with bases on earth and "in heaven." The pope was an armed landlord, too, and depended on revenues from his estates (bishops also owned estates, and monasteries were little ecclesiastical kingdoms). The pope exercised imperial authority over moral standards and the salvation of souls throughout his heaven-conferred empire, over which he claimed the right to rule as God's "vicar," or representative on earth. Papal disapproval of lending at interest retarded the recovery of the economy in Western Europe and explains why Jews, who were not subject to church law, were such valued citizens as bankers and traders. Bishops were powerful in their own right. Some were entitled to vote in the selection of kings. They operated from cathedrals that were at least as impressive as the palaces of local lords, and, like those palaces, cathedrals were filled with art meant to convey the image of power to the viewer. The cathedral in Mainz, Germany, for example, has more statues and reliefs of bishops and archbishops than of kings, lords, and nonclerical saints.

The church's leverage over kings was exercised primarily through its imperial authority to offer or withhold the means to achieve eternal salvation. A ruler who displeased the church could find an "interdict" imposed on his territory; no one in it could be baptized, have a church wedding, or receive communion or last rites before death. Every Catholic believer in the community was thereby put in grave danger of going to hell for eternity, encouraging kings to stay in line to avoid this terrible punishment. Kings chafed under clerical restraint and gradually resorted to earthly weapons to kidnap, threaten, and even kill troublesome priests—and popes. As the Middle Ages waned, some kings became "protestants"—protesters—and heads or sponsors of national churches. Perhaps the most famous was Henry VIII of England, who retained the religious beliefs he had been taught as a child until the end of his life but saw breaking away from the authority of the Catholic Church as the only way to escape papal interference with his goal of having a legitimate son to inherit his kingdom.

Political scientists refer to this complicated, overlapping, and unstable configuration of territories and governance as a "heteronomous" system. By this they mean not only that it was complicated, overlapping, and unstable but also that its elements were not equivalent. A little like Heisenberg's electrons, elements even changed character depending on how they were observed. Medieval agents were far from functionally identical, and corporate identities were complicating factors. A vassal family of powerful knights might marry a daughter to a king and have sons in the church. Even after priestly celibacy became a convention of the Catholic Church in the eleventh century, powerful clerics had mistresses who bore children, some of whom became scholars, military leaders, artists, merchants—and popes. Who or what anybody or anyplace was depended on particular spaces of appearance. A bishop could be more powerful than a king, as Lothar II, king of Lotharingia (855–868), found out when he tried to divorce his wife. The local archbishop objected, forcing Lothar to go to Rome to beg for a dispensation from the pope, a fruitless trip that brought on the king's untimely death.[14]

The situational quality of heteronomy is important in theory and in practice. Heteronomy makes it impossible either to think of medieval "units of analysis" as interchangeable or to deploy them in relatively simple models like the balance-of-power theories we discussed in chapter 3. In practice, the multiple identities that heteronomy gave persons and territories made it difficult for anyone to domesticate them. Surveys, social security numbers, and birth certificates couldn't even be imagined—who would have issued them?

Becoming Modern

The transition to modernity is, in part, a transition to rationalized hierarchy headed by large institutions like states and corporations. Paradoxically, it also is a transition to greater equality, offering individuals more choices in their personal lives. Under the orchestration of nation-states and entrepreneurs, land gradually became privatized, bounded, bought, sold, taxed, and regulated; resources were counted, exploited, and taxed; people were counted, regulated and taxed; and, in the process, personal identities were reorganized and regimented.[15] Nationality—who belongs to which state—was created under international treaties during the nineteenth and early twentieth centuries and enforced by passports and immigration controls.[16] People were required to adopt and use family names. Birth certificates were issued, along with the other paperwork identifying each of us and where we belong. Even "national forests" were regimented: surveyed, logged, and then replanted in straight rows of uniform trees. These and the many other organizing policies of centralizing states made it easier for governments to count and manage their human and natural resources. Governments (the ministers in charge of the state, along with the bureaucracies that actually do the work) became larger and better able to penetrate, observe, and control. This transformation occurred as nation-states and the capitalist economy developed symbiotically to create the modern world. As we discuss more fully in chapter 7, the state also was "made" through war.

As hierarchical states developed, equality increased. This occurred as unruly elements of identity were taken out of the public sphere and privatized, leaving a larger range of life choices up to individuals. States often regulated the market for such choices but ceased making them directly. Consequently, economics and religion moved from the public to the private "sphere." What to wear and where to live, choices we think of today as nobody's business but our own, also were privatized, giving modern people greater individual freedom than their medieval counterparts. But all good things come at a cost. The expansion of individual choice comes at the expense of ready resources for collective action.

Individualism

Modern persons define many of their own "statuses," and, with sufficient resources, social mobility is not only possible but expected. We call this "individualism," but the term is paradoxical. On the one hand, it reflects the fact that within the limits of their resources, people choose for themselves what to believe; whether and whom to marry; where, for whom, and how hard to work. Individualism is the bedrock of liberalism, but, as we argued in the previous chapter, what can be chosen is limited, while the range of choice depends on one's resources. Indeed, gauging differences in resources is how we make distinctions among persons. Modern individuals no longer are defined by their families, where they were born, or hereditary occupations, but by how much money, education, and income they have. Consequently, most modern persons are liberal *and* social individuals.

On the other hand, individualism comes at the expense of lifetime membership in stable communities of obligation. We need communities because the social individual depends on networks of mutual support, but liberal individuals have to construct and maintain these networks pretty much on their own. The conflict between liberalization and the needs of social individuals is encapsulated in the difference between the abandoned spouses and throwaway kids who populate daytime TV, and the hired man in Robert Frost's poem who defines home as "the place where, when you have to go there, they have to take you in.''[17] Modern families can be as supportive as the idealized picture on *Leave It to Beaver* (or as unsupportive as on its satirical twin, *The Sopranos*), but individuals must make this happen without help from institutions like female subordination and lifetime employment, two linchpins of the medieval order that also are unspoken assumptions about the lifestyles depicted in these TV series.

One puzzle is how this radical new orientation emerged from the presumably closed medieval world. What we find is that this world was far from closed. Assumptions about gender relations are stood on their head by the evidence of powerful women and female-run communities, while social status generally was more fluid than we tend to think. Women found many ways to exercise authority, both individually, as property owners or ''saints,'' and collectively in convents, some of them parallel *poleis* housing educated and powerful women.[18] Knights were early ''secular'' individualists, younger sons and lower-class men whose ruthless talents in combat offered many ways to get money and rise in status. As shown by analyst Leo Braudy, the church domesticated knights materially, by channeling their activities away from Europe to the Crusades to capture Jerusalem, and ideologically, by promoting the heroic value system we call ''chivalry''; both helped to bring knights under religious, social, and political control.[19]

In contrast to the knights' marauder style of individualism, philosopher Isaiah Berlin suggests that individualism is based on individual rights to privacy—rights to choose for oneself. He sees individualism as arising from the rediscovery of classical civilization in the Renaissance and the assertions of morally responsible individuality that marked the Protestant Reformation.[20] The Enlightenment, which sought to replace superstition and tradition with science and reason, was the third major intellectual movement in European history that changed how people looked at themselves and their rights.

C. B. Macpherson weaves the revolutionary ideas of the Reformation into a story of economic, political, and philosophical developments that brought changes in values and institutions to Europe and made individualism—''negative liberty''—a social and political practice.[21] Negative liberty emphasizes the right of the individual to think and act for herself as long as her actions do not interfere with others' rights to do the same. Institutional expressions of negative liberty include markets and secularism, the two kinds of privatization we mentioned earlier in this chapter. The institutions and values most responsible for defining and establishing the rules for modernity are also those connected to the mutual construction of capitalism and the nation-sstate system.

Macpherson says that Hobbes and another seventeenth-century philosopher, John Locke, along with worker-activists such as the Levellers, changed our values by introducing the novel idea of ''possessive individualism.'' The hallmark of a society based on possessive individualism (a ''market society'') is the alienability of land and labor. This is a legal regime for dividing land into sellable parcels and people's bodies and skills into sellable services and making them private property. This makes both accumulation (the collection of wealth-producing assets by private individuals) and liberal—"market"—society possible. Market societies allow the relatively advantaged to deploy their superior resources to command superior gains. In market societies, economic activity is disconnected from particular persons and places, and is thereby "disembedded" from customary social constraints.[22]

Individualism naturally attracted people from social classes expecting to gain power and wealth from its acceptance. But it also attracted groups like the Levellers, whose members lost security but, in their view, gained morally and politically from its acceptance. The Levellers understood personal autonomy as a private property right, basing it on the idea that a free man owns himself. If you own yourself, you can decide whether to sell your labor and/or limited access to your body to a buyer who does not own you or have to be responsible for you as a person. Such "alienation of labor" is a basic requirement of capitalism. Without it, employers would have to house, feed, educate, and care for their workers. In a modern economy, workers must provide these things for themselves.

Although alienation of labor and commodification, which we discussed in previous chapters, detached the economy from the rest of social life, even highly privatized economies remain enmeshed in political and social structures. Businesses don't run schools for everyone's future employees or build roads to take everyone's goods to markets; banking systems and stock markets have to be regulated and supervised by the state to prevent market rigging and theft. If there were no laws against pollution, we'd all be choked by poison gases, liquids, and solid wastes generated by people and corporations that would not want to pay to dispose of them properly, no matter how much they injured others. Indeed, when you think about how many local, state, and federal agencies produce systems and services to support industry and agriculture, you can see why the modern "private" economy is far more dependent on the services of the state than the "traditional" economies it replaced.

Secularism and Sovereignty

A similar disembedding of religion from social life detaches religious authority and practice from political systems. The result is a secular society. Quasi-religious rituals (like saying the Pledge of Allegiance or singing "God Save the Queen") train citizens to venerate the state, while religion as such is protected by rights guarantees. In a secular state, citizens are not required to be religious at all, much less to be members of the ruler's religion of choice or to support any religious organizations with their taxes. These principles are set out explicitly in Thomas Jefferson's arguments for Virginia's 1779 statute for religious freedom. Jefferson and James Madison argued for even stronger religious freedoms than the First Amendment guarantees in the U.S. Constitution, not because they themselves were unreligious but because they believed that state support of religion would corrupt both religion and human reason.[23]

Secularization is a foundation of the modern state system because of its intimate connection to sovereignty. Sovereignty for a state is equivalent to individualism for a person. Individualism as negative liberty, the idea that my rights end a millimeter from your nose, has its counterpart in negative sovereignty. Most definitions of sovereignty start where we did earlier in this chapter, with the proposition that a nation-state is a bounded territory that preserves its autonomous existence through its own efforts. A state governs itself by creating rules and institutions that give the state and its agents a monopoly over the legitimate use of violence on its territory,[24] which is a major change from the past, when mercenaries and free lances could be hired by anyone to challenge someone else's right to rule.[25] Under these arrangements, states are responsible for protecting their populations from outside attacks and from domestic criminality and unrest. Mature states also supply populations with goods and services, like roads, health care, and airports, that are necessary for modern life. The obligations of sovereignty have interdependent internal and external dimensions. State capacity to keep the peace domestically depends in part on state capacity to defend against outsiders. State capacity to engage in cooperative relations with other states allows citizens to trade, travel, and invest safely overseas.

A state's right to do as it likes domestically is termed "negative sovereignty," an analogue to individualism that says a state can do whatever it wants as long as it doesn't interfere with another state. The rules and values that institutionalize negative sovereignty are among the strongest constituting the nation-states system,[26] yet there are limits to negative sovereignty in practice. The new U.S. national security strategy, which we discuss further in chapter 7, challenges it directly as a system norm. Even earlier, powerful states ignored negative sovereignty when they saw it as in their interests to intervene in the affairs of weaker states. Before the announcement of the new Bush Doctrine, however, few did this openly. Despite the real flaws in negative sovereignty (such as its use as a screen for human rights violations),[27] serious repercussions would result from its disappearance. Among the most important is a likely increase in the frequency of war.

"Positive sovereignty" refers to the legitimacy (authority and social support) a state can claim as an effective defender of domestic rights and provider of goods and services that ensure the general welfare. You will recall from chapter 1 that in *Leviathan*, Hobbes imagines that the State of Nature ends when a state and its subjects agree to a social contract that gives the ruler the right to make and enforce the law. This is Hobbes's image of domestic legitimacy. Another is the idea of popular sovereignty saying that states are the joint property of their citizens. The United States started out as a nation-state based on popular sovereignty. Its constitution begins with the words "We the people of the United States," not "The government of the United States" or even "The United States," to reflect that understanding. In older nation-states, as people struggled to win more rights from their rulers, they gradually converted their status as subjects into citizenship, while the originally artificial notion of social contract became identified with constitutions and laws guaranteeing rights and entitlements to citizens by virtue of their membership of the political community.[28] Today we envision legitimacy as the state's reward for protecting civil liberties and acting as a disinterested referee among equally protected citizen-competitors.

Negative sovereignty and secularism were parallel developments incorporated into the rules of the game governing relations among European states beginning in the seventeenth century. Negative sovereignty was a strategy to prevent kings from excusing their invasion of other states by saying that they just wanted to "save" religious minorities from persecution. The Treaty of Augsburg in 1555 instituted the doctrine of *cujus regio, eius religio*—in effect, whoever governs a country gets to pick its official religion. This principle defines religion as a purely domestic concern between a king and his subjects. Failure to live up to it led to the bloody Thirty Years' War, resolved in the treaties of Westphalia (1648), which reconfirmed secularism and negative sovereignty as constitutive principles.[29]

After 1648, secularism developed as a principle of domestic politics, too. When religion became less likely to cause wars, rulers were less likely to see religious (and other) minorities as potential traitors. Religious majorities were less compelled to convert religious minorities by force and no longer were permitted legally to terrorize or kill them. A growing sense of security led to laws requiring legal toleration and norms encouraging prudent politeness. Both made it easier for people to live together peacefully (most of the time). Religious toleration did not guarantee complete political equality where states had official religions and enforced laws in their favor. It did encourage removing religious dissent from the list of capital crimes and helped to shrink the scope of legal discrimination against religious minorities. Even so, some religious groups today—most notably Jews but also Roman Catholics, Muslims, Mormons, and others—continue to experience official and unofficial discrimination in various jurisdictions.

Secularism and the toleration it institutionalizes is "cosmopolitanism" at home. Together, secularism and toleration offer freedom to make personal life choices by discouraging the state (and the neighbors) from interfering. Yet they also increase the vulnerability of a society to corruption, in part because they reduce the authority of social structures, like the church, that worked with the state to enforce universal beliefs and standards of behavior. This problem invites new ways to think about sin and virtue.

We tend to equate corruption with sin, and this also was true in earlier times, when greed was regarded as a "deadly" sin and a source of spiritual corruption.[30] But when the Renaissance rediscovered the heroic values of antiquity, some people began to think that greed might not be so bad after all. Greed's character changed in their minds from a "passion," a sinful compulsion that should be resisted, to an "interest"—in this case, a rational desire for self-advancement. This change in meaning accompanied the acceptance of individualism and its emphasis on personal achievement, a kind of heroism, as a social value.

Yet excessive individualism could be oppressive. Royal "absolutists" like Louis XIV, whose identification of the state with himself is the epigraph beginning this chapter, measured their individual achievement by seizing more territory, taming barons and bishops, and acquiring the capacity to control their realms without local intermediaries in power-over terms. Both Protestant and Catholic kings asserted a divine right to rule. They appealed to businessmen-clients for financial support, offering in exchange protections (privileges) and tax relief (immunities) that strengthened new institutions associated with capitalism.[31] Religious dissidents protected by toleration often complained about overly powerful kings and their favored wealthy clients, but few argued that self-interest was bad. Many were businessmen themselves. Some believed that work was equivalent to a calling, and that making money in this world was a sign that they would be saved in the next.[32]

Personal achievement became a sign of virtue at the same time that power-seeking kings needed to be brought under control. This is how greed as self-interest became a political resource. Political theorists made distinctions between "rational interests" (which were OK) and "irrational passions" (which were not). A rational interest in profits might be used to counter an irrational passion for glory—make money, not war! (This is a sentiment that Kant would recognize.) By the eighteenth century, interests were seen as diffuse and multiple, able even to act as checks on one another, while commerce was touted as a more constructive mode of competition than warfare, domestically and internationally.

This conception of checks and balances was consciously imported into the structure of the state with the adoption of the U.S. Constitution in 1789. James Madison, writing in *Federalist 10*, identified competing interests as a brake on state power. He envisioned the legitimate state as one able to act as an impartial referee among competing interests. Similarly, the First Amendment to the U.S. Constitution (ratified in 1791, along with nine others spelling out citizens' rights and liberties) forbade both the establishment of a national religion and interference by the state in individual religious preferences and practice. While one could argue that the lack of state capacity in the new and diverse United States made a privatization strategy logical and necessary, Madison's (and Jefferson's) belief in the ability of people to make good judgments in constitutionally protected spaces of appearance also helped ensure that basic decisions about religion, along with commerce, would be left to individuals.

International System or International Society?

Checks and balances are integral to balance-of-power theories. What we've called "basic" balance-of-power is an eighteenth-century, power-over recipe for keeping any state from becoming so "corrupt" that it takes over the whole system. Balance-of-power envisions an anarchic environment in which nothing matters other than how many resources a set of actors, each seeking to dominate others and yet escape domination by them, can bring into play. It is what many people mean when they talk about the "international system."[33] A good thumbnail description would be "politics as physics."

"International society" is a power-with concept. We still are talking about states but in a different kind of rule-bound system. International society is not governed by "natural" laws but by rules that states determine collectively for themselves. The framework of international society is international law. Along with diplomacy, this includes written and unwritten conventions, treaties, customs, and rules that states use in their dealings with one another; international law also includes the institutions that states set up to enforce those rules, and the norms and values that give the international law regime shape and coherence. Negative sovereignty is a system norm, meaning that state autonomy is a value that states accept and support, even if they don't live up to it all the time. An interesting example is the recognition of the sovereignty of foreign embassies located inside another state; under the conventions of international law an embassy is a little piece of the country it represents. Refugees try to get into friendly embassies because governments rarely dare to ignore this sovereignty convention by sending their national police in after them.

International law also connects the nation-states system with capitalism. Much of international law comes out of treaties regulating economic relations between states. NAFTA (the North American Free Trade Agreement) and the WTO are modern examples of this strand of international law. When you think about these bodies, consider how they envision the various state participants: as equal parties. Every state is supposed to obey the same rules. The norm of sovereignty says that all sovereign states have equal sovereign rights and therefore are equally responsible for obeying the rules and equally entitled to the benefits of doing so (there are practical problems with this assumption that we explore in chapter 9). Each agreement outlines the terms of member access to one or more bodies authorized to resolve disputes under the rules, and describes conditions under which rule violators lose their equal access to the trade regime the treaty defines. Such arrangements make trade treaties "self-enforcing." Loss of equal access to international markets is a high price to pay for an illegitimate resort to power-over.

"But that is not all!" as the Cat in the Hat used to say. When you look at them more closely, you can see that these agreements aren't just *saying* that all states are equal. They are *requiring* them to be equal in important ways. States that belong to these organizations must harmonize their trade laws to conform to international standards outlined in the agreements. If a state subsidizes farmers who grow key crops or industries that are its economic and political mainstays, it has to end these protections because they are unfair to foreign competitors.

Fairness toward all is a good general principle, but problems arise when protections for workers are automatically defined as unfair under trade treaties. For example, under NAFTA, a state with environmental protection regulations that keep out foreign or domestic investors who want to construct polluting industries can be sued for damages by the foreign investor for infringing her right to make a profit (this is governed by NAFTA's infamous Chapter 11, a rule that we think should be changed—see chapter 9). Yet in spite of such drawbacks, membership in international trade regimes appeals to states at all levels of development. Nearly every state in the world wants to get into the WTO, while, in spite of the horrors of Chapter 11, the governments of most countries in Central and South America want NAFTA to be expanded to include them as well. The costs and benefits of membership may be unequal with regard to individual countries and different groups within each country, but the benefits they envision encourage governments and populations to accept these costs.

One example of this complex cost-benefit analysis comes from Kuwait, a rich oil-exporting country in the Persian Gulf where a diverse parliamentary coalition composed of Islamists (religious fundamentalists), economic neoliberals (market fundamentalists—we'll talk about market fundamentalism in chapter 9), and aspiring democratizers (political liberals) supports harmonizing Kuwait's laws with the provisions of the WTO. Kuwaiti Islamists, like the Puritans of early America, are businessmen who see the international economy as an avenue for religious renewal and economic freedom. Neoliberals, who may be secularists or Islamists, want to get the state out of the economy, a very big issue in a country where the state owns the largest industries and controls the vast majority of national income and wealth. WTO rules would make it harder for the Kuwaiti state to resist privatizing at least some of its holdings. Kuwaiti democratizers see the rules of the WTO, especially requirements that the state open its economy equally to all investors (including Kuwaitis) and conform to transparent accounting and trading rules designed to minimize corruption by eliminating the secrecy necessary for under-the-table deals, as the only way to get an authoritarian state under control (checks and balances again). Very different motivations lead these often bitterly opposed parliamentary factions to the same conclusion—that conforming to WTO rules would be good for Kuwaitis.[34]

Altered States

As international agreements proliferate, and transnational firms dominate more and more trade and investment worldwide, some people worry that states are losing authority, and some express these fears as opposition to globalization.[35] "Globalization" is a catchall term that describes a very large number of rapid changes whose overall effect is to connect people and resources more directly, making all of us more vulnerable to events happening beyond our control.[36] To some critics, globalization represents the end of the nation-state as the most powerful actor in world politics. They fear that corporations and banks are undermining the ability of states to serve their populations, and see other offshoots of globalization, like mercenary military forces and international terrorism, as direct threats to individual welfare. We'll discuss the economic and technical aspects of globalization further in chapter 9, and terrorism in chapter 7. Here we'll touch on some of the pathologies of contemporary states.

Positive sovereignty depends on state capacity. It is not merely authority but, just as much, a state's capacity to enforce that authority throughout its territory. As Robert Jackson points out, before WW II nation-states had to demonstrate capacity before their sovereignty was recognized by their peers. Decolonization created new nation-states that were formally independent. From the beginning, they enjoyed negative sovereignty as a reflection of new international values, whether they had demonstrated much capacity or not.[37] But many were only "quasi-states," with little in the way of positive sovereignty. They had unrepresentative governments, a legacy of divide-and-rule tactics adopted by colonial powers. Their leaders clung tightly to power because they had few internal grounds for exercising it. They sought benefits for themselves and members of their group rather than to serve the people as a whole. Where governments with positive sovereignty deficiencies controlled natural resources that were widely dispersed, warlords were tempted to seize them and use them to challenge the regime. An example is Charles Taylor, who seized control of diamond mines in his attempt to take over the government of Liberia, then held by another warlord, Samuel Doe. Other states with rich resources also started out with weak institutions, but if their leaders could claim legitimacy on other grounds, such as tradition or success on the battlefield, they could deploy those resources to build capacity and more popular support. Examples include the oil-exporting monarchies of the Persian Gulf.[38]

A poorly institutionalized state is little help for a ruler in trouble, because its many vulnerabilities offer protected spaces within which criminals and political entrepreneurs can operate in relative safety.[39] States that cannot control criminality or suppress rebellion are failed states. Some are the prey of warlords who try to capture and hold as much of the dying state as they can. Journalist Misha Glenny, an observer of the demise of the former Yugoslavia, calls such offspring of failed states "para-states."[40] Seizing choice morsels of the parent body, leaders of para-states are vicious heads of entourages that delight in inflicting violence. Some para-state leaders control substantial resources acquired from the dying/dead "parent" state. In the former Yugoslavia, for example, the Serb remnant inherited the bulk of the army and its weapons, giving the para-states of Serbia proper and the territory held by Serbs in Bosnia a military advantage over other fragments of the expiring country. Another example is Chechnya, still nominally part of the Russian Federation, where warlords acquired weapons from the collapsing Soviet military when the former Soviet Union became a failed state.

The inclusion of Yugoslavia and the Soviet Union in the ranks of failed states shows that this condition is not limited to Robert Jackson's postcolonial quasi-states. Any state can become a failed state if its institutions decay and it ceases to serve and protect its people. Any state can crumble into para-states if leaders are ruthless enough and followers vicious enough to kill as many people as stand in the way of their taking what they want. A failed state is a Hobbesian world; a para-state is even worse. Clea Koff writes:

> Why . . . [do] governments decide to murder their own people? . . . I think the answer is self-interest. Particular people in a government of a single ideology with effectively no political opponents have supported national institutions that maintain power for themselves. What muddied the waters were the "reasons" the decision makers gave for their political agendas. Take Kosovo: were the killings and expulsions in the 1990s really meant to avenge the Battle of 1389, as Serbian president Slobodan Milosevic was fond of stating? Or was it because mineral-rich parts of Kosovo can produce up to $5 billion in annual export income for Serbia? Or take Rwanda: did Hutus kill their neighbors *and* all their neighbors' children simply because they were Tutsi, as the government exhorted them to do? Or was it because the government promised Hutus their neighbors' farmland, land that otherwise could only have been inherited by those very children, and those children's children, ad infinitum?[41]

Are States an Endangered Species?

All states impose burdens on citizens, and any state can fail, imposing even larger ones on both citizens and the neighbors. Critics of Anglo-American capitalism charge corporations and banks with taking resources needed by states to protect and provide, arguing that globalization is a process that creates failed states. Some speculate that globalization might be ending the era of the nation-state as the most powerful actor in world politics. For critics of capitalism who also are critics of states, this presents a dilemma: failed states show us a world no one wants to live in, yet states with capacity also can be oppressive and dangerous. Another school of critics is more positive. Whatever else globalization is doing, they say, it also is expanding civil society, individuals and groups operating at home and in the world to exercise checks on states as well as on one another. As potential and actual sources of community involvement in collective human destinies, they are integral elements of "the international community"—states, firms, groups, and persons, all of whom embrace cosmopolitanism as a way of life. This view of civil society is most common in Anglo-American communities and, to a lesser degree, elsewhere in the West.[42]

As we noted earlier, one of the two primary strands in the history of oppositional civil society is religious. Religious activists defied power holders, directing their critiques against established churches and absolutist states. Some also rejected cosmopolitanism and toleration as subversive values that undermine faith and virtue. Similar patterns can be found among contemporary religious movements. The other main thread of opposition to the absolutist state is economic and cosmopolitan, based on the experiences of long-distance trade and led by business interests seeking protection and rights. Today's economic activists are similar to their predecessors, too. Among the demands of both kinds of oppositional movements then and now is that the state recognize whole categories of activities—religious beliefs and practices, business organizations and decisions—as private matters rather than public—that is, state—concerns. Unlike the frontispiece of Hobbes's *Leviathan*, where the king is "the" person signifying the state and his subjects are merely little corpuscles inside his body (but not his head), opposition movements demand rights to "bodies"—and "heads"—of their own, as individuals and as members of nonstate collectivities.

Institutions of domestic civil society—churches, firms, banks, and a wide array of voluntary associations like the Red Cross and the YWCA—are venues organized by citizens to assert and pursue their interests. It is not surprising that business and religious groups have been prominent in oppositional civil societies for so long. Medieval businessmen were clients of kings, but this relationship always included some antagonism. You will recall that traders depended on rulers for safe passage to and from the Champagne fairs. When Champagne and Brie were absorbed into France, traders not only were not protected but were actually harassed and harmed. Another example consists in those among the artisans enriching the quality of life in Samarkand who had been kidnapped and brought there by force rather than coming on their own. Kings routinely borrowed money from wealthy clients, and, especially before government bonds became formalized through parliaments and investment regimes, they just as routinely defaulted on their loans.[43] Organizing to protect themselves against bad behavior by rulers was a perfectly reasonable response by traders and bankers to the risks of doing business in and with states.

Religious groups challenged states from a different framework of interests, mostly by objecting to encroachments on the authority of religious leaders but sometimes in response to the persecution of individuals. They had an advantage over business groups because they could claim divine protection, just as kings claimed a divine right to rule. Religious leaders were more dangerous to rulers than business leaders. They were personalities in their own right, and some—think of John Calvin and Martin Luther—were a lot more popular than many kings. They challenged the legitimacy of states through negative portrayals, like Saint Augustine's description of a corrupt Roman empire in *The City of God*, and positive examples of enlightened rule, such as the government Mohammad established under his leadership in Medina, which attracted adherents from elsewhere on the Arabian Peninsula, including from among Mohammad's former opponents. Continuing a tradition of "godly governance" going back to Moses, John Calvin set up a religious utopia in Geneva, while many of the early settlers in North America crossed the Atlantic hoping to found communities that would approximate the kingdom of God on earth. John Winthrop's career epitomizes the dual forces of religion and business as foundations of civil society.

Winthrop led the group of settlers who came from England in 1630 to establish a trading company in Massachusetts. The charter of the Massachusetts Bay Company authorized its stockholders (called "freemen") to elect a governor and other Company officials every year. The Company was not allowed to make laws that did not conform to the laws of England, but otherwise there were few restrictions on its procedures.

> [T]he stockholders, taking advantage of the omission in the charter of any specified meeting place, carried the Company lock, stock, and barrel to Massachusetts Bay, where they turned the charter into the constitution of the colony and opened freemanship, without any requirement to purchase stock, to all free adult males belonging to a Congregational church.[44]

As historian Edmund Morgan observes, this was a revolution that created a republic on the other side of the Atlantic, one whose governing principles were greatly at odds with those of the "mother country" the colonizing freemen had left behind. The Company charter required annual popular elections for what effectively were political leaders, and, as amended, it made populist churches the cradles of citizenship. The risks from such acts of independence were not lost on Winthrop, who served as the governor of Massachusetts Bay during most of its early history. During those years he tried to convince freemen to make as few laws as possible at their quarterly meetings so the king and his advisors might not notice that they were doing things that were "repugnant to the laws of England."[45] But the colonists demanded their democratic rights under the charter, insisting that the rule of law rather than the will of their governor apply in Massachusetts. The freemen prevailed (especially during a three-year period when Winthrop was not the colony's governor), and it is not surprising that the authorities back in England soon noticed the revolutionary nature of the Massachusetts experiment. Eventually, though not in Winthrop's lifetime, the king took the government of Massachusetts away from the freemen.

The Massachusetts Bay Colony highlights how the interests of religion and business served as dual foundations for civil society around the world. From the religious perspective, the colonists were idealists fighting for justice and righteousness. Idealism was the wellspring of their energy and determination to make new lives in the "New World." But the freemen also were stubborn and intolerant. They were hardheaded, insisting on making laws even though they knew it could get them in trouble with the king. They also were hard-hearted. Minority zealots were willing to fight to the last breath against the majority, which, equally zealous, was quick to punish doctrinal nonconformity. The majority banished dissenters like Roger Williams, who left to found his own colony of Rhode Island and Providence Plantations, and Anne Hutchinson, whose eviction led to her death at the hands of the native peoples the colonists were dispossessing.

Yet the colony also was democratic and rule bound. Its procedures were set out in a contract that not only specified "stockholder" rights but also community institutions—a governor and a "general court" composed of all the freemen meeting quarterly to make the laws for the Company. (It was this right, to make the laws that governed their lives and activities, that the freemen refused to give up, even though by insisting on the letter of that right they jeopardized and eventually lost it.) The contract was a constitution and in its form and operation can be seen as a direct precursor of the national compacts of modern states. Constitutions are contracts that limit the reach of governments. Unlike the Massachusetts Bay Company Charter, most constitutions offer at least limited protection to dissenters and nonconformists. It is the contract as a product of political action, rather than religious ideals, that constitutes the primary structure of regimes of toleration, making cosmopolitan life—plurality—possible.

Possible, but not guaranteed, which is why civil society is as important now as then, and why it extends beyond religious dissidents and corporations to embrace other groups, including some organized across national boundaries. The Puritans' ideas about freedom and equality traveled from England to Massachusetts and Rhode Island and back to England, where they underpinned the first-ever modernizing revolution in the mid-seventeenth century.[46] Calvin's Geneva experiment attracted the attention of philosophers whose ideas contributed to two eighteenth-century revolutions, the first in British North America and the second in France. As Alex Colás has observed, ideas of freedom and the often small but always enthusiastic groups that spread them were integral to the success of people seeking to establish representative governments during the early modern period.[47]

In chapter 3, we saw contemporary evidence that civil society in this sense is alive and well. Jiřina Šiklová and Martin Luther King organized with like-minded partners to stand against authoritarian regimes and unjust legal systems. These and other activists are prominent in the global fight for human rights. Just as in the seventeenth century, civil society groups promoting human rights are organized across political boundaries. Human Rights Watch, Médecins sans frontières (MSF—Doctors without Borders), and Amnesty International are full of individuals committed to exposing rights violations and mobilizing international pressure to make them stop.[48] With nonstate corporate actors like the Catholic Church and ad hoc groups such as Let Freedom Ring, human rights activists organized a series of demonstrations against human rights violations by the Chinese government during the 1997 visit of Chinese president Jiang Zemin to the United States. Human rights activists have saved millions indirectly through their lobbying and publicity campaigns, and hundreds of thousands directly through aid projects that, for groups like MSF, also provide the entrée for observing conditions on the ground.

Analysts differ on how important human rights elements in international civil society are today, especially since the terrorist attacks on the United States in September 2001. Michael Ignatieff asked in 2002, "Why criticize Russia's war against Chechnya when Chechen jihadis are fighting America in the mountains of Afghanistan"?[49] One year later, the U.S. military asked a similar question—why criticize terrorist groups like the Mujahideen-e-Khalq Organization (MKO) when it is attacking Iranians, residents of another "axis of evil" power?

Indeed, U.S. military leaders in Iraq signed a cease-fire agreement with the
MKO in April 2003 that allowed it to keep all its weapons, including hundreds
of tanks and thousands of light arms, just as long as it did not attack U.S.
forces.[50] The United States was publicly embarrassed and renounced this agreement a few weeks later, showing some remaining effectiveness on the part of
human rights activists in a post-9/11 world. Even so, Ignatieff's question is
reflected in how much human rights worldwide have been diminished since
then, including in the United States, and how little the United States has done
to rein in the MKO despite the U.S. show of responding to human rights concerns.

If idealistic human rights activists are on the defensive around the world,
where is civil society's strength, and is it enough to challenge state power effectively? This can be answered by going back to the source—religious and business interests. We examine the activities of some contemporary religious
activists in greater detail in chapter 9, but here we'd like to note a few reactions
to the dominance of business in civil society, nationally and internationally.

The prominence of businesspeople and business groups in civil society
reflects their superior social and economic resources. Yet the record of these
actors as promoters of human rights is ambiguous, as is their effectiveness in
promoting the economic development they themselves tout as their contribu-
tion to human society around the world. Indeed, statistics show that a majority
of people living in low-capacity states that rely primarily on "the market" for
"development" have experienced little, if any, of its promised benefits,[51] while
we all live in societies where the growing power of business has led to increasing inequality and the destruction of traditional institutions.[52] Large corporations, with governments' blessings, invest in impoverished areas, taking
advantage of cheap labor to produce goods for rich countries' markets. But as
we showed in chapter 4, that a country is rich does not mean that its people are.
The migration of manufacturing is just another way to describe the migration of
jobs. Michael Moore's 1989 documentary *Roger and Me* is an often horrifying
snapshot of how outsourcing automobile production from the United States to
Mexico devastated one small U.S. city.

The dominance of business interests in civil society carries other risks. In
the United States, pro-democracy Republicans and Democrats in Congress call
this dominance both a cause and an effect of political and economic corruption
and have struggled for years to limit contributions to electoral campaigns. Even
more troubling is the impact of business dominance on democracy itself. Analyst Kevin Phillips sees wealth becoming more and more of a substitute for the
human resources that voters represent to politicians.[53] Especially when voter
turnout is low, politicians can get what they need to be (re)elected by serving
the interests of a few large donors rather than having to accommodate the
many interests of the electorate as a whole. The result is crowding out—the
wealthy few have direct access to decision makers who depend on their lar-
gesse, while the middle-income many can't get in to see the officials making
decisions that could affect their whole lives.[54]

Another question is whether civil society itself is democratic. To answer that we need to look inside civil society groups and also at their behavior as part of larger political systems. Inside, we know that many such groups are not democratic at all. Quite a few churches and most businesses are like little kingdoms, bureaucratic hierarchies ruled by clerics and CEOs who are checked only by government and market forces.[55] Civil society organizations also are exclusive—you had to belong to a Congregational church to vote in the Massachusetts Bay Colony, just as you must belong to the Sierra Club or the National Association of Broadcasters to vote in these groups. Exclusivity limits democracy outside, too. Civil society organizations work for the interests of their members, which means they often work against the interests of nonmembers. The U.S. Chamber of Commerce opposes unionization and other movements for workers' rights; the Ku Klux Klan opposes the rights of nonwhites, along with Catholics, Jews, and other groups the Klan calls "anti-American." Insofar as civil society groups are parts of a larger system of checks and balances, one that is regulated by a higher authority (so that business owners can't shoot union organizers, and vice versa, and the Klan can't burn down people's houses or lynch people they disagree with), this self-centeredness is fine. But without an authority to make and enforce "rules of engagement," "civil society" is just another term for "vigilantes."

States and Their Rivals

The nation-state today is far stronger and commands more resources than its medieval predecessors. Even so, individuals and groups still manage to challenge state authority with some success. Human rights activists bring state crimes into public view and mobilize large international coalitions to apply political and economic pressure to offending governments. Economic agents supply investment, trade, and jobs that improve the lives of many, and use their clout to gain advantageous positions in the undeveloped economies of weak states. Just like the Puritans, today's militant religious activists defy states in the name of God, often in causes many see as just.

A trend that is gaining attention as a result of the Iraq war is the growing involvement of private corporations in organized violence. Preinvasion studies of these "new mercenaries" accepted too readily the flawed neoclassical argument that mercenary forces are inherently cheaper than military organizations maintained by states (they aren't); they did identify moral issues arising from creating an industry whose interests lie in perpetual war.[56] A serious problem in a world where only states are bound by international law is the difficulty of controlling private military forces. One example is the decision of four contractors working in Iraq to save time by driving through Falluja against military orders. That cost all four their lives and touched off a major wave of violence that two Marine battalions were needed to subdue. Another example is the role of contractors in torturing prisoners at Abu Ghraib.[57]

Mercenaries play both/all sides of a conflict in their search for profits, and much of what they do is criminal—they are neither subject to nor protected by the rules of war. Consequently, whether they take their skills into wars or criminal enterprises like the drug trade or human trafficking, mercenaries enjoy substantial impunity.[58] Perhaps the greatest danger from the return of mercenaries to so many enterprises of violence in the world today is that it refutes the state's claim to be the only legitimate wielder of force. When states themselves go to the market to buy mercenary services and enter into treaties (make contracts) with terrorist—freelance—organizations, they dissipate their own legitimacy.

These new trends make the study of civil society even more complicated than it was in the past. Nearly all the elements of modern civil society are regulated by states, just as the Massachusetts Bay Company ultimately was regulated by the king of England. Yet the actions of John Winthrop and the other freemen show that determined individuals and groups can challenge a powerful state directly and undermine its authority over the long term. Also, while it is true that the expansion of human rights in the New World through the American revolution—and the U.S. Constitution—arose directly from actions taken by the freemen of the Massachusetts Bay Company, other actions by the colonists violated human rights. They took the lands and lives of the native peoples they found in Massachusetts,[59] viewing them as outside of their communities of obligation and therefore as exploitable and expendable. Colonists banished fellow freemen even though they knew that ejecting dissenters from the community would deprive the exiles of their property and expose them to mortal danger. To argue that civil society in any era is either a benign or a malignant force is simplistic. Like states, civil society can be good or bad depending on what it does.

The civil society debate is a symptom of a much larger change in how we view world politics. It represents a different vision of the distribution of power and authority than leaders and citizens in the developed countries at the top of the global food chain are used to. Unlike modern assumptions that place the state at the center of world politics, the postmodern thrust of the civil society debate counts nonstate allies and opponents of states as autonomous international agents. This debate and the events that produced it are signs that the heteronomy that made the medieval world so interesting and so difficult to control is not a thing of the past but a characteristic of the present and, perhaps even more so, of the future.

6

People and Borders

Mr. Bush promised, as his father once did, to draw a line in the sand. But how do you draw a line in a maze?

—Maureen Dowd

Borders are lines that divide. They separate things from one another (especially countries) and keep things together (especially people). Sometimes borders are easy to cross. At other times, they are impossible to cross. This seems odd, for the borders that divide countries and people are largely imagined. Oh, sometimes they follow rivers or mountains, but there is nothing inherent in geography that says "here" and not "there." Borders are social constructions. Human beings draw them and, having done so, regard them as "natural" features of the landscape. Borders are imaginary and could be anywhere, but they have real effects: border crossings, fences, barbed wire, guns, mines, "Your passport, please."

This chapter is about the lines that divide us and contain us. We begin with a discussion of what borders do—that is, what social function they perform. In the second part of the chapter we examine how borders come into existence, especially between countries. How is it that lines are drawn where formerly there were none? After that, we consider how borders in politics contain and connect while imposing separations between what is recognized as political activity and what is not. In the fourth part of the chapter, we look at what might be called the "in-between spaces": frontiers, borderlands, limnality, what the Greeks called *metaxu*. Finally, we ask whether borders should be regarded not as demarcating the safe from the dangerous but rather as lines that make possible both pluralism and diversity. In this sense, they are more about connections than separation.

What Is a Border?

Borders are everywhere. They tell who is "in" and who is "out." They divide places, separate people, and sometimes appear where there were no borders before (occasionally, they disappear, too). Cyprus, for example, is divided by a "Green Line" that runs through the capital city of Nicosia. On one side of the lines are Turkish Cypriots, on the other side Greek Cypriots. The border has been there for almost thirty years. Before the line was drawn, Turkish and Greek Cypriots intermingled peacefully and lived next to one another; since then, they have been separated and more or less at odds. That pattern can be found the world over: a line is drawn on the ground, and people on either side are kept apart.

But why are there so many borders? Who draws them? Why are they in the places where they are? Can they be changed? And what happens when they do change? At a very early age, children learn about borders and difference, when they discover who belongs to their household and who does not; who is family and who is not; who can be trusted and who cannot. Borders are as much about order within as disorder without. As the child grows older, she discovers that borders are fundamental to an ordered and disciplined social life. They are central to the maintenance of social institutions and the consent we give to them. Revisiting Hobbes, the sovereign rules inside; no one rules outside.

At one time or another, we become conscious of these invisible lines that divide some people from others, snaking through neighborhoods, schools, towns, religions, races, ethnicities, income groups, and classes. Crossing such lines can be socially difficult, if not physically impossible. Sometimes such crossings are deadly. Think of Shakespeare's *Romeo and Juliet*, of the war between the Capulets and Montagues, of the very thin line that divides virtually identical families.

Those who cross such lines do so at their own risk. The risk could be to life and limb, but more often it is to "belonging." If people outside the border seem different from those inside, then those inside must be the same (or, at least, similar to one another). Sameness extends beyond appearances; it also includes beliefs and practices. Indeed, beliefs and practices are more important than appearances—the antagonists in *Romeo and Juliet* are identical to each other except in what Sigmund Freud calls "the narcissism of small differences." Each believes that his house is the greater, even though the houses hardly differ at all. Romeo and Juliet cross the line, finding their differences so minor that they don't matter but, trying to defy convention, lose their lives.

Sameness becomes a refuge, a "source of help, relief, and comfort," as the dictionary puts it. Sameness helps to produce an individual's identity, providing a pattern for behavior that identifies a person as belonging to one group and not another. The in-group is differentiated from all other groups, and the reenactment and reproduction of in-group patterns becomes instrumental to the maintenance of difference. Group members are admonished if they deviate from them and are punished if they do so consistently.

Thus, if someone dares to cross a border defined as inviolate and returns without injury, that very act of crossing becomes a threat to group identity and cohesion. It demonstrates that crossing is possible, even at considerable risk, and that the beliefs and practices on the "other side" are not so all-corrupting and dangerous that they cannot be tolerated. By the same token, however, if someone dares to cross and does not return, that act reinforces the necessity of maintaining the border. Having "gone over" the line, that person has also "gone over" to those across the line.

Ultimately, the very existence of that imagined line serves to keep some in and others out. Group members discipline themselves; they do not need someone to threaten them in order to stay in line. They act in prescribed and expected manners so as not to be named a threat to group identity and cohesiveness. Violators are punished, marginalized, or even ejected from the group. In earlier times, such a fate could be tantamount to a death sentence; today, it may have devastating psychological results. We seek solace and security in groups, it would seem, and to be a member of no group is to lose that sense of safety and belonging.[1]

Think about the borders in your life, about the beliefs and practices that separate your in-group from others. As a student, you might be regarded with disdain by "townies," and you might return the feelings. Does your college compete in sports with some other school nearby? Is the rivalry an intense one? Do you take care to not to wear the "wrong" colors on the day of the Big Game? What happens if you do? Now consider how those differences are magnified and reinforced between countries, in language, in customs, in appearances, in practices. Make a list of those differences and try to explain why they matter.

You will discover that they do not matter, yet they make all the difference.

A Short Genealogy of Borders

The primordial border must have been one that divided kin groups from one another, a line inscribed in lineage and blood. Kin groups are communities, and although they might have shared a language and culture with other groups nearby, and traded and intermarried among groups, kinship corresponded to territory and survival. Many societies had elaborate systems for categorizing kin and nonkin, and complicated rules about who could marry whom. The effect was to maintain and reinforce distinction. In some societies even today, the marriage of a son or daughter into another kin group could mean his or her permanent departure from the natal community.

Eventually, some parts of the world started getting crowded relative to available land, and villagers found they needed to mark the boundaries of their community of obligation more carefully. People inside the community were entitled to food, protection, and respect, while those outside did not share these entitlements. Yet the borders of kin-based communities were fluid, expanding when resources were plentiful or new members appeared who could offer valued services, then shrinking in times of shortages and stress.[2] Today, citizenship defines similar communities of obligation

Over time, as cities, kingdoms, and empires emerged, borders came to signify rule and to distinguish among centers of power: on this side, my king; on that side, your king. Rulers took food, taxes, and labor from those who lived on their side of the border, and these extractions were used, in turn, to maintain power. Between the centers of power and the lands they governed were "borderlands," frontiers, zones where control was never complete and often changed hands. We shall return to the topic of borderlands later in this chapter.

Many of the borders between modern-day countries are a consequence of what we might call "historical accidents"; others are the result of the types of primordial kinship practices described above and in chapter 5. Rulers sought to build alliances and expand their territories through marriages between families. In some cases, one king or queen ruled over widely separated bits and pieces of land, but all were subsumed under the same center of power.

Such alliances were rarely stable, and lines of succession were often in dispute. In Europe, the result was centuries of war leading to the further division of some territories and the unification of others. In Central Europe as late as the end of the seventeenth century, there were still something like five hundred German states; France, by contrast, had been welded together from more than a dozen formerly independent territories. It was not until the final few decades of the twentieth century that most of the world's borders were firmly fixed, and, even now, some remain in dispute, and a few have yet to be drawn.

Oddly, however, borders did not become barriers until the twentieth century. Before then, it was relatively easy to cross them without much in the way of official restrictions. The passport did not come into general use until the turn of the twentieth century, and many countries were indifferent to migration across borders for many years after. There were several reasons for the change to a more vigorous policing of borders.

First, until late in the nineteenth century, most countries were overwhelmingly rural. Industrialization in Europe and other parts of the world, and the privatization of commons, pushed people off the land and into growing cities. Cities were the places where uprisings and revolutions began. Rulers became concerned about who was living in the cities they governed, where they came from, what they did, and the ideas they held.

Second, growing involvement by the state in the management of the national economy—for both growth and defense—and the provision of social welfare created the need for more information about who lived where, their socioeconomic status, their ability to pay taxes, and their needs for social service.[3] Governments became concerned about the demographics of the people living within their jurisdictions, and this led to further measures to control flows into and out of countries.

Third, mass migration, especially to the New World, expanded dramati-

cally during the nineteenth century.⁴ Millions of people left Europe due to famine, oppression, and war. This altered the demographics of sending and
receiving countries and introduced new languages, practices, and ideas, especially into receiving countries. By the 1920s, most states had installed rigorous
immigration controls that limited the number of new arrivals and required that
they meet certain specifications regarding their health, wealth, and intelligence.
States began demanding passports, visas, and all the other paraphernalia of
border crossing. After World War II, with its displacement of millions throughout Europe and Asia, movements across borders at first increased and then
slackened as the borders of both new and old states crystallized under the
pressures of the cold war. But this, too, was a short-lived phenomenon.

By the last decade of the twentieth century, the obsession with national
borders had been overtaken by their gradual diminution under the pressures
of globalization. It began to seem as though goods, capital, environmental pollution, diseases, refugees and migrants, drugs, guns, culture, and ideas could
all cross borders without much restriction. The European Union and other
regional organizations, such as the Gulf Cooperation Council, became more
open internally. Nationalist claims to exclusive rights over territories and people were seen by many as a bane of human civilization; their harmful effects
were evident in the civil and social wars in ex-Yugoslavia, Central Asia, the
Middle East, and Africa. Some pronounced "the end of the nation-state,"
although the evidence supporting this claim remains rather thin.

The Borders Outside

At the same time that national borders seem to be losing their power to contain
and exclude, new borders are being drawn everywhere. These, however, are not
lines on the ground; rather, they are lines in the mind. Anthropologist Benedict
Anderson wrote a book about nationalism with the title *Imagined Communities*.⁵
During the last decade of the twentieth century, such communities proliferated.
Scholars named this unexpected phenomenon "identity politics." Identity-
based groups drew borders between themselves and others. Sometimes these
borders differentiated on the basis of ethnicity and at other times on the basis
of lifestyle and cultural practices. We will return to this topic below.

The attacks on New York and Washington on September 11, 2001, appear
to have reinvigorated the status of national borders. There is much more scrutiny of who is in and who is out, who is trying to enter, where she comes from,
and what she might wish to do. The American state, in particular, is seeking to
reinforce its borders without obstructing economic flows into and out of the
United States. The results are rather surprising.

In one sense, the United States no longer has real borders. This is the case
not because lines on the ground are not policed and protected, but because
America's presence, and its interests, are so pervasive in so many parts of the
world. Despite the economic downturn and decline in stock prices that began

in 2001, America's economy remains the largest in the world. U.S. corporations have subsidiaries and strategic allies in all parts of the globe. According to Chalmers Johnson, the U.S. Defense Department "acknowledges some 725" bases around the world, outside of the United States.[6] U.S. culture, products, and influence have colonized many places, even those where the presence of American corporations and citizens is invisible or absent.

Borders serve, more and more, to separate *classes* of people rather than *nationalities*. The wealthy have no problem crossing borders; they and their money are welcome everywhere. Criminals with sufficient funds are also able to cross borders without too much trouble; for the right price, they usually can acquire the necessary identity documents. Only those without money and power find borders to constitute a significant barrier to movement; and they are far likelier to be subject to search and arrest by the states whose borders they have crossed.

But the poor usually discover that there are as many, if not more, borders within the societies in which they live. Economic stratification makes the well-off and the poor strangers to each nother. The rich of different countries find they have more in common with one another than with their impoverished conationals. The poor discover that, even though they live in the same social space as the wealthy, they are denied access to many places within that space.

Such denial is effected in many different ways. Sometimes there are physical barriers, such as the gates and fences that encircle a growing number of communities. Often there are guards, police, and cameras keeping an eye on who is present in what quarters. Those who are deemed to be "out of place" can find themselves hustled back whence they came. At other times restrictions are imposed through appearance, dress, manners, practices, and possessions— such as cars. Many such borders are not there in any visible sense; people simply "know" where they can go and where they cannot, what they can do and what is forbidden.

The Borders Inside

Not all borders keep people apart; many keep them together. First, as we saw above, borders contain nations within the spaces we call "nation-states." Of course, there are very few true nation-states in the world, that is, states whose populations include only one nationality.[7] Even in the most ethnically pure states, very visible borders are drawn between people grouped by class, race, and various markers of ethnicity (such as religion). Second, there are very distinct borders between what is accepted as political and "public" and what is nonpolitical and "private." This second type of internal border helps both state and society to maintain order and stability. Third, there are borders within which we are socialized as both children and adults, lines that both connect and divide in everyday life, such those drawn between bodies and genders.

Internal Borders

Prior to the creation of today's nation-states, much of the world was divided into empires or protostates made up of inherited properties. Each had at its core a dynasty that supplied the head of state and chose the allies and advisors who made up the ruling class. Other interests allied themselves with the rulers and constituted one or more elites.[8] Inhabitants of cities, towns, and other territories were subordinated to varying degrees to the rulers of these territories. Nationalism proved to be a potent force for maintaining cohesion among the peoples of multinational empires.[9] But it meant little to individuals and groups who aspired to their own seats of power and populations resistant to cultural assimilation. In the last half of the twentieth century, most of the colonies of European powers were granted independence as autonomous nation-states. Near the end of the century the last large empire in Europe, the Soviet Union, dissolved; the binational state of Czechoslovakia separated peacefully into two independent states; and Yugoslavia, a multinational state plagued by both power seekers and religious minorities seeking dominant status, divided into a set of secessionist daughter states and warring para-states.

Despite the "ethnic cleansing" marking the redrawing of state boundaries in Europe, few nation-states, old or new, are ethnically homogenous. Quasi-state borders were products of imperial history, drawn according to criteria that had no relationship to where people actually lived or to whom they might be related. Some tribal and ethnic groups were combined into one country; others found themselves residing in and even in control of more than one. In Africa especially, the borders of postcolonial states were sacrosanct under decolonization agreements.[10] Almost everywhere, state borders cannot be changed except through war or internationally recognized secession.

As we noted in chapter 5, among the legacies of imperialism is that, in many new states, one ethnic group was granted or acquired power at independence, after which it ruled the state as its own nation. Which group was left in charge was a result of the administrative policies of the imperial power. The result was that people from other groups were left at great disadvantage, not only because they were shut out of political power but also because those who controlled the machinery of government also controlled the machinery of the economy. They were the ones who could create property rights and themselves acquire title to the best land and resources. They could issue work and business permits and make rules imposing restrictions on who could receive them. They could allow activities that favored some groups, and forbid those that favored others. If the differences between groups became great enough and the borders hard enough, violence and civil war could break out.

Consider the case of Rwanda, a small country in Central Africa that was once a colony of Belgium. When the Belgians arrived in Central Africa, they found the region's residents engaged in two occupations: farming and herding. The Belgians believed there were physical as well as historical differences between farmers and herders. The Tutsi were taller, handsomer, and lighter skinned, claimed the Belgians, who thought that the Tutsi possessed European blood. The Hutu were imagined as shorter, less attractive, and darker. In fact, the distinction between the two groups in terms of appearance and origin was not a hard and fast one. Many Rwandan families had Tutsi and Hutu members.

The Belgians favored the Tutsi and exaggerated differences between the two groups by giving more resources and greater opportunities to the Tutsi elite. Because the Tutsi were a small minority, they depended on the Belgians to keep them in their high position, a situation that was just fine with Belgium. But shortly before independence, the Belgians orchestrated a "revolution" that transferred power to the Hutu, who greatly outnumbered the Tutsi and resented them for their greater wealth and privilege. The result was a state and government that, over the following three decades, became more and more authoritarian, and a politics marked by recurrent pogroms and rebellions. The worst episode of violence occurred over a three-month period in 1994, triggered by unknown persons who shot down the plane carrying the Rwandan president, Juvenal Habyarimana. He was returning from a conference in Burundi, a neighboring state with similar ethnic tensions. Eight hundred thousand Tutsi and moderate Hutu were killed in a campaign of genocide masterminded by a large remnant of the Hutu-controlled state.[11] Because of the ethnic differentiation between Hutu and Tutsi and the violence that arose from it, the social borders between the two groups became more "real" than the national borders separating Rwanda from its neighbors. People were forced to keep to their own group because crossing over meant risking injury and even death. Hutu Rwandans asked well-placed friends to conceal their Tutsi relations; others betrayed family members and friends to demonstrate their loyalty to Parmahutu, the genocidal para-state.[12] Similar social borders have hardened in other places. Examples include Sri Lanka, Kashmir, Israel/Palestine, and what was once Yugoslavia.

Borders between Public and Private

The second way borders keep people together within countries is quite different, and depends on the distinction between "public" and "private." Nowadays, the public sphere is usually considered to be the realm of politics and the political. The private sphere is restricted to familial and market matters (sometimes a border is drawn between family and market, too). In liberal societies the state is in the public realm, and it is not supposed to meddle in the affairs of the private realm. This is discussed further below.

The public-private distinction became important in a different way with the rise of the European nation-state and capitalism. Before that, land and business interests took measures to encourage the sovereign to keep out of affairs of family and business, so as to protect their property and persons. In return, they paid taxes, most of which were locally set and collected, and supported the sovereign in various ways from sending armed men to fight his wars to lending him money to finance them. As the state became more involved in governing the economy, and as law and relations among states became critical to states' interests, the bourgeoisie also demanded regularized representation in the government. While it might be granted, it was usually highly limited. Under some regimes, representation existed "on paper" but mattered not at all. Whether representation began in the Middle Ages or in modern times, it was not extended to include everyone until well into the twentieth century.

The private was the realm of human activity in which the state had no legitimate interest and state intervention was supposed to be kept to a minimum. Prior to the development of capitalism, states were heavily involved in regulating the economy and social life. With the rise of the bourgeoisie in Europe, a struggle developed over control of wealth, property, and the economy.[13] Who would protect the new middle class against expropriation by their rulers? The capitalist market and private property were the answer: by "disembedding" the economic from the political, limits were put on the state's tributary rights. As time passed this distinction was "naturalized," so that by the time of Adam Smith, the market was imagined as a primordial human institution ruled by an "invisible hand." Despite the extensive state support and regulation necessary to make capitalism work, markets were depicted as working automatically, kept civilized through norms, manners, and rules that everyone knew and everyone observed.[14] In today's liberal societies the border between public and private serves a very political function. It prevents politics from becoming too active and populist by justifying the privatization of decisions about matters affecting society that elites prefer to decide by themselves. If everyone were entitled to participate in making political decisions about the market, capitalism as we know it would be impossible because each of us would demand that our individual interests be served.

This did not (and does not) mean that the state does not intervene extensively in *political economy*. Like the British monarch surveying the activities of the Massachusetts Bay Company, America's founding fathers—there were founding mothers, too, but we rarely hear of them—recognized the threat posed by too much decision making. They were virtually all men of property who desired to protect their possessions from expropriation by either the state or the people. In the first instance, they made sure that the laws of the new United States were friendly to property owners and protected their possessions, including slaves. Beyond this, elites clashed repeatedly over how much the state should be involved in governing the economy, although they all agreed that the public sphere should be relatively limited. In the second instance, they carefully drew borders around the public sphere and limited popular participation to selected segments of the people.

Modern liberalism was not possible in a system in which human beings were property and had no control of their labor. Thus the quarrel over slavery in the United States, even more than the earlier clash over whether or not to have a central bank, became so furious that it took a brutal civil war to resolve it.[15] Over time, the right to vote was extended to minorities and women but, by the end of the nineteenth century, nearly always in a manner that kept these people out of the public sphere. As a result, the "government of the people, for the people, and by the people," as Abraham Lincoln so eloquently put it, has always attached limits to the "of," the "for," and the "by." The abolition of slavery democratized politics by freeing the slaves and making them citizens, but the implementation of the post–Civil War "settlement" granting person- hood to corporations closed politics back down again by shifting important decisions about the economy out of politics and into "administration." The emergence of the American regulatory state during the late nineteenth and early twentieth centuries was directed toward this very end: emerging out of the Progressive movement, regulation focused on limiting the power of corpo- rations, even as elites opposed those Populists who wanted to break capital through greater state intervention into the economy.[16]

This has never meant, of course, that the border between the public and private realms has been impermeable. On many matters, people involved in the public sphere have found reasons to interfere with and regulate the private, not only with respect to economics but also by restricting certain forms of sexual relations between consenting adults and exercising various forms of control over the bodies of both women and men. From the private sphere, some citizens have found it in their interest not only to become active in affairs of state but also to use the state to enrich and empower themselves through insider deals. The recent upsurge in corporate crimes as a result of inadequate state regula- tion of market activities illustrates how the private can use the public for its own benefit.

What are the practical consequences of this border between public and private, and how does it serve both to connect and to divide? All societies are organized around "imagined" principles and norms. These are rules of belief and practice that serve to define the "virtuous" life within the society. If people subscribe to these principles and norms and agree that they are fundamental to social life, and if people behave accordingly, people support the status quo organization of the society. This is the case *even if those rules give advantage to some and not others*. The trick is to get people to accept the rules as "natural" and immutable, as facts that cannot be changed.

The principle that some things are private and others are public seems inviolable in economics, even though it is challenged constantly with regard to personal status issues like marriage and reproductive rights. Yet the location of the border between politics and the economy is accepted in Anglo-American societies as natural, unchangeable, and fundamental to the maintenance and success of society. Whereas conflicting interests on personal status issues like the regulation of marriage and reproduction loom large in national debates, conflicts between economic interests are treated as illegitimate ("class war- fare"). This is because to acknowledge them would undermine the society itself.

So the border between public and private unites society along one axis while dividing it along another. Borders can be curious things.

Borders between Bodies

At a very early age, children learn who is in and who is out, what is in and what is out, whom to connect with and whom to avoid. Our bodies are borderlines: boys and girls, men and women, fathers and mothers, friends and strangers; color, religion, morals, values, beliefs. All of these categories and differences are internalized at such a very early age that they seem "natural." Each individual, each body, has a role. Those who transgress their assigned roles are regarded as "unnatural," as aliens (in the sense of not belonging), as sinners.

Why do such borders develop, and what keeps them in place? It would be relatively easy to explain them as biological—as some do—and say that humans by nature are territorial and categorizing animals. Claiming that such behavior is natural is tantamount to saying it cannot be changed: if we are that way "by design," we might as well learn to live with it. But the historical evidence suggests that what appears to be fixed among humans is almost never so. Even in collectivized societies and among pairs of identical twins, people differ from one another in many ways. In fact, even gender is much more fluid than commonly believed.

While it is impossible to explain exactly how social distinctions and hierarchies were first put into place, we know they are not rigid because we have so much evidence of how they have changed over time. The development of agriculture probably had enormous consequences for group organization. Permanent settlements and established households emerged. The allocation of use rights to land created borders. Customs and rules were formulated that made distinctions of all kinds. Hedges were planted, ditches dug, and fields patrolled. Hierarchies were created within villages. Succession and inheritance made men interested in being able to identify their children. Only by exercising control over a woman could a man be sure that her children were his. How or when this pattern began to develop we do not know, but it seems to have been the source of patriarchy as a specific type of social relation through which older men dominate women and younger men. At first, such domination existed only within families and kin groups; later, it became the model for authority over the village, the city, and the state.[17] At some time, somewhere (perhaps in many places), armed men seized the reins of power and began to put into place rules that differentiated not only between male and female but also among families, language groups, physical types, and other characteristics. Those differences served to enhance the power and authority of some and disempower others. As such borders were drawn and redrawn their origins were lost, making them seem natural because they had "always" been there. Boundaries became even more fixed with the invention of writing, which inscribed rules and rituals and, as we can see with the Bible and other "scriptures," created permanent artifacts that served as sources of tradition and authority that were highly resistant to challenge.[18]

The category of "race," for example, so deeply embedded in American politics and political discourse, has no biological basis. All human beings can interbreed, the touchstone of genetic similarity. Different physical characteristics among human groups have less to do with genetics and more to do with patterns of migration and isolation whose long-term results were to scatter genes across many groups or sequester them among a few.[19] But although "race" is a biological fiction, it is a political convenience. Centuries of Euro-American "science" justified assertions of superiority by some groups who looked at others as less than human.[20] Even after the biological bases of racism had been demolished, racial distinctions remained. To recognize that persons from other groups deserve equal treatment threatens hierarchies and norms founded on distinctions between rich and powerful and poor and weak. Yet the distinctions that separated people by color, religion, lineage, and language united as well as divided. Thus, in the United States before the Civil War, the poorest, most ignorant white was deemed superior to the wealthiest, most educated black, simply by virtue of race. That very small grant of recognition to poor whites by the rich and powerful cemented a social coalition that even today has not disappeared entirely.[21]

Borders are, in other words, a product of power. This is evident in relations among countries. When those on the other side of the border are named "enemy," social hierarchies are created, legitimated, and reinforced, even if the border has no material significance with regard to the people who live on each side. Similar principles are applied at every level of human social organization (think of sports competitions between cities or schools), extending even into the family. Borders separate us and keep us together at the same time.

In between Borders

Because borders are not natural—they are "social constructions," in the language of social theory—they are not immune to change, regardless of how "timeless" they might appear. Indeed, the very distinctions that borders are meant to establish and reinforce are also sources and sites of contradiction. Borders are produced and maintained by power, but they are always blurring and dissolving because of how power tries to maintain them and how the less powerful try to evade them. A useful way to think about this paradox is through the concept of borderland. At its most literal, a borderland or frontier is the space straddling a border, where distinctions between the two "sides" are difficult to make. For example, many residents of national borderlands are bilingual and reflect other social and cultural characteristics of the societies on both sides. The politics and economies of the two sides tend to be integrated in many ways in a borderland, and people routinely move back and forth across the line on the ground. Borderlands are multicultural; they are sites where borders are constantly being constructed and just as constantly being destroyed.[22]

The American Southwest is an archetypal example of such a borderland. It comprises areas that less than two centuries ago were part of Mexico, extending from Texas to California and several hundred miles into what is now the United States (there is a corresponding zone of Americanization on the Mexican side of the border). Within that region, both English and Spanish are spoken. Many U.S. Latinos of Mexican origin live in this borderland, where, in some ways, "American" culture is the foreign one.[23]

The United States has long been a destination for Mexican migrants, both legal and illegal. Mexico is a poor country, and the border is a long way from the center of power in Mexico City. Work was available in the United States, along with already long-established communities of Spanish and Mexican origin, stranded north of the border after the American territorial conquests. U.S. policies like the *bracero* program, which welcomed temporary workers from Mexico, along with the creation of the *maquiladora* zone along the border, served to make crossing it easier and more attractive. As a result, the U.S.-Mexican borderland has been extended deeper and deeper into both countries, including at "outposts." With numbers comes recognition, as with wealth comes power. The border is dissolving.

Yet, there is a continuous effort to reconstruct the border. The United States is motivated by the fear of some of its citizens that their power and prerogatives are under threat from immigration. Calls to halt immigration are usually couched in terms of jobs, welfare, and the economy, but they are equally motivated by threats to long-established hierarchies and social divisions. The U.S. government repeatedly strengthens patrols at the U.S.-Mexico border—since September 11, 2001, it has done so at all international borders—in response to these constituent demands. At the same time, however, the very organization of economic and political life in the United States encourages both border crossings and expansion of the borderland.

On the Mexican side, the effort is directed toward policing the borderland as a geographic region, and the nation-state as a site that is acutely permeable. The state's strategy has been to regulate property ownership so that foreigners are barred from owning economically desirable coastal property and land adjoining the U.S. border. Mexicans who became naturalized U.S. citizens found themselves treated like foreigners because Mexico did not permit dual nationality. Since March 1998, the laws were modified to divide citizenship from nationality. Now Mexicans holding U.S. citizenship can apply for Mexican nationality, which exempts them from property-ownership restrictions but does not allow them to exercise basic citizenship entitlements, like voting and running for political office.[24] Some Mexican Americans resent those restrictions and have been lobbying to have them rescinded. The government is in a delicate position. Migrants to *el Norte* remit billions of dollars every year that help to support the Mexican economy, and countless others regularly cross the border (although for those without the appropriate documents, this has become more and more difficult). The president of Mexico, Vicente Fox, meets some of the migrants' criticisms by demanding greater protection and rights for Mexicans in the United States. (Movements of people and relationships between the European Union and North Africa have a similar character.)

Under the pressures of economic and cultural change, borders become porous, even fluid, and borderlands emerge. Borderlands and frontiers are not limited to the areas along international borders but also include various aspects of social life and practices. Indeed, one could say that in historical terms, fluidity and change are the norm rather than the exception. Stable social systems tend to be stagnant; fluid social systems tend to be dynamic.

What types of changes are we talking about, and what might they involve? When pressures are intense and the rate of change is great, virtually all institutions, from the family to the state, can incorporate "borderlands." Old or conventional ways of doing things become dysfunctional; social arrangements are disrupted or destroyed; adaptation to new conditions becomes necessary. Consider, for example, how globalization has affected the family. Rather rigid borders have been drawn between the "private" realm of the family and the public realm outside. As with other borders, these serve to contain the family as well as to keep out certain types of external influences.

But things change, and stuff happens. The economic and cultural circumstances that make a particular family form normative in society do not stay the same. For example, as it became more and more difficult for middle-class American families to survive on a single income (something that had never been possible for the poor and never a concern to the wealthy), wives and mothers entered the labor force in larger numbers than ever before. Social movements contributed to cultural changes that broadened popular acceptance of working women and households whose adult members did not conform to the traditional social norm. Today, a family might consist of two women or two men with or without children, or three or more adults with or without children, or single parents, or unmarried couples—or any number of other arrangements. Although legal struggles over status, entitlements, and protections continue, the borders have been breached.

This does not mean that new types of family are regarded with equanimity by those in positions of political and economic power. Remember that borders contain and keep out. When borders are breached, new ideas, practices, and expectations come in along with the other intruders. If they were to spread, they could upset old orders. The hierarchy of power in a society depends on keeping socially destabilizing ideas and practices contained. The borderlands in which change manifests itself become a threat to that power. Hence, the backlash against alternative forms of family constitutes an effort to reimpose the old borders and discipline those who would try to cross them.

When borders become fluid and dissolve, just as when new forms of family emerge or different languages are spoken in everyday life, authorities worry that society will change or collapse. Enemies are sought in the quest to reinforce borders and reestablish order. Yet, human life is a chronicle of change. What's so bad about that?

7

People and War

The prospect of war is exciting. Many young men, schooled in
the notion that war is the ultimate definition of manhood . . .
willingly join the great enterprise. The admiration of the crowd,
the high-blown rhetoric, the chance to achieve the glory of the
previous generation, the ideal of nobility beckon us forward. And
people, ironically, enjoy righteous indignation and an object
upon which to unleash their anger. War usually starts with collective euphoria.

—Chris Hedges

If the prospect of war is exciting, then the problem of war may be insoluble.
As we have seen, scholarly and policy literatures are full of theories describing why wars happen. Our discussions of structural theories based on balance-of-power models describe one of the two currently dominant explanations
in American political science of why wars begin. More recently, a large school
has developed around the other theory favored by U.S. analysts, the "democratic peace thesis." This is the proposition that democratic countries don't start
wars, at least not against other democracies. We also noted a number of criticisms of both theories.

In this chapter we look more systematically at war. In general, we believe
that war is overdetermined. Wars are justified for many reasons, while conventions of warfare and therefore the causes and conduct of war change over time.
By necessity, no one theory can fit all cases. As we have noted repeatedly
throughout this book, particular wars must be confronted on their own terms
and in their own times if we are to understand why and how they came about.
We are especially skeptical of theories about war that do not incorporate ways

to assess the responsibility of policy makers. This is because, even though we believe that wars are overdetermined, we also believe that they are not accidental.

We also believe that some theories, often in combination, are better than others in explaining war. General propositions thus can be devised that explain why wars are more likely to occur in some situations than others. Finally, we believe that theories of war should be widely discussed and debated to help us understand violent conflict, limit it, and perhaps even prevent it in the future.

What Is War?

People use "violent conflict" as a synonym for "war," but we want to refine our definition to exclude some forms of group violence and include a concept that frequently is not seen as war despite its association with what we'll call "regimes of punishment." When we speak of war, we mean the deliberate application of organized violence by one or more states. "Deliberate" and "organized" mean that this activity is planned, rehearsed, and directed. "Violence" means to inflict harm, and it may be acute or structural. "Acute violence" refers to agents applying direct physical means (guns, bombs, knives, fists, machetes, fire, etc.) to hurt, damage, and destroy people and property. This is the conventional view of war as fighting. The requirement that states or state agents direct and apply this violence distinguishes war from other violent acts that might be similarly destructive, such as riots; be similarly organized, such as gang conflicts; or kill lots of people, such as the Oklahoma City bombing or the 9/11 attacks. None or. that list qualifies as war under our definition, because none is a state project.[1]

Wars also are fought via the manipulation of structures. Examples of "structural violence" include regimes such as boycotts (refusals to buy from) and embargoes (refusals to sell to), both key elements of "economic sanctions." We extend this understanding to include "structural adjustment" policies, such as IMF demands that debtor nations give a higher priority to foreign lenders than to domestic needs. Structural adjustment may not be acknowledged as violence by the agents who impose it, yet it is experienced by targeted leaders and populations as "war by other means." As a result, it is little or no different from the embargoes and boycotts more conventionally seen as acts of war.

Means and Ends of War

Since 1648, the date of the treaties of Westphalia inaugurating the modern international system, the conventions of great power warfare have changed significantly. As a result, how we explain the causes and outcomes of war must change as well. One change is actually a return to the past.

From prehistoric tribal feuds through the wars of antiquity and the Middle Ages, [the] threat [of extinction] was directed at all members of the enemy people, not just its soldiers. While the cabinet wars of the eighteenth and nineteenth centuries restricted violence to the direct participants on the battlefield, the scorched-earth policies of twentieth-century total war once more universalized the threat. Limited warfare, conducted by a professional military apparatus and carrying no real or imagined peril to the populace at large, was thus a phenomenon that lasted a mere two centuries.[2]

Here historian Wolfgang Schivelbusch traces a complex trajectory. During the sixteenth and seventeenth centuries, wars in Europe were "total." Everyone on the other side was a potential target.

Total war is very old. The destruction of entire communities and the expropriation of valuable resources has been a—if not the—primary objective of warfare through most of recorded history. In Homer's story, elaborated by Euripedes, the Trojan War ended with the destruction of the city, the slaughter of its male inhabitants, and the capture of Trojan women to take back to Greece as slaves. Similar tales are recounted in the Hebrew Bible and Thucycides' history of the conflict between Athens and Sparta.[3] Civilians and their property were targets in other ancient wars, such as Genghis Khan's sweep through Asia into eastern Europe, the Hundred Years' War, and the seventeenth-century religious wars, whose conclusion inaugurated the nation-states system. What is remarkable is "limited war," what Schivelbusch means by "cabinet war."

Limited wars are competitions for status and authority between rulers and states. During their heyday they were won or lost based on the relative effectiveness of professional armies. This is what Kant means by war as a contest among kings and what Clausewitz means when he says that war is the continuation of politics by other means.[4] If diplomacy failed to get a ruler what he wanted, he could deploy his forces like chess pieces to achieve political objectives, from "adjusting" boundaries to influencing dynastic succession. A limited war has limited ends and applies limited means. Its prominence in eighteenth-century Europe allowed Kant to envision war as a moral enterprise in which ethical rulers could draw lines between acceptable and unacceptable tactics. The image of war as a rational pursuit that can and ought to be limited by codes of conduct sped the development of the "rules of war" that make up a significant body of international law.[5]

An international system "adjusted" by limited war presumed that the principals shared interests in their own survival as individuals, their populations and lands as their personal property, and the set of relationships among them that constituted the international society of the time. Interstate conflict during the brief era of cabinet warfare resembled contests among knights in medieval tournaments more than contests among rulers, invaders, and would-be rulers in ancient, medieval, and most contemporary wars. Philosopher Anatol Rapoport notes that military forces might not even engage in a cabinet war. "The object of the campaign frequently was to reach a situation (by proper maneuvering) in which it could become clear that one's own side had a strategic or tactical advantage." At that point, the side likely to lose could capitulate with honor.⁶ A winner was declared, the objective achieved, and everyone went home.

Unlimited wars also were fought during the era of cabinet warfare, but not in Europe. Total war was waged by Europeans against indigenous populations in Africa, Asia, and the New World to take over their land, enslave or exterminate their peoples, and expropriate their possessions. Also, in Europe itself, the transition from cabinet war back to unlimited or "total" war was more ragged than Schivelbusch's thumbnail sketch indicates.

Napoleon mobilized a huge citizen army from the French population and harnessed the French economy to support his drive to establish an empire. Until he was defeated, Napoleon, along with his enthusiastic citizen-soldiers, swept through Europe like a latter-day Genghis Khan. Even earlier, the American Revolution offered a foretaste of the power of nationalism applied to warfare. Rebellious colonial leaders saw their struggle (quite realistically) as a life-or-death fight. Much to the surprise of the British, the colonies' ragtag and part-time citizen forces defeated an army of professional officers, "impressed" (involuntary) naval forces, and ground troops composed of peasants rented from landlords/warlords like the Landgrave of Hesse-Cassel (where the term "Hessian" as a synonym for "mercenary" comes from).⁷ Toward the end of the nineteenth century, the citizens of Paris mobilized to continue fighting after Napoleon III had surrendered at Sedan in September 1870.⁸ This "second phase" of the Franco-Prussian War lasted for less than five months, but it represented a radical democratization of military forces in European societies. Along with the importation of industrial technology into war fighting (generally seen as beginning with the U.S. Civil War), the democratization of war further blurred the distinction between civilians and military forces.

Twentieth-century wars relied even less on professional military forces. Industrial technology operated by unskilled and semiskilled citizen-soldiers (and soldiers mobilized from colonial populations) was applied on the battlefield. "Maneuvering" in the style of cabinet warfare grew more difficult, and major power wars became far more deadly. As the image of war moved from contests between rulers to struggles between "nations," national pride and the struggle to survive returned war aims to demands for the "unconditional surrender" of the enemy.

Given this transformation of ends and means, limited war became untenable. One of the oddest twentieth-century conflicts in terms of what was left of the distinction between limited and unlimited war was the American phase (1965–1972) of the Vietnam War (1930–1975). With some notable exceptions (like the treatment of U.S. prisoners of war by the North Vietnamese and the U.S. "Christmas bombing" of Hanoi in 1972), both sides generally adhered to international conventions setting rules of engagement between U.S. military forces and the military forces of North Vietnam. Meanwhile the territories and the civilian populations of Laos, Cambodia, and South Vietnam (the nominal U.S. ally) were brutally ravaged.⁹

Technology undermined cabinet warfare by making the democratization of warfare possible. The implications of this transition are revealed in a short book by historian Noel Perrin on the two-hundred-year Japanese ban on guns imposed by the Tokugawa military elite.[10] The Japanese were repelled by the way that guns reduced warfare from a highly specialized art to unskilled mayhem, undercutting the status and value of daimyo (lord) and samurai (knight) in state and society. A similar idea of war as an art infused the image of cabinet war. But no nation, including Japan, could afford to treat war as an art when national survival was at stake. Although a gunless Japan managed to win a war against an armed Korea, when Commodore Perry made his second visit to Japan in 1854 with seven U.S. warships, Japanese elites demanding military modernization ousted the Tokugawa and, soon after, ended the power of the feudal warrior classes.

War and Modern Technology

The impact of technology on warfare became clearer with the advent of larger guns, automatic weapons, chemical weapons, and the ability to drop bombs from the air. Most soldiers needed only easily acquired skills to be able to use this technology. Armies could field citizen-soldiers with confidence, while their ''blunt instrument'' reach brought combat conditions to every living thing within a range far greater than that measured by a sword or the distance a horse could run at top speed. Coupled with the large-scale mobilization of populations and resources and the application of sanctions and other forms of structural violence, the total wars of today are far more deadly and destructive than total wars before the cabinet-war era.

Industrial technology continues to effect systemwide changes in conventions of warfare. One such change is the application of industrial machines and techniques for the mass production of death and destruction. During WW I, the set-piece battles on the western front, eastern campaigns like Gallipoli, and submarine warfare demonstrated the power of automatic weapons, artillery, and torpedoes to kill tens of thousands efficiently. The mass production of death expanded radically with the routine air delivery of bombs to cities during WW II. Aerial bombardment killed millions of persons and laid waste to vast expanses of territory. Industrial technology also was applied to genocide, the deliberate attempt to eliminate a specific group of human beings.[11] Some suggest that industrial technology was not necessary for Rwandan Hutus to slaughter eight hundred thousand Tutsis and Hutu moderates in only one hundred days in 1994. Yet technology in the form of hate radio played a very important role in the Rwandan genocide, mobilizing killers, broadcasting lists of targets, and directing truckloads of *genocidaires* to places where Tutsis had sought refuge. Mary Ann Tétreault and her colleague Harry Haines argue that the skillful use of electronic media by the state marks a fourth technology-driven transition in conventions of warfare in the modern period, marking a shift from modern to "postmodern" war, which we discuss below.[12]

Although war and warfare change over time, these few examples show no sharp break dividing war into eras, although we can make fairly clear distinctions among different types of war. For example, limited war continues today, a function of the power differential between the United States and the countries it (and the Soviet Union) attacked during and after the cold war. To a superpower such wars are limited, but for its adversaries they are total, "asymmetric" wars recalling the imperial invasions of earlier times. Other contemporary wars, including "civil" conflicts (wars between contenders living in the same nation-state) and genocide campaigns aimed at eliminating an entire group of people may be symmetrically or asymmetrically "total" in that the aim of at least one side is to destroy enemy leaders, their resource base, and the independent existence of the enemy population.

The return of total war explains why civilians are military targets. They are killed in large numbers "accidentally," part of the "collateral damage" inflicted in the process of killing enemy troops and destroying enemy infrastructure. They are killed in even larger numbers on purpose: to eliminate support for fighting forces; to erase evidence of war crimes like theft, torture, and rape; to demoralize troops and governments; to demonstrate the power of terrorists; and, in genocidal conflicts, to eradicate members of a target group.[13] Direct violence may be augmented by structural violence aimed at reducing an opponent's capacity to wage war or resist occupation. By its nature, structural violence makes an entire society its target. Finally, most of today's wars are industrialized to some degree, especially those involving major powers. Major powers mobilize armies that operate machine technologies like railroads; tanks and automatic weapons; bombs; aircraft; chemical, biological, and space weapons; and sophisticated systems of command and control. Modern war thus adds blunt-instrument, industrial efficiency to the premodern objective of destroying one's enemy.

Wounded Warriors

The glamor of high-tech war machines and the perspective from which we view them—the killers', not the victims'—divert us from seeing soldiers as casualties. Most people don't like to think of dead and wounded young men and women. In the current war in Iraq, this natural uneasiness supports the Bush administration's strategy of directing popular attention away from U.S. casualties through press policies forbidding coverage of the return of bodies to Dover Air Force Base and discouraging stories about the wounded. Official U.S. policy is to refuse to record the number of Iraqi casualties at all. During the Vietnam War, U.S. and Vietnamese wounded and dead, enumerated in weekly body counts, were constant reminders of the human costs of war and served as focal points of antiwar rhetoric. By refusing to count the dead and wounded, the Bush administration masks this human cost.

But it doesn't go away. Dead and wounded soldiers have families whose primary breadwinners are disabled or destroyed as the result of war. Theda Skocpol has found that the first "welfare" program in the United States (and one of the first welfare programs anywhere) was a system of pensions for Civil War veterans and their families.[14] The number of fighters in that war was very large, nearly 4 million, and produced correspondingly large numbers of military casualties: 560,000 dead and 412,000 wounded. The figures for WW I are even more harrowing: a total of 8 million dead, 22 million wounded, and 2 million missing, from all sides.[15] Military casualty totals for WW II vary radically depending on the source, as do estimates of civilian casualties. We are probably safe to assume that between 25 and 30 million military personnel and a somewhat larger number of civilians were killed.

The dead and the visibly wounded are not the only casualties of war. For many, having to kill is a more difficult prospect than having to die. Watching others die violently may be even more affecting, whether one is responsible for those deaths or not, and perhaps especially when the deaths appear to have been caused by leader carelessness or betrayal.[16] Soldiers have a term for the effect of battlefield violence on individuals: such persons are said to have a "thousand-yard stare." Emotional reactions to combat severe enough to be disabling were common during WW I, but military organizations, civilian societies, and even doctors didn't want to admit that what ailed these men was a natural emotional reaction to the horrors of war. They preferred to think of it as a physical ailment—which they called "shell-shock."[17] But there are other mental reactions. Some fighters discover that they actually enjoy hurting or killing people,[18] a taste that if not suppressed or controlled can be expressed as criminal behavior, addiction, or suicide. P. W. Singer notes that unemployed military personnel who enjoyed their former jobs or simply cannot fit back into civilian life are eager recruits for the new firms selling military services.[19] Perhaps the most common long-term emotional effect of war fighting is a different kind of addiction, to the adrenaline that stimulates effective fighting and escape from danger. War memoirs are full of the difficulties of adjusting to the boredom of civilian life.[20]

War and "War"

In recent years, "war" has become a synonym for other kinds of campaigns. The "war" on cancer, declared by U.S. president Richard Nixon, is an obvious example of a nonwar "war." (We'll continue to distinguish between such campaigns and war as we defined it at the beginning of this chapter by using quotation marks for the nonwar "wars.") Some, such as the U.S.-led "war" on drugs, occupy the frontier separating "war" from war. Military equipment and advisors are sent to attack farmers and drug lords and sometimes the political enemies of host regimes. The mix of policing (aimed at criminal activities) and civil conflict (between political opponents) makes such conflicts hard to classify. The 9/11 terrorist attacks on New York and Washington have confused the issue even more. Despite the attackers' "declaration of war," the attacks themselves were criminal acts performed by civilians. Al Qaeda is neither a state nor an aspiring state, and its actions are not warfare: they are crimes. The U.S. government responded by declaring a "war" on terrorism, but it fights it primarily by policing—examples include passenger inspection at airports, expanded surveillance and espionage activities, new regulations for international economic transactions, and close cooperation with other police organizations. The United States also declared war on Afghanistan and Iraq, nations it accused of harboring and aiding terrorists.

Both "war" and war are useful to leaders. The "war" on terrorism waged by the United States has increased the power of the executive branch to a degree that would have been unthinkable before September 11. It justified reorganizing government departments to give the president greater control over personnel and policy at the expense of workers' rights and checks and balances exercised by Congress. Civil-liberties guarantees were curtailed or ended for citizens as well as aliens, reducing personal autonomy and protection from state violence and challenging the autonomy of courts. Budget priorities were reorganized to favor expenditures on military and quasi-military activities, which are national monopolies directed by the executive branch, at the expense of programs like education and health care, operated by states and localities. The external "war" on terrorism also incorporates war components that expand government authority and centralize state power under executive control, and undermine targeted foreign governments ("regime change").

War increases the power of states and their leaders, and historically it has been integral to nation-state building. Charles Tilly describes early nation-states as protection rackets, warlord operations offering protection in return for loans and taxes.[21] Successful war making enlarged the power of the state by bringing new territories with all their resources under state control. War making left warlord kings, who had raised effective armies, with the means to subdue internal rivals and crush political opposition. Military expenses could be paid from booty and then from taxes, efficiently collected by states with effective intelligence and surveillance agencies. Most critically for the shape of the modern world order, strong states commanding vast resources could offer special protection to key economic elites who, in return, supported the governing elites by paying "protection rent."[22] This is a share of the excess profits a business makes when the state awards it a monopoly or attacks its competitors.

This alliance between kings and entrepreneurs explains why nation-states and capitalism evolved together as mutually supporting systems and also why the modern world system experiences recurring "hegemonic" wars. These large-scale interstate conflicts establish the dominance of a core state over the "international system" of nation-states. The winner not only is strategically dominant but also gets to impose economic regimes that favor its national interests and the interests of key elite supporters of its regime. Hegemony thus extends the length of time winners can claim the fruits of victory.[23] Postmodern war is analogous. It funnels state resources to the core constituencies of the leadership of the state, strengthening the leaders' hold on power by attracting votes from enthusiastic consumers of war-as-spectacle.[24] There are so many reasons for wanting to get to or stay at the top of the international hierarchy of power that we can see why nations and leaders might risk total war to do so.

Waltz and His "Images" of War

In an influential 1958 book, political scientist Kenneth Waltz divides theories of war into three "images," or categories. The first image finds the cause of war in human nature; the second image locates it in particular regimes or kinds of regimes; and the third image sees war as the inevitable result of system structure.[25] Waltz himself believes that international system structure, which he describes in Hobbesian terms as "anarchy," is the primary engine driving states to war. He dismisses other theories—such as the democratic peace thesis (a second-image theory) and psychological/theological theories, such as the notion that wars arise from the deliberate choices of particular individuals, from popular pressure on the state to attack an enemy, or from mankind's propensity toward evil (all first-image theories)—as "reductionist."[26]

But systemic theories like those based on balance-of-power models also have problems. How the balance of power is envisioned—as a power-over mechanism that operates by itself, as a mitigated system that incorporates "international society," as the policy of a leading state, or as a convenient way to interpret a mixed bag of events and decisions (in other words, as an artifact)[27]—shapes predictions and explanations. Niall Ferguson's Realist examination of the causes of WW I combines a first-image analysis of the role of Edward Grey on the British side with a third-image analysis of systemic pressures on the German side. Together, these analyses lead him to conclude that WW I was "unnecessary"—and yet it happened. Ferguson says this was because Germany felt compelled by the Franco-Russian alliance and its inability to keep up with British naval expansion to launch a war against France and Russia. Germany's leaders feared they were falling behind strategically and saw attacking in 1914 as a "now or never" proposition. But the decision of Britain to send its army to France was discretionary. Britain did not need a war with Germany to protect its naval supremacy, and it could have delayed making any military response until it was too late to send the British Expeditionary Force (BEF) to France.

Indeed, Ferguson says that Britain's decision to send the BEF made the war a "world war" rather than one limited to continental Europe. Although a limited war on the continent might have "adjusted" quite a few borders, Ferguson believes it was unlikely to have produced revolution in Russia, the sudden creation of a large number of new—weak—nation-states from the carcasses of the Austria-Hungarian and Ottoman empires, and a second world war two decades later. Ferguson's analysis challenges the Waltz third-image model by making third-image factors contingent on first-image causes. Other theorists explain the failure of events to unfold the way systemic models predict as the result of errors of perception by policy makers; some, like Robert Jervis, incorporate the likelihood of making such mistakes directly into their theories.[28]

As Ferguson's complex analysis shows, perhaps the greatest problem with any theory of war is the attempt to explain war as having only one kind of cause. Even though war is evident in what we know about virtually every human culture throughout time[29]—or throughout as much of time as we have records about—it is as hard to explain war as having a single cause as it is to explain marriage, another social practice that is evident in all cultures and throughout recorded history. Systems theorists can say that war is the result of competition for scarce resources by rival human groups, just as they can say that marriage is the result of biological competition to reproduce the species. But how this happens and what form it takes in any era is a function of values, structures, and the particular agents involved. As a result, more complex theories are needed to explain war than any one "image" can generate.

Ethics and War

In most conventional IR theories, ethics are either entirely absent (balance-of-power theories); are mentioned but discounted (the first moral principle of statesmanship is to preserve the lives and property of citizens no matter what it takes); or construe the behavior of the theorist's country as morally superior—war is someone else's fault, and all we are doing is defending ourselves (the subtext of the democratic peace thesis). Theories that do attempt to address ethical and moral concerns are marginalized, relegated to lawyers, clergy, women, and others charged with being too "soft" to face "reality." This logic of ethics is laid out by Hobbes, who says, "To this war of every man against every man, this also is consequent; that nothing can be unjust. The notions of right and wrong, justice and injustice, have there no place. Where there is no common power, there is no law; where no law, no injustice."[30]

There are two key elements in the Hobbesian position. One is that in a situation of total war (a "war of every man against every man") all means are ethical. The other element points to the reason why this is so: in the absence of law, there is no "right and wrong." Hobbes says that this is why a strong state is necessary for domestic peace: only a strong state can legitimately apply the force that ensures the security of all. His position has been generalized by Realists such as Hans Morgenthau to hold for the international system—in the war of all states against all states, there is neither right and wrong nor a way to prevent war. The duty of the statesman is to ensure the security of the nation, and duty requires that he be prepared to defend it by whatever means he must. While Morgenthau dreamed of an international regime capable of protecting people against war, he was not optimistic that such a regime would come about any time soon.[31]

The most prominent twenty-first-century Hobbesians, popularly known as neoconservatives, returned to power during the George W. Bush administration. Their position corresponds to what scholars refer to as "hegemonic stability theory." It says that a hegemonic power is necessary for international stability and world order. Putting this theory into practice in accordance with U.S. interests is the basic idea behind George W. Bush's national security strategy, which gives the United States the right to initiate wars or otherwise topple regimes that threaten its vision of a world order based on political and economic marketization.[32] The U.S. invasions of Afghanistan (2001) and Iraq (2003) were guided by this strategy,[33] along with the ongoing "war" on terror. The strategy also informs attempts to effect "regime change" in places such as Iran, Syria, Cuba, and Venezuela, where, so far, it has been unsuccessful, and it guided the administration's support of rebels in Haiti who brought down the government of Jean Bertrand Aristide in February 2004.

"Softer" proponents of hegemonic stability theory, such as Robert Gilpin, Robert Keohane, and Joseph Nye, see the role of the hegemon more benignly.[34] Keohane calls the neoconservative position "the crude basic force model"[35] and attacks it by saying that the most successful hegemons were not dominating but rather nurturing, motherly states that provided economic and security services to weaker partners. Like Gilpin, Keohane sees self-interest, not force, as the primary motive for cooperating in a stable hegemonic regime, another power-with model. In his 1984 book *After Hegemony*, Keohane suggests that U.S. allies should continue to support the United States–led international regime even though U.S. power seemed to be in decline. This was because the subordinate states continued to benefit from security and economic services underwritten by the United States. This view is known as "neo-Realism."

A very different vision of world order comes from "Idealists." At their extreme, Realism and Idealism as theoretical and ideological points of view constitute two "ideal types," schematic models of how the world operates. Some of the differences between Realism and Idealism lie in the units and levels of analysis that each one uses. Realists see states in conflict as their units of analysis and the system of international anarchy as their level of analysis. All other actors are subordinate to states, the "power-maximizing" units whose competition creates the international system. Idealists see the world as composed of many units, not only states but also individuals, firms, churches, and a whole range of public and private organizations. They are envisioned as operating within relationships constructed and maintained by their own efforts. In consequence, although Idealists' level of analysis is the individual, their units of analysis are medieval in their variety. Idealists also see choice as variable, motivated not just by the desire to have more power but also by moral and practical concerns. Like politics in the Middle Ages, idealist models of politics are hard to boil down into a few basic propositions.

Idealists also operate from wider frames of inclusion than Realists. Realists follow philosopher Friedrich Nietzsche in their idea that "the world is horrible and fundamentally unintelligible; the bad thing was to pretend that it has an intelligible rational structure *or* anything to make us optimistic about political progress."[36] As a result, they have a narrow view of who is entitled to the state's protection—its citizens or subjects—and what they ought to pay for it—total loyalty and whatever material resources the state demands. Idealists operate from what Kant called a "cosmopolitan" perspective. Idealists see all human beings as entitled to dignity and respect, and view politics as decision making based on human reason. Idealists condemn group loyalties such as nationalism, religion, ethnic identity, and economic interest as inherently emotional and divisive. To them, only reason allows us to arrive at a politics that is "active, reformist and optimistic, rather than given to contemplating the horrors, or waiting for the call of Being."[37] In other words, Idealists believe that reasonable people can collaborate to create a world order based on human rights rather than group rights, one that includes strategies for containing "global aggression and [promoting] universal respect for human dignity."[38]

Martha Nussbaum shows how Kant's image of cosmopolitanism grew out of the ethical and political views of ancient Roman thinkers, including Marcus Aurelius, who ruled the Roman empire from 161 to 180 C.E.[39] Known as one of the "five good emperors," Marcus showed that cosmopolitan ideals were compatible with effective governance, refuting the claims of Realist theorists that a humane politics based on the articulation of common purposes and committed to peaceful relations could never succeed. Marcus and those who share his views hold that aggression is wrong and that force should be used only in self-defense. This "Stoic" position in Western thought shaped concepts of human rights, the development of international law, rules of war, and repeated attempts to create international institutions that might be sufficiently shielded from the emotional demands triggered by group loyalties to pursue the common purposes of human beings.

Kant contributed to this tradition throughout his writings. In *Perpetual Peace* he offers a short list of practical rules to help reasonable leaders avoid violent conflict.[40] One encourages transparency by renouncing secret treaties; another promotes mutual respect among nations by forbidding states to interfere in the constitution and government of other states, assassinate their leaders, foment domestic unrest, encourage treason, or break agreements with them. Another rule encourages respect for citizens by forbidding territories and populations from being treated like the personal property of rulers. Two rules attack systemic pressures for war, calling on states to abolish standing armies and to refrain from borrowing money to support aggression against another state. We could summarize these rules as advocating honesty, openness, mutual respect, responsibility, and cooperation.

As we noted in chapter 1, Kant argues that to have an international system based on rules like these requires that the parties to them have representative governments incorporating a separation between legislative and executive branches—checks and balances. This is why Kant is regarded as an early proponent of the democratic peace thesis. But Kant's vision of the international system is more complicated than that. It also requires what he calls "a federation of free states," international institutions in which sovereign states come together in a diplomatic forum to determine how to achieve the common good: "peace can neither be inaugurated nor secured without a general agreement between the nations."[41] This is a formula for discussion and negotiation. It describes neither a world state that could become a global despotism, nor a world of perpetually warring states. In other words, perpetual peace is a project, not a destination. Kant's essay suggests ways to move that project along.

Kant has many descendants. Prominent among them are feminist theorists like J. Ann Tickner and V. Spike Peterson, who argue that the Hobbesian perspective that dominates contemporary security policy actually creates global and national insecurity: recurrent "total" wars, genocide, pollution and resource depletion, climate change, and a world economy in which inequality is growing by leaps and bounds while resistance to the degradation and suffering it causes becomes deadlier every day.[42] If reasonable people can agree that these are problems, can we engage in Kantian dialogue to resolve them? Perhaps, but first we'll also have to deal with the fact that many people profit from war, and some also enjoy it.

Postmodern War

The impact of technology on the causes and conduct of war reaches a new peak in "postmodern war." Chris Gray defines postmodern war as a product of technology and culture leading to a "limited definition of rationality and science as an institution to replace valor."[43] In their recent paper, Mary Ann Tétreault and Harry Haines expanded that view but also disagreed with it in significant respects. They do agree with Gray that postmodern war is a product of war-fighting technology, including pure robotics and "cyborg" (bionic) technologies that allow human beings to do such things as "see" in the dark and stay awake for days at a time. Electronic technology is key to postmodern war. It promotes the illusion that policy makers are invulnerable while, in practice, it allows many fighters to remain at safe distances from combat operations. Prosecutors of war can focus destruction on the buildings, vehicles, and even individual persons who are their actual targets; this gives the prosecutors a sense that what they are doing is morally correct because injury to the "innocent" is minimized. Meanwhile, for the war's "consumers" at home, news broadcasts from the front echo what for some is a lifetime of experience playing war games via computer and "reality" simulation.[44]

Tétreault and Haines see postmodern war as part of a high-tech culture, but, unlike Gray, they believe it comes not only from technology but also from new understandings of how to produce personal and historical memory through the use of electronic media.[45] "Historical memory" is what "everybody knows" about past events, not only a particular version of what happened but also how to link that common knowledge to contemporary events. An example is how arms inspections in Iraq ended in 1998. "Everybody knows" that Saddam kicked the arms inspectors out, but that isn't what happened. In reality, the inspectors were withdrawn by the United Nations when chief arms inspector Richard Butler complained that Saddam was not cooperating with them.[46] By revising this story in October 2002, at the precise time that UN arms inspections were resumed, the spinners created expectations that the inspections would fail.

Historical memory is deeply implicated in postmodern war, which resembles cabinet war in that its defining quality is artistic performance. Its target audience includes populations as well as leaders. Being able to manipulate experience and memory is critical to its political success because such conflicts are wars of choice—they are not necessary for national survival. Unlike cabinet war (or medieval tournaments), postmodern war is not a duel. It is a team sport in which both promoters (political leaders) and "fans" (voters) must be protected from direct exposure to violence so that they will continue to play. Like modern war, postmodern war is an expression of nationalism, the source of the "team spirit" that supports rising defense budgets and the (re)election of armchair-warrior leaders by armchair-warrior voters.

Commercial media are crucial allies of governments fighting postmodern wars. Because such wars are fought by choice, leaders must market them to sustain the illusion that they are necessary, thereby justifying their high cost. Commercial media face pressures that make them the natural partners of governments in this enterprise. Mass marketers of news are as interested as political leaders in minimizing context and simplifying stories, because it helps them to attract the largest number of consumers, particularly in the demographic group most cherished by advertisers: young men. Competition for readers, listeners, and viewers also encourages standardization, stories based on stereotypes that appeal to the prejudices and expectations of target markets.[47] Cost pressures dictate doing this as cheaply as possible, such as by eliminating expensive background pieces, along with facts incompatible with story "genres" and style conventions that make reported events intelligible and palatable to naive consumers.

Examining coverage of antiwar protestors during the American war in Vietnam, for example, Daniel Hallin found that the few stories centering on out-of-the-mainstream groups and ideas (i.e., protesters and antiwar messages) tended to marginalize the actors and belittle the policies they advocated.[48] This treatment reinforced the out-of-the-mainstream status of dissenters and their identity as "bad guys." The depiction of bad guys is stylized in other ways. Terry Thompson discovered floating signifiers—symbols detached from their real-world settings—in CBS television news coverage of Eastern Europe during the 1980s. These stories featured pre–WW II footage of marching Nazi troops as "illustrations" of contemporary life fifty years later (and in different countries).[49]

Visual presentations are more effective at creating historical memory than print or audio messages. "Pictures" stick in people's minds. Because the same pictures are seen by millions of persons, they validate themselves by increasing the number of "witnesses" to the stories and events they portray. Television is more powerful than film in this regard because more people are exposed to it, and they view it in settings where they rarely engage critically with what they are seeing.[50] The power of television to create historical memory that conflicts with history was revealed in polls taken in the fall of 2003. Persons who relied on commercial television for news about the third Gulf War (GW III)[51] harbored significantly more misconceptions and outright errors of fact about the conflict and its causes than those who relied on newspapers and noncommercial radio and television.[52]

Another trend is especially disturbing to those interested in resolving international conflicts peacefully because it promotes the enjoyment of war as an entertainment "product." The widespread consumption of video "war games" blurs boundaries dividing virtual from actual events. As representations of battlefield violence in the news comes closer in appearance to the parallel universes generated by video games, war news is both more absorbing and less shocking.[53] Viewers of the popular general Norman Schwarzkopf's nightly TV reports during the second Gulf War (GW II) could justify their consumption as fulfilling the responsibility of citizens to stay informed while they enjoyed the thrill of participating in a video game they had a real-world stake in winning. Representations allowed viewers to occupy the positions of actors dropping bombs on "targets" indicated by crosshairs imposed over vague images of "facilities" and "installations," or to watch "tracer" images of "their" Patriots knocking out "enemy" Scuds. These images delivered excitement, validation, and political support as coalition forces prepared to move on the ground.

The parallels between civilian video and television consumption and modes of wartime news coverage developed further during GW III, when "embedded" journalists individually accredited to military units became the analogue to civilian "reality TV." Confined to their small units, embedded journalists could "see" and report only on narrow yet highly emotional events, offering a perspective that drew viewers into vicarious participation on the front lines.[54] Even more than GW II "pool" reporting and Schwarzkopf briefings, embedded reporters limited viewers' perceptions of the war by shrinking its context. The multiple news stories fragmented understanding of the policy frame of the conflict, reducing it to genre representations of combat units, each with its obligatory complement of embattled all-American "kids" up against a faceless and terrifying enemy. To portray a war in terms of its experience by identified and identifiable extensions of the viewers' personas limits viewers' initiative to question it as policy.

Curbing Knights and Knaves

"The prospect of war is exciting." Yet the reality of war is something else again, especially as the toll of injured and dead, devastated homes and infrastructure, and the taxes and reduced services that pay for it all displace the initial excitement like a hangover after a wild party. Realist leaders deal with this by building up a preponderance of power so that no one will dare to attack them, but that strategy triggers the security dilemma.[55] Whenever any country beefs up its armaments, other countries see it as preparing to attack and arm themselves in response. Even hegemons are not immune to unpleasant consequences when they add to their arsenals. As an Iranian scholar of our acquaintance once put it:

> The greatest irony of nuclear weapons is that security for country X requires insecurity for country Y. Naturally, and as a corollary, as country X continues to [improve] its nuclear (and other) weapons instead of abiding by international agreements to work towards disarmament, and as it claims that as a Great Nation it is not bound by international law or the UN Charter [but rather] has the "moral clarity" to wage wars of aggression with impunity, country Y will inevitably conclude that its security requires obtaining equal or better weapons. This isn't a matter of envy on the part of country Y; it is a matter of survival.[56]

The charms of war so appealing to people who clothe their drive for power as a story of the forces of good battling the forces of evil do not attract people who recognize the common humanity shared by fighters on both sides.[57] One of the most evocative stories of a personal transition from Realism to Idealism is recounted by Vera Brittain, a young woman just beginning her university studies as WW I descended on Europe.[58] Vera, like her brother and his friends, was caught up in the excitement of the war, and Vera left Oxford to become a volunteer nurse caring for wounded troops. First in London hospitals and then on Malta and in France, Vera encountered thousands of mangled and dying soldiers. While she was overseas, she also nursed badly wounded German prisoners of war and found herself shocked that she could think of them—the enemy—as sharing a common humanity with her own wounded and dead countrymen.

During the war Vera lost her fiancé, two close friends, and, as the war was drawing to a close, her only brother. Throughout the book she published fifteen years after the end of the war, she rails bitterly at her loss of these and other things, like her youthful enthusiasm and her sympathy with those in her country who had not experienced the war directly, as she had.

But Vera did not give up. She returned to Oxford, graduated, and embarked on a public life as a speaker and writer. Although at first it made her feel disloyal to the memories of the dead, she found new interests and formed new friendships. Eventually, she married and had children, finding a life she had once believed that the war had foreclosed to her forever.

As Vera's career flourished, she began to use her position as a public figure to work for peace, speaking all over England about the virtues and shortcomings of the League of Nations and, through novels and reporting, writing contemporary history in stories of individual lives caught up in world-shattering events. In her memoirs she tells about traveling in Central and Eastern Europe shortly before her marriage. She was repeatedly struck by how people living in the countries she visited were as bitter as she was about all they had lost in the war yet, unlike her, found their feelings hardened in response to nationalistic appeals naming outsiders as the source of their pain. Her way of reaching some of these isolated people was to share her own experiences. She told one of the directors of the Krupp corporation, a man with a war wound who had made his hostility to his visitors obvious, that she had nursed German soldiers during the war.

> "German soldiers!" he exclaimed. "You mean—prisoners?" "Yes," I replied, "At Étaples." . . . This experimental information had been the mere impulse of shamed nervous tension, but had it been most carefully calculated, it could not have proved more effective. . . . [T]he alarming director became positively communicative, and pointed out to us the square where the Essen riots had broken out, and the tree-shaded park which had once been used for testing munitions. . . . Later, he took us through the spacious workrooms that had once been used for the manufacture of field artillery, and showed us how swords were now, literally, being turned into ploughshares in their modern guise of typewriters and surgical instruments.[59]

Even then, in 1925, Vera sensed the seeds of another war in Europe rooting themselves in the misery and hostility of the people she interviewed. As that impending war drew closer during the 1930s, she became a committed pacifist. She remained so throughout WW II despite hostile criticism from friends and strangers alike. When that war was over, Vera and her associates founded the Campaign for Nuclear Disarmament, and she continued her peace activism until she died in 1970.

Vera Brittain's international activism in pursuit of her vision of Stoic cosmopolitanism was noteworthy for how much of her life and energy it consumed. Yet Vera's quest for intellectual openness and flexible institutions sturdy enough to support negotiation and cooperation is not unique. In response to the horrors of modern and postmodern war, thousands, even millions of others have worked and continue to work to establish and preserve islands of common ground on which people and nations can stand together and work out differences among themselves without going to war.

It is too simple—even naive—to say that human beings ever can abolish war. The need to defend populations and habitats from predators is likely to persist as long as there are people willing to stop at nothing to achieve their goals. Yet, at the same time, the prospect of war as a response to fear and ignorance, as something to pacify citizens or distract them from the failures of their leaders, or merely as a source of excitement and entertainment is, as Kant believed, a problem resolvable through reason. In his first inaugural address, Franklin Roosevelt appealed to reason when he said, "The only thing we have to fear is fear itself." Chris Hedges appeals to the common ground human beings share as mortal, and moral, beings. He ends his book on war this way: "[Love] does not mean we will avoid war or death. It does not mean that we as distinct individuals will survive. But love, in its mystery, has its own power. It alone gives us meaning that endures."[60]

8

People and Justice

The law, in its majestic equality, forbids the rich as well as the poor to sleep under bridges, to beg in the streets, and to steal bread.

—Anatole France

W hy are there so many poor and hungry people in the world? Why are so many people killed because of their religion, race, or ethnicity? Why do powerful countries invade weak ones? Why do women continue to suffer from patriarchal oppression? In short, why is there so little *justice* in the world? Is global justice possible? What would it involve? What would be required to achieve it?

Most of us know injustice when we see it, yet, what, exactly, is justice? Justice might have as many definitions as there are people in the world, but how might we define it? In this chapter, we examine the concept of justice in the world, how it is defined, and the ways in which it is (not) practiced. Justice, or its absence, is closely linked to three topics we have already discussed at considerable length: power, the state, and capitalism. Injustice is an age-old problem, of course, but its particular manifestations in contemporary life are not merely a consequence of some inherent flaw in human nature. As we discussed in chapters 6 and 7, injustice also is linked to structures and regimes that discriminate against particular people and groups. In a world in which some modicum of justice is both feasible and desirable, the causes of injustice lie in our institutions and the practices they foster. Certainly, people do commit unjust acts against other people, and must bear responsibility for the consequences of those acts. Nevertheless, if we understand ourselves as "social individuals" whose awareness and behavior are strongly motivated and directed by norms and principles, it becomes clear that injustice is more than merely the malicious acts of bad individuals.[1]

Theorists of justice and injustice fall into several distinct camps. One is most concerned with the problem of *distributive justice*, that is, how are income and wealth parceled out among members of a society, and what can be done to make this division fairer? A second school focuses on *rights* and *recognition*, that is, how do the legal and cultural status of a group contribute to the injustices it suffers, and what might be done to overcome these conditions? A third group addresses *structural sources* of injustice, the social and institutional norms and practices that perpetuate injustice even as people fight for redress. None of these three schools is purist; there is considerable overlap among them. Much of the literature on justice—both distributive and social—addresses abstract situations and focuses on human rights, mostly for the individual. A growing literature argues that specific groups must be accorded rights in order to achieve both social and economic justice. Here, we develop the notion of "respect" to go along with rights and recognition. That is that, if we acknowledge the need for respect of others as foundational to justice, we must also acknowledge the consequences of our everyday behaviors and consent in reproducing conditions of injustice.

Defining Justice

At its most basic, justice can be defined as getting what one deserves—the root of the phrase "just desserts." The idea here is that we all engage in activities for which we seek some kind of reward or remuneration; our due is what we deserve for what we have done. Thus, we expect to be fairly paid for our work, fairly recognized for our status, fairly rewarded for our achievements, fairly treated whoever we might be. Those who commit crimes and are tried and convicted, thereby receive their just desserts—"criminal justice" implies exactly this. But we know that justice is not always meted out fairly. Some receive more than their due, while others manage to avoid paying for their crimes. The distribution of rewards and punishments is often unfair. Why?

Although we tend to regard luck as playing a major role in this distribution of good and bad, chance does no more than exacerbate already existing tendencies and conditions. Those who are well off or have "connections" receive their due (and more!) when others do not. Criminals represented by highly skilled—and expensive—lawyers are more likely to walk free than those relying on the overworked employees of legal aid or, worse, on third-rate lawyers who depend on court appointments for subsistence. Significant accomplishments go unnoticed in the absence of a good publicist or extensive networks—how many of you had heard of Shireen Ebadi before she received the Nobel Peace Prize in 2004? We know of what justice consists; what we don't know is why it seems so difficult to accomplish.

But it is not so simple to devise general rules of justice that everyone agrees are fair. After all, what if expanded social services enjoyed by all were to result in less private wealth? There are three basic ways to think about this problem. First, we could simply decide that resources and wealth should be allocated to decrease the gap between rich and poor. Second, we could try to formulate a set of rules governing society that would grant to every individual equal rights and access to opportunities and institutions. Finally, we could actively try to enhance the access and opportunities of those who have been disadvantaged by the existing rules governing society.

Justice as Distribution

In the early 1970s, during a famine in East Bengal, Peter Singer wrote a famous article entitled "Famine, Affluence, and Morality."[2] In the article, Singer criticizes the relative lack of provisions for the relief of others by inhabitants of rich countries and by their governments. Singer's primary argument is that "if it is in our power to prevent something bad from happening, without thereby sacrificing anything of comparable moral importance, we ought, morally, to do it." His reasoning is based on what we can call "marginal utilitarianism." Singer believes that we should minimize the amount of pain in the world, and famine and starvation certainly cause a great deal of pain. Furthermore, the solution to starvation is straightforward: famine relief in the form of food shipments from rich countries to poor ones. Therefore, every individual ought to be sending money for famine relief, and should do so until his situation becomes equal to that of the people receiving the relief, as long as doing so does not create a greater moral sacrifice. In other words, it would not be moral to starve your children in order to feed others, but it would be immoral to live in luxury while others were starving. At the extreme, Singer seemed to imply that the greatest level of global justice could be achieved only by the near-equal distribution of the world's wealth. There are some obvious problems with Singer's proposal, some practical and others philosophical. Singer ridiculed the amount of aid that was actually being provided by the United States and Europe. He thought that charities provided competent means of getting relief to where it was needed, but, in practice, in the absence of coordination, some sufferers would receive a great deal of assistance while others would get little or none.[3] In general, however, Singer disapproved of the notion of "charity" because, he wrote, people and groups compete with each other in the hope of receiving credit for "moral" behavior, a point with which other analysts agree.[4] Even governments send aid to appear morally correct and also to benefit their economies. But, as Singer emphasized, moral acts should not be contingent on any kind of return, material or other.

Regardless of these practical considerations, Singer's proposal raises a troubling question: What do we owe morally to those who are neither family nor members of any of our communities of obligation, such as fellow citizens? We help kin without question because the ties of blood are strong; we help conationals because we live in the same society and we are tied together through common history, rituals, and institutions. Must we help those whom we don't know and with whom we don't share attributes such as religion, language, or culture? According to Singer, yes. He drew a comparison between a child in danger of drowning nearby and people in danger of starving far away to demonstrate this point. You would not fail to jump into the water to save the child, even if the child were a stranger and the rescue came at the cost of ruining your new suit or dress. Singer argues that the second case is similar; if people unknown to you are dying far away and you can do something to save them, you are morally obligated to do so.

Not everyone agrees with Singer's reasoning. A year or so after Singer's article was published, Garrett Hardin issued a riposte to Singer. Hardin was a biologist best known for his *Science* article "The Tragedy of the Commons," which argues that shared resources were inevitably abused. The title of Hardin's rebuttal is "Life Boat Ethics: The Case against Helping the Poor."[5] Like Singer's, Hardin's argument is utilitarian, but he draws the relevant lines (or borders) differently, claiming that we have no obligations to those who live outside of our country. Hardin is particularly concerned about global population growth and its impact on humanity's prospects for survival; in this, he is Malthusian in his reasoning.[6]

Imagine, writes Hardin, that you and some number of people are adrift at sea in a lifeboat with sufficient food and water to last until you are rescued. In the water around you are a large number of people who can still swim but eventually will drown if they are not saved. Imagine further, he continued, that the lifeboat represents your country and the people in the water represent the poor of the world in need of help. You could, of course, save those in the water, but at what cost? The lifeboat is already full. If too many additional people climb in, it will founder and everyone will be tossed into the water to drown. You could save a very few, but then you would have less food and water for each person and it might not last until you were rescued. And how would you decide whom to save? You can't very well interview people as they are going under!

Completing the metaphor, Hardin argues that the people of wealthy countries, secure in their lifeboats, cannot afford to feed the billions of poor and hungry, swimming in the sea. First, the rich simply do not have enough food. Second, helping the poor would only encourage them to have more children, creating an ever-growing demand for food. Eventually, as Thomas Malthus argued in 1778, population would outstrip agriculture, and everyone would starve.[7] Better to let the poor fend for themselves by halting immigration into the rich countries, and by providing aid only to one's needy and deserving conationals. We have no moral or other obligations to anyone who is not a bona fide, legal citizen or resident of our country, according to Hardin. He insists that the only acceptable approach to distributive justice is what is fair and acceptable to us and our descendents; we cannot rectify the injustices of the past or injustices in other countries. Indeed, Hardin writes:

We Americans of non-Indian ancestry can look upon ourselves as the descendants of thieves who are guilty morally, if not legally, of stealing this land from its Indian owners. Should we then give back the land to the now living American descendants of those Indians? However morally or logically sound this proposal may be, I, for one, am unwilling to live by it and I know no one else who is. Besides, the logical consequence would be absurd. Suppose that, intoxicated with a sense of pure justice, we should decide to turn our land over to the Indians. Since all our other wealth has also been derived from the land, wouldn't we be morally obliged to give that back to the Indians too?[8]

His answer is, self-evidently, "No!"

But Hardin's conclusion is not quite so self-evident as he claims. Consider that a significant portion of the wealth of the United States came from the surplus value produced by slave labor prior to the Civil War. Over the intervening century and a half that wealth has been reinvested many times and, through both economic growth and compound interest, has come to be an enormous sum. (One dollar invested in 1860 at an annual interest rate of 4 percent would today have compounded to more than $80. Even with inflation, this is a substantial increase.) It does not seem wholly unreasonable to imagine that the descendants of U.S. slaves ought to receive some sort of reparations (similar, perhaps, to what West Germany paid to Israel as reparations for the Holocaust), even though it could never fully compensate for the injustices of slavery. Or consider the issue of Palestinian properties confiscated without compensation since 1948 by Israel. These confiscations made major contributions to the prosperity of that state, while today millions of Palestinians live in deep poverty. Why shouldn't Israel provide reparations to them, and why shouldn't Jewish refugees from Arab states be compensated for the loss of their properties, too?

Singer and Hardin illustrate the poles of the debate over justice as distribution, and one can imagine all kinds of positions in between. But what is critical about this debate is its singular focus on material goods. To repeat one of the questions raised above: Is it fair that some people have so much and others have so little? Neither of these two authors is especially interested in explaining how things got to be so unjust or asking whether we have any responsibility for the actions of our ancestors or our governments. Other philosophers of justice acknowledge our inability to do anything about the past, but believe that simple redistribution is not the answer to injustice, either. They seek sets of social rules according to which justice can be achieved and which, to some degree, will function more effectively than Singer's morality and Hardin's self-interest.

Justice as Fairness

The late John Rawls, considered by some to be the most eminent theorist of justice during the twentieth century, believes that "justice is fairness."[9] Rawls recognizes that societies are organized in ways that tend to institutionalize injustices, but he also thinks it would be possible to determine and follow fundamental principles that would increase the level of fairness in a society. Once its members recognized the centrality of such principles in seeking and achieving just outcomes, they would willingly accept those principles and the outcomes, however unequal the results. Rawls devised a thought experiment that, he argues, makes it possible to establish the necessary conditions for justice. He calls the experiment "decision making from the original position, behind a veil of ignorance."

Imagine, if you will, a situation in which no one knows anything about his own situation: his wealth, education, lineage, skin color, nationality, and so on—and we use "his" in this case because Rawls ignores gender as a category of analysis; his people are all men. This is the "original position." The "veil of ignorance" guarantees that all decisions about distribution will be made "disinterestedly," that is, that people will make decisions based on what is right rather than on what would be best for themselves. The decision to be made is about the riches of a society or the world. How should they be divided up, and what are the rules that will ensure that the division is fair?

Rawls concludes that it is likely that such a group of people would decide to divide the wealth into equal shares. How each might use his share, what each individual's condition might be in the future, and the constitution of other rules are of no importance in establishing the initial rule. Individuals are not equal in intelligence and capabilities, but they should not be penalized for what are accidents of birth. Over time, of course, some people might find ways of turning their share of riches into fabulous wealth, while others might see their initial endowment disappear. But outcomes were not of concern to Rawls; procedures were.

Clearly, the real world is not like this, and people's views of what is and is not fair are heavily influenced by their personal "original positions." Individuals are born into families, some poor, some wealthy, and their life chances and opportunities are shaped even earlier, by their genetic endowment and events during their fetal existence. After birth and as we grow older, we become aware of our own and others' endowments and learn that they are unequal. Some can use their endowments to increase this inequality even further. The result might be unfair, but if they have done nothing illegal to obtain their wealth, is it unjust? Moreover, why should anyone agree to rules that might diminish her share of the wealth? In contrast, someone who is poor in comparison to others is likely to see things very differently. Fairness, it would seem, is in the eye of the beholder.

But that trivial conclusion is not the point of Rawls's thought experiment. His goal in devising this scenario is to derive principles of justice about which everyone can agree, regardless of their initial position. Rawls concludes that two principles follow from such a deductive exercise: first, an equality of basic rights, and second, what he called the "difference principle," which regards any inequality as unjust unless its removal makes worse the situations of the worst-off members of society. Here we can see an echo of Singer in Rawls's argument.

There are numerous complications to Rawls's arguments that need not concern us here, but the fundamental point is that his reasoning was of a purely theoretical nature. Rawls seems to have hoped that recognition of these rules of fairness would stimulate discussion and lead to the principles they rest on becoming the basis for justice in society, but he offered no program to make them so. Fairness as conceived by Rawls was not, moreover, the same as equality. An equal division of resources might not, in fact, be fair, because some might make greater sacrifices than others (think of inequalities in the household division of labor or the greater risks and responsibilities carried by soldiers as compared to civilians during wartime). At best, one might seek to equalize opportunities and be willing to leave the rest in the hands of individuals.

Rawl's arguments, published more than thirty years ago, have generated a vast literature, both supportive and critical.[10] What is most important, perhaps, about the original position and the veil of ignorance is that Rawls limited their application to liberal societies, that is, those that are both democratic and capitalist. He believed that it is only in such countries that the individual is central to the beliefs and practices leading to both justice and injustice. Only in liberal societies, he argued, can the individual even begin to conceive of himself in the original position and behind the veil of ignorance, a situation devoid of power, hierarchy, and history. We know, however, that even in liberal societies the original position is a fiction. It is not so much that the theorist himself fails to fulfill the requirements of the thought experiment as that he has failed to recognize the lack of connection *between* the thought experiment and action. As experience shows, even liberal societies were unable to envision rules reflecting the original position, because liberal elites are unwilling to assume the veil of ignorance.

Justice as Rights

Another approach to justice that relates tangentially to Rawls's original position and also to liberalism argues for the provision or availability of "human rights" to all individuals.[11] Conventionally, such rights are divided into categories: civil, political, social, economic, and cultural. *Civil* rights are linked to citizenship and include freedom from discrimination. *Political* rights, such as the right to vote or run for office, enable full participation in the institutionalized political processes of a country. *Social* rights allow an individual to participate in society to the greatest extent possible and include the right to an education. *Economic* rights provide access to those activities and goods that ensure livelihood. Finally, *cultural* rights permit groups to identify themselves as distinct, in some fashion, from the society in which they live. Theoretically, a society in which all these rights are available to every individual and group would be a society in which everyone is treated fairly and has access to goods and opportunities that would redress inequalities.

Human rights occupy a rather problematic position in the search for justice, however. Although explicit political and civil rights have their origins in events such the seventeenth-century revolutions in England and the eighteenth-century revolutions in the United States and France, economic and social rights are more recent, both cause and effect of the rise and evolution of the welfare state. The sources of all these rights are the focus of continuing debate. Originally, political and civil rights were regarded as "natural law," which is how they are presented in the American Declaration of Independence and Constitution. Political rights, described by Isaiah Berlin[12] as "positive liberty" (or "freedom to"), include rights of free association, free press, and access to the public square. Civil rights, which Berlin calls "negative liberty" (or "freedom from") had to do mostly with the freedom of the individual from control by outsiders, not only the sovereign, with his capacity to violate the body through such practices as torture, but also the neighbors and the church, which is why freedom to choose a religion (or no religion) and the right to choose a spouse, a domicile, and a job belong here. These freedoms relate to one's right to a private life.

The individual in a liberal society cannot function autonomously if she is overly constrained by rules and laws, but she also cannot function if her rights are not protected by rules and laws. Thus, at the extreme, these two sets of rights are in conflict. Full expression of positive liberty erases negative liberty for everyone else; full expression of negative liberty erases the public sphere for everyone. As with all rights, there are conflicts that must be addressed and settled by each and every society. To take just one example, consider the practice of male and female circumcision. These are cultural practices among certain religions, marking a bond to the society and a rite of passage. Yet, circumcision can also be seen as a form of child abuse and a violation of the individual rights and bodily integrity of children.

The other sets of rights—social, economic, cultural—arise from the observation that civil and political rights are of little use or benefit to those who are poor, hungry, homeless, and unemployed, and to those who belong to groups that are the focus of organized discrimination and even violence. In liberal societies, people are supposed to be able to satisfy the needs for food, a home, and employment through individual initiative. The United States, for example, does not recognize social, economic, and cultural rights as rights, arguing that state and society have no responsibility to provide them. We shall return to this issue below. Groups in liberal societies presumably are granted no exceptional privileges on the basis of ascriptive characteristics such as race, ethnicity, or gender, even though we know that some groups in civil society enjoy exceptional privileges for other reasons, such as social class or political connections.

Are human rights really "natural"? Recall that in Hobbes's State of Nature, men were completely free of limits but were also completely insecure. They were not threatened with torture by some ruling king, but they lived under constant threats from others. Indeed, the rights of individuals could not exist without a sovereign who is above the law to enforce the law. Hence the paradox of such rights: while they are constraints imposed on the state, they are also granted and protected by the state. While the theory calls these rights "inalienable," in practice, what the state giveth the state can taketh away.

In order to address this apparent contradiction, human rights have been embedded in a set of international conventions and agreements, such as the Universal Declaration of Human Rights (UDHR),[13] the International Covenant on Civil and Political Rights (ICCPR),[14] and the International Covenant on Economic, Social and Cultural Rights (ICESCR).[15] The United States has signed the UDHR but, as a declaration by the UN General Assembly, it is not a treaty and not binding, although it does set out norms and aspirations that have influenced the writing and passage of subsequent binding treaties. Thus, it is unfortunate that, even though the United States did sign both of the two international covenants, it has ratified only the ICCPR and is highly unlikely to ratify the ICESCR. While various rights agreements have been ratified by countries whose actual practices leave much to be desired, they, like the UDHR, still represent constituting elements in a human rights regime whose status transcends the individual states that are parties to them. Yet implementation remains in the hands of individual states, and the international mechanisms for evaluating state performance are run by states that rarely criticize themselves. More disinterested assessments of actual practice come from nongovernmental organizations such as Amnesty International and Human Rights Watch, which also condemn these practices when necessary.[16]

Even countries that actively promote human rights find it hard to balance various rights against one another. The provision, in particular, of economic and social rights requires either a high rate of economic growth and widespread prosperity to "trickle down" to all, regardless of status and position, or a substantial degree of redistribution that is fiercely resisted by the wealthy. Inasmuch as capitalism's efficient operation depends on a certain degree of inequality in a society—otherwise no one would sell her labor—there are real structural impediments to providing greater access to resources—think of admissions to Harvard, for example. Moreover, resistance to taxes suggests that there are limits to the public provision of social and economic rights. Even social programs directed at the poor come under criticism by the middle and upper classes, as contemporary Venezuelan politics illustrates, leaving many governments with little interest in pursuing this battle. To put all of this another way, while the fulfillment of all five sets of human rights would theoretically result in a reduction in injustice around the world, merely acknowledging such rights without recognizing the tensions among them has little effect on the problem of injustice.

None of this is meant to suggest that human rights are irrelevant; they play a critical role in the struggle for justice, and their pursuit, as much as their enforcement, is central to eliminating injustice around the world. Yet the troubling relationship between human rights and the state is visible in many places. Among the most important is the liberal state's reluctance to enforce civil and political rights where the market is concerned, visible in the sometimes violent suppression of popular protests against WTO rules and practices. This suggests that justice must be based on more than principled statements. Moreover, the individualized nature of life in liberal societies, in which the bonds of kinship and interdependence have been weakened (see chapter 2), exacerbates for many those social and economic conditions that are so central to the problem of injustice. Consequently, it would seem that, if the onus for redressing these conditions falls on the individual, she should be able to acquire the tools and capabilities to do so.

Justice as Opportunity

Redistribution is politically treacherous; rights are difficult to enforce fully; and the original position requires a strong moral commitment to justice. Members of liberal societies, moreover, tend to argue that no one can or should guarantee the equality of outcomes. They say that the best that can be done is to try to ensure that no one is blocked from efforts to overcome the disadvantages she might have been born under. Amartya Sen is probably the most articulate proponent of this position, making his arguments in the language of freedom.[17] As he puts it,

> The constitutive role of freedom relates to the importance of substantive freedom in enriching human life. The substantive freedoms include elementary capabilities like being able to avoid such deprivations as starvation, undernourishment, escapable morbidity and premature mortality, as well as the freedoms that are associated with being literate and numerate, enjoying political participation and uncensored speech and so on.[18]

Sen argues further that freedoms that include civil and political rights cannot be achieved if the substantive freedoms guaranteeing social and economic rights are lacking. But he also recognizes the obstacles to simply providing substantive freedoms, and the many failures that have accompanied "development" projects intended to do just this.

Consequently, Sen focuses instead on what he calls "capabilities," that is, "expansion of the 'capabilities' of persons to lead the kind of lives they value—and have reason to value."[19] Capabilities differ according to an individual's situation and needs, but they constitute something like an autonomous capacity to act in ways that enhance her quality of life. Here, "quality of life" is not simply income but the combination of factors, both material and intellectual, that enables a person to live a full and fulfilling life. They include such things as low infant mortality, access to family planning, adequate food and housing, employment at a living wage, literacy, numeracy, and other skills acquired through education, full participation in political and community activities, and so on. While Sen's concept of "development as freedom" is highly utilitarian, it does not seek to maximize aggregate utility. That is, the distribution of capabilities among individuals is more important than the greatest happiness for the largest number.

Yet Sen is critical of the basic principles of distributive justice, which rest largely on income and wealth. Although he acknowledges the virtue of economic growth as essential to achieving development, he does not believe that growth alone is sufficient. Examining the People's Republic of China and India—in particular, the state of Kerala in India—Sen points out that the development of capabilities that can be found in both China and Kerala is lacking in other parts of India. Kerala, it should be noted, has one of the lowest average per capita incomes in India. What, then, accounts for the difference, and why does Sen offer the case of a "poor" society as a "good" example?

We have to acknowledge that neither India nor China is an exemplary provider of rights, and that both currently suffer from a growing gap between rich and poor. But whatever their shortcomings, both Kerala and China have been strongly committed to social development through the provision of education (especially for women), employment, health care, food, housing, and land reform. Interestingly, perhaps, both also were governed by communist parties during the period in which these capabilities were developed. In China, in particular, claims Sen, this laid the foundation for the subsequent introduction of markets and the enormous economic growth rates of the past two decades.[20] While Kerala remains quite poor, and many of the social services once provided by the state have disappeared, it still remains one of the most socially developed states in the Indian Union, and its level of urban communal violence is among the lowest in the country.[21]

Sen argues that although his program for development requires a high degree of state involvement, it is nevertheless a liberal one, committed to individual freedom, and also is a capitalist one, dependent on growth to support and guarantee full access to capabilities. Sen makes no arguments about outcomes and whether they should be equalized; people should be free to do with their capabilities whatever they wish. Individuals simply must be able to recognize and seize opportunities when they appear, and the rest will be, as they say, history.

Not everyone who values Sen's approach to justice, development, and freedom is quite so sanguine about outcomes, however. John Isbister points out that "unequal outcomes in time create unequal opportunities."[22] As he explains the problem,

> This reasoning [about justice] leads to the possibility that equality of opportunity actually *requires* equal outcomes. This possibility exists because we live our lives over a period of years, our generations overlap, and our societies continue over time. My opportunities are determined in large measure by the resources—including economic, educational, technological, and moral resources—given to me by my parents and by my society. If my par-

ents and my society are vastly different in their access to these resources from yours, you and I will be unequal at the starting blocks. Until each person has an equal opportunity to develop his or her talents—something that cannot exist while the distribution of outcomes in the world remains unequal—we cannot be equal at the starting line.[23]

Addressing this contradiction clearly requires some means of restoring equality of opportunity. That means, at the least, a larger allocation of resources to public goods. Even with that, the social capital comprised of the various networks and contacts enabled by privilege and family history would still remain with the individual. Some argue that shifting the provision of goods from the private to the public sphere amounts to an infringement on people's freedom, since what they have acquired fairly is being taken away unfairly. Isbister does not subscribe to this argument, made by libertarians and economists such as Milton Friedman, but he quotes Philippe Van Parijs, who says that "real freedom is not only a matter of having the right to do what one might want to do, but also a matter of having the means for doing it."[24] Thus, while Isbister supports Sen's basic approach, he also favors a progressive tax policy so that the income ratio between the richest and poorest is reduced to about eight to one.[25] He would also impose a steep inheritance tax so as to minimize inequality at the beginning of life.[26]

There is an additional complication here that is worth considering, one that goes beyond both the veil of ignorance and Isbister's case against generational advantage. Justice as opportunity internalizes the idea that, if provided with the appropriate tools, anyone can be successful on his or her own terms. Yet, it is clear that many people with substantial capabilities do not succeed in their efforts to excel in particular areas; by some estimates, nine out of every ten new businesses in the United States fail within their first year. Similarly, many very bright and well-trained individuals find themselves rejected by medical, legal, or graduate schools, through no particular fault of their own. We assume that those who fail are individually responsible for their failure, and that such an outcome is fair and just, while those who fail may feel they have been discriminated against. Both are too simple as explanations.[27] They disregard, once again, the *social* nature of success and failure as well as fairness and injustice, and the fact that rights are often in tension and conflict.

Recall our discussion of the social individual presented in chapter 2. There, we saw that the individual is very much a "product" of the many social relations, over both space and time, that she has with other people, with things, and with institutions. We can call these relations a "social network." Social networks are built up through the many activities that we undertake, in school, work, and play. They constitute what is often called "social capital," in the sense that we invest energy and commitment into developing such relationships and realize various forms of "return" on them. Building a strong relationship with professors can be important if you will need letters of recommendation for graduate or professional school, or for a job application.

Having good relations with your boss will help you advance through the company. The people your parents know from school might be valuable connections for you as you search for work, and so on.

It should not have escaped your notice that the social capital inherent in networks of this sort correlates strongly with status and wealth. The poor may have as many relationships as the rich; the difference is that rich people's networks have greater scope and capacity, and more members with resources to use in influential ways. That, in turn, builds up more social capital and gives the rich a further advantage. Moreover, social capital can be turned into financial capital through these networks—think of that first job someone gets through a friend of the family. None of these relations can be measured easily (as opposed, say, to years of education or scores on achievement tests), yet they can be as important to success as any opportunities offered to you or capabilities you might possess. So how could we fold them into the notion of "justice as opportunity?" And how might we redress the inequalities that arise because some people have impoverished social networks compared to others?

The short answer is: "We can't." The long answer is: "Perhaps we can, but not without time and tolerance." Affirmative action represents one approach to redressing social inequalities, but it is badly flawed. We are used to hearing that affirmative action gives minorities and women an unfair advantage over equally or better-qualified white men. But this is an incorrect argument: affirmative action selects out specific *individuals* who are deemed representative of the best of a particular group and gives them an advantage over other specific individuals in other social groups. This is pretty routine practice among the already privileged in all walks of life (that job you got from a family friend did not go to someone else). It does not, however, mean that the position of the group as a whole is improved compared to that of other, more-advantaged groups. A successful individual might have a high income and live in a great neighborhood, but this doesn't do anything for anyone else in her natal social group. The average income of the group will rise if hers is included, but there is no personal benefit from her inclusion for those at the bottom of the distribution.

The argument for affirmative action rests on the assumption that providing meritorious individuals from disadvantaged groups with access to institutions rich in networks and potential social capital will improve the situation of the disadvantaged groups as a whole. The reasoning is that as larger numbers of disadvantaged individuals improve their positions—through opportunity—a sort of "trickle down" to others in that group will follow. Yet, there is now a growing understanding that middle-class African Americans can coexist comfortably with and in remarkable isolation from a growing impoverished black population. The successful middle class might raise the average, but it does not improve the lot of the worst off.[28] Justice is not served.

Moreover, to what are people entitled? Those who are born rich may squander much of their wealth, yet we consider them entitled to do so. Those who are born poor but with much promise may never succeed, simply for lack of support. Is it fair that the hand we are dealt when born has so much effect on our lives? And when we have to make choices about comparably qualified candidates for, say, admission to medical school, on what basis do we decide? Is it better to support those who have come from a relatively impoverished home in the hope that their eventual success will generate broad social benefits? Or should we select those who meet specific technical criteria such as minimum grade point averages and test scores? Which candidate is most entitled to admission?

This was the issue in the case of Allen Bakke, who was denied admission to the medical school at the University of California, Davis, in 1973 and 1974, even though his scores were higher than those of a number of minority candidates who were admitted under an affirmative action program. The supreme court of California ruled that he had been discriminated against and should be admitted. Eventually, the case made its way to the U.S. Supreme Court, which also found in Bakke's favor.[29] Since that time, similar cases have been brought; in more recent ones, the Supreme Court has been more equivocal about affirmative action programs, but the fact is that the courts should not be left to rule on these matters; they are issues for political debate and ought to be decided in the public square.

Is there a better way? One possibility might be to develop an institutional infrastructure specifically for those groups that are disadvantaged, whether as a result of poverty, race, ethnicity, or all three. Special projects and funds might provide large endowments (rather than specific program or project funds) to institutions serving disadvantaged groups. Imagine, for example, if schools and colleges serving minority and disadvantaged students in the United States had access to resources such as those available to prep schools or Harvard! Unfortunately, the resources to fund such endowments would have to come from somewhere—presumably taxes—undoubtedly evoking bitter opposition and loud cries of "injustice!"

Justice as Recognition, Respect, and Dignity

Yet another approach to the problem of injustice can be found in the concept of "recognition." Nancy Fraser, in particular, has been a strong advocate of recognition, although in recent years she has also argued that it is of little use without some degree of distributive justice.[30] Fraser is especially concerned about social justice, that is, some kind of equalization in terms of both distribution of resources *and* respect from others. Connected to the discussion about social capital and networks above, social justice would amount to the incorporation of disadvantaged groups into the social relations of the dominant group. This would entail not assimilation but what Fraser and others call *recognition*. With respect to discrimination against women, she writes,

> From the recognition perspective . . . gender is a status differentiation. A major feature of gender injustice is androcentrism: the authoritative con-

struction of norms that privilege traits associated with masculinity and the pervasive devaluation and disparagement of things coded as "feminine," paradigmatically—but not only—women. When these androcentric norms are institutionalized, women suffer gender-specific status injuries, including sexual assault and domestic violence; objectifying and demeaning stereotypical depictions in the media; harassment and disparagement in everyday life; and exclusion or marginalization in public spheres and deliberative bodies. These harms are injustices of misrecognition. They are relatively independent of political economy and are not merely "superstructural." Thus, they cannot be remedied by redistribution alone but require additional independent remedies of recognition.

She goes on to argue,

> Treating recognition as a matter of justice has a second advantage as well. It conceives misrecognition as a status injury whose locus is social relations, not individual psychology. To be misrecognized, on this view, is not simply to be thought ill of, looked down on, or devalued in others' conscious attitudes or mental beliefs. It is rather to be denied the status of a full partner in social interaction and prevented from participating as a peer in social life as a consequence of institutionalized patterns of cultural value that constitute one as comparatively unworthy of respect or esteem. This approach avoids difficulties that arise when misrecognition is understood psychologically.

Because redistribution will not afford redress of the injustice associated with misrecognition, which itself cannot address the injustice associated with redistribution, Fraser argues for a "two-dimensional" approach to justice. At the heart of her approach is what she calls "parity of participation." As she explains it,

> According to this norm, justice requires social arrangements that permit all (adult) members of society to interact with one another as peers. For participatory parity to be possible, I claim, at least two conditions must be satisfied. First, the distribution of material resources must be such as to ensure participants' independence and "voice." Second, the institutionalized cultural patterns of interpretation and evaluation must express equal respect for all participants and ensure equal opportunity for achieving social esteem.

In other words, without access to the resources necessary for a valued life, the individual has neither time nor opportunity to interact in society. And without the respect and legal basis for participation, redistribution is not likely to make much difference in terms of social justice.

While Fraser is on to something here, she has also fallen into the old "ought-is" trap: she is arguing for a social change in consciousness and practice without specifying clearly how that might be accomplished. What's more problematic is the tautological nature of this two-dimensional framework: each cannot accomplish justice in the absence of the other, yet neither seems likely to come about unless the other happens first (well, perhaps redistribution could precede recognition, although recognition would certainly cost less). Political philosophers rarely are responsible for seeing through their proposals and projects; their job is to conceptualize the conditions under which a particular objective might be achieved. Where, then, is the lever that could "move the world?"

Communitarianism vs. Cosmopolitanism

Let us return, for a moment, to the contrasting approaches of Peter Singer and Garrett Hardin. Singer, you will recall, argues that every human being is deserving of help, whether a conational or not, and that each of us should help others until we are no better off than they are. Hardin argues that we have obligations only to our families and conationals and should not help others lest we cause our "lifeboat" to founder. Singer's approach is an extreme version of *cosmopolitanism* (or, perhaps, what Karl Marx calls "species being"). It is extreme because it accords equal respect and dignity to *all* human beings, whereas Kant distinguishes between obligations to one's community and hospitality to the stranger (see chapters 1 and 7).[31] As a political philosophy, cosmopolitanism involves a good deal more than matters of justice;[32] as it applies to justice, there are several ways to articulate it.[33] The approach of particular interest is taken by Onora O'Neill, who writes about the *obligations* associated with justice, even to those who are "distant strangers."[34] We will return to this argument shortly.

Communitarianism draws lines outside of which we have no moral obligations and need not be concerned about justice; it is similar to Hardin's views in that it draws those lines generally as the borders of *nation-states*. Hence, communitarianism is an approach that is consonant with contemporary world order, and its proponents are unconcerned about people who live and die in faraway lands. Indeed, while there are differing approaches to communitarianism, we can say that, in general, the limits to justice ignore even proximity and potential suffering. Thus, an individual who is among us but not of us has none of the rights or privileges granted to members of the community. We are not even obligated to take in someone who has grounds for fearing persecution, torture, or death if she is returned to her homeland.

International law mandates that such individuals be granted asylum if they can prove their fear is justified. But those who might leave their home countries for what are judged to be purely economic reasons have no grounds for requesting asylum, and it is the host state that decides whether a refugee is political or economic. In a communitarian system, consequently, injustice is often committed on any number of fronts: there are the conditions that create the injustice in the first place; there are the conditions under which those who seek to escape unjust conditions must live; and there are the conditions that make a supposedly moral distinction between "political" and "economic" injustice, with the latter deemed to be of no import. Evidently, communitarianism can not only accept but even encourage injustice.

Let us return, then, to the obligations of justice. O'Neill counterpoises these obligations to a "rights-based" approach that relies, in effect, on individuals claiming rights and demanding that others—whether fellow citizens, state authorities, or international agencies—fulfill them. More to the point is that the rights discussed earlier in this chapter are discussed in the abstract: people deserve them but there is no ensuring, even in the best-off societies, that they will be met. Obligations, by contrast, are imposed on or accepted by each individual, whose duty is to see that they are fulfilled. And, as O'Neill puts it,

> There are reasons enough to show that obligations provide the more coherent and more comprehensive starting point for thinking about ethical requirements, including the requirements of justice. Although the rhetoric of rights has a heady power, and that of obligations and duties few immediate attractions, it helps to view the perspective of obligations as fundamental if the political and ethical implications of normative claims are to be taken seriously.

Even if we are not sure to whom we owe obligations, she argues, "we at least begin with a practical task."[35]

O'Neill does not go quite so far as Singer in defining the extent of our obligations, and she is willing to consider a mix of strategies and tactics beyond simply giving until we have no more to give without causing ourselves moral or physical injury. But what is important about her approach is that it requires *agency:* we must act in order to be just and achieve justice, and we must do so regardless of states, governments, and even conationals. Better yet, we should do so with others, as a collective political project. As Arlo Guthrie once said (in a somewhat different context), "If you want to end war and stuff you got to sing loud."[36] If we want to have justice, we have to sing together.

How Far Do Our Obligations Extend?

Much of this chapter has been concerned with justice in an abstract context, as something that we all desire but about which we disagree. Although the conflict between communitarian and cosmopolitan approaches to justice might seem the most antagonistic, the real guts of the problem are to be found in *structures* that we tend to regard as "natural" but that are not, and that reproduce again and again the very social relations that are the source of injustice in the first place. We discussed structures and naturalization earlier in this book when we considered people and economy (chapter 4). Here, we examine the injustices perpetuated by particular structures, not all of them economic, that lead to the acceptance of injustice as "natural."

Consider the notion of reparations to the American descendants of slaves, discussed above. This is an idea that has been around since the first rumors that "forty acres and a mule" would be given to the newly freed slaves at the end of the U.S. Civil War. In recent years, the proposal has surfaced as a means of rectifying the long-standing socioeconomic gap between the majority of African Americans and the majority of whites.[37] While it is difficult to estimate the appropriate value of reparations, somewhere between $1 trillion and $10 trillion is a reasonable estimation of the fair value of the wages earned but never paid to black slaves.[38] Whether or not this sum is absurdly large or insultingly small is not important; the critical question is whether such a payment is fair and obligatory. Many people, when confronted with this question, respond that they bear no responsibility for what happened centuries ago, and nothing is owed to the descendants of slaves. Besides, who would get the money, how would you know who is legally entitled, and how could we possibly pay for it? Another, somewhat smaller, group of people respond, "That was then. Slavery was legal, and the slaves were freed. We cannot change the past." A few legalistically inclined observers claim that slavery has caused no injury to anyone now alive and therefore that no one is owed any compensation.

Recall Garret Hardin's argument about the theft of land from Native Americans, quoted earlier. Disregarding for a moment Hardin's cynicism, does this point to his conclusion? He writes,

> Clearly, the concept of pure justice produces an infinite regression to absurdity. Centuries ago, wise men invented statutes of limitations to justify the rejection of such pure justice, in the interest of preventing continual disorder. The law zealously defends property rights, but only relatively recent property rights. Drawing a line after an arbitrary time has elapsed may be unjust, but the alternatives are worse.
>
> We are all the descendants of thieves, and the world's resources are inequitably distributed. But we must begin the journey to tomorrow from the point where we are today. We cannot remake the past. We cannot safely divide the wealth equitably among all peoples so long as people reproduce at different rates. To do so would guarantee that our grandchildren and everyone else's grandchildren, would have only a ruined world to inhabit.[39]

We think not. No one is speaking of some kind of infinite redress, only something proportional to the original injustice. What Hardin and others attempt in making arguments such as "We are all descendants of thieves" is to naturalize both theft and injustice as inherent to human nature and society. Yet, as even Hardin acknowledges, our current prosperity is due in no small part to the original capital in land, labor, and resources provided by both Native Americans and slaves.

The same argument can be extended to virtually all rich countries, whose wealth is not simply the result of prudent investment, technological innovation, and brilliant entrepreneurship, but also a product of colonialism, exploitation, and theft. The "fact" that, in the absence of such historical crimes and injustices, the world would be a much poorer and, perhaps, even less just place today is hardly a basis on which to excuse the acts of our ancestors. Where we are able to rectify such injustices, we are obligated to do so in the name of cosmopolitan justice.

Carol Robb makes an interesting argument about the notion of "debt" to preceding generations that belies Hardin's claims that we have no obligations to those whom we might have dispossessed or treated unjustly. She argues that we are obligated to "make payment on the social mortgage," which is "the debt all must pay back to a society in recognition that one inherits wealth in the form of goods or knowledge or technology from those who have gone before or who walk with us now."[40] Robb claims, in essence, that there is no such thing as a purely "private" return on investment or property; that all human activities, whether social, political, or economic, are built on foundations laid down by others.[41] Even at 1 percent, the interest on current social wealth would amount to a goodly sum that could go a considerable way toward redressing historical injustices.

How far must we go to fulfill them? And how to go about it? O'Neill does not provide more than general guidelines, and there is no sign that she concurs with Singer's dictum. She does, however, offer the following:

> Kantian economic justice does not point simply to increasing average income or wealth, let alone achieving economic uniformities of any sort. Like other aspects of justice, it is a matter of limiting relative power and powerlessness, so securing the external freedom within which people can seek to obtain the means to lead their lives. . . . If justice is fundamentally a matter of securing external freedom for all, reforms which build a more just transnational economic order might have to regulate and police international markets, transactions and relations so that the conditions that make some local markets and transactions and domestic social relations relatively secure even for the weak obtain more widely.[42]

Accordingly, we are obligated to work toward the kinds of institutional changes that will facilitate and foster the conditions under which all people can pursue a valued life.

Justice for the People!

In our discussion of the many approaches to the problem of injustice, there is one point that we have, so far, failed to discuss: the relationship between global politics and justice for people. After all, if the sources of injustice are to be found in the actions of states, the operations of markets, and the structures of societies, what can a focus on individual justice accomplish? This question points back to an earlier discussion about the nature of social change and how it takes place. Some argue that what is most important is a change of perspective: once enough people start to demand justice, states and corporations will have no choice but to comply. Others believe that technology is key: if biotechnology can increase world production of food, fewer people will go hungry and injustice will decrease. A few still place their hopes in class struggle and the changes that would accompany revolution against capitalism and the state.

We regard these arguments, taken separately, as something like the old parable of the blind men and the elephant. Each man touched a different part of the elephant and imagined it to be a different kind of animal from the ones the others reported sensing. Justice demands that we believe all our fellow human beings to be worthy of dignity and respect; that we act in ways that facilitate and foster dignity and respect among human beings; and that we provide the material necessities that enable people to live dignified lives worthy of respect. Indeed, we are obligated to do these things and also to help to construct a discourse that will propagate justice and embed it in institutions at every level of life. In chapter 10, we will return to this obligation and the political action necessary to meet it.

9

People and Globalization

I'd like to teach the world to sing in perfect harmony.

—Roger Cook and Roger Greenaway

We've talked a lot about globalization in this volume, and now it's time to look more closely at what "globalization" means. Its most basic definition—this version is taken from economist Joseph Stiglitz—is "the closer integration of the countries and peoples of the world which has been brought about by the enormous reduction of costs of transportation and communication, and the breaking down of artificial barriers to the flows of goods, services, capital, knowledge, and (to a lesser extent) people across borders."[1] Political scientist James Mittelman says that globalization is "[d]riven by changing modes of competition [such that it] compresses the time and space aspects of social relations. [It] is a market-induced, not a policy-led, process,"[2] but, as we discuss in this chapter, there are many engines of globalization in addition to the market, and globalization occurred long before "the market" as we know it existed.

Globalization takes many pathways. It brings people and places closer to one another at a faster and faster rate, forcing both to adjust to the continual change demanded by its disruption of social space. Strangers come to new lands to exploit resources that formerly were out of reach; people change jobs, locations, and identities repeatedly in a single lifetime. Some argue that this makes the global economy more stable and efficient than national economies, but others note that it also increases individual insecurity.[3] As we saw in chapter 7, economic competition is an element of modern and postmodern warfare. In consequence, both globalization and the resistance it evokes can be intense and violent.

Globalization Then and Now

These qualities of globalization were evident in the late nineteenth century, the only period of hyperrapid incorporation into global capitalism closely similar to what is happening today. Then as now, globalization grew out of new transport, communication, and command-and-control technologies. Karl Marx and Frederick Engels describe the rapidly globalizing nineteenth-century world as one where "all that is solid melts into air."[4] Karl Polanyi traces the role of nineteenth-century globalization in creating what today we call "the Third World," where local cultures were shattered by a combination of market mechanisms and crushing tax burdens imposed by imperial powers:

> The catastrophe of the native community is a direct result of the rapid and violent disruption of the basic institutions of the victim (whether force is used in the process or not does not seem altogether relevant). These institutions are disrupted by the very fact that a market economy is foisted upon an entirely differently organized community; labor and land are made into commodities, which, again, is only a short formula for the liquidation of every and any cultural institution in an organic society.[5]

Globalization is thus a complex process of economically led cross-cultural integration. Trade, finance, and investment are its biggest engines, and local structures and cultures are its victims. Globalization's results include the centralization of governance, cultural homogenization, and the redistribution of wealth and income within and between nation-states.[6]

Despite the prominence of capitalism in both phases of modern globalization, we should not think of this process as either totally modern or merely economic. Older forms of "contact" affect people's lives and life chances, too. Trade and markets have always connected peoples, as studies of the transmission of infectious diseases like plague and influenza show.[7] War, conquest, colonization, and enslavement are globalizing processes that, like trade and investment, initiate or speed up the redistribution of power and wealth among persons and countries.[8] Natural disasters like floods, droughts, and earthquakes also trigger population migration and wealth redistribution, sometimes with a little help from human beings in positions to take advantage of the misfortunes of others.[9] One example familiar to Americans is the great famine in Ireland (1845–1850), when potato blight wiped out the food crop that most Irish peasants depended on. Landowners reaped a bonanza. Food prices soared across Europe, and landlords exported grain that the domestic population could not afford to buy. More than one million peasants starved to death, and as many migrated to the New World in search of a better life. The pattern of starvation and migration was repeated during the great El Niño famines of the late nineteenth century.[10]

The movement of people, goods, and money depends on the movement of information. Superior information increases the ability to command and control events at a distance, not only in trade and diplomacy, but also in war fighting. During the eighteenth and early nineteenth centuries, locally based British East India Company (BEIC) employees policed the boundaries between their trading enclaves and the hinterlands surrounding them pretty much as they chose.[11] Company military forces continually expanded BEIC territory along this "turbulent frontier," justifying each added increment as necessary to ensure the security of what they had taken before. Although the British government, which had chartered the company, was ultimately responsible for its actions, it had little to say about how it conducted its military operations.[12] The inadequacy of British command and control of the BEIC was exposed when British-trained Indian troops rebelled against the company in 1857–1858. Spurred by egregious violations of the religious sensibilities of Hindus and Muslims, they rose up in the bloody "Sepoy Mutiny," which spread rapidly to disaffected groups in major cities like Delhi.[13] After two years of fighting and thousands of deaths, London took direct control of India.

Today's technology allows political leaders to supervise military activities closely, even if they are taking place thousands of miles away. The command authority for U.S. troops fighting in Afghanistan was located in Tampa, Florida, conveniently close to Washington yet no more isolated from the battlefields than Saigon-based general William Westmoreland had been during the Vietnam War. Paradoxically, this increase in state command-and-control capability comes along with the proliferation and mass marketing of communications technology in the private sector—"command and control" does not guarantee "control" outside of "command." The commercial availability of telecommunications and air travel democratizes globalization and challenges the ability of states to restrain the movements of ideas, people, and goods undertaken privately. The same infrastructure that allows states to command and control armies half a world away allowed terrorist organizers equally far from action fronts to devise and coordinate a set of suicide attacks on two large U.S. cities using planes owned by commercial airlines. The instigators of these attacks showed how easily globalization can thwart state power, repeatedly eluding the armies sent to capture them by slipping quickly and quietly from one country to another, leaving little more than a trail of videotapes behind.

Globalization includes the movement of virtual "goods" such as images, designs, symbols, and money from their cultures of origin to somewhere else. The dispersion of virtual goods also precedes modern times. Textile and pottery designs migrated widely among "primitive" people. A particularly good collection for observing the impact of cross-cultural contact on textile design is held by the Museum of the American Indian, recently transplanted from New York to Washington, D.C., which has many textiles from widely separated places that feature similar motifs and patterns. Another example is the blue and white "Delft" tableware patterns manufactured and sold by Dutch potteries. They were derived from Japanese pottery designs, and both were influenced by the earlier diffusion of the Blue Willow design from China, itself a product of the demand for high-quality Chinese porcelain from new Muslim elites in Europe and west Asia and only later sold in Chinese markets.[14] What is different about the dispersion of virtual goods today is how quickly this happens. Textile designs in the pre-Columbian Americas traveled "on foot" and in small boats; Blue Willow pottery designs circulated throughout Asia and Europe on pack animals and ships. The Internet offers a much faster way for designs to get around.

Social critics from the twentieth-century Frankfurt School argued that the same mass production techniques that gave us the Model T Ford (and its successors) now are routinely applied to the manufacture of cultural artifacts.[15] But, as with pottery and textiles in the past, the films, music, and television programs produced by large media companies do more than standardize citizen-consumers. They also offer ways for individuals to express their own values and aesthetics in symbols that are intelligible cross-culturally.[16] Even complicated ideas like human rights take similar meanings in the minds of persons from widely disparate cultures.[17] So while it is true that commercial values and pop culture are spread by modern communication technologies, they travel with additions, contentions, and reinterpretations, thereby constituting a far larger repertoire of values and cultures than whatever might have come in the original package.

Structures

Structures of globalization are complex regimes incorporating technology, organization, and sets of norms, values, and rules that are codified and enforced by international and national bodies. During the first round of El Niño famines in India, for example, Edward Robert Bulwer Lytton, Britain's viceroy of India, used military technology to keep distressed populations from stealing food; British law to prevent private charities from giving food to the starving; the rail system to collect and export "surplus" food from India to earn foreign exchange for his pet project, a war in Afghanistan; and his power to tax to trigger foreclosures on drought-stricken land, enabling wealthy Indians and Britons to purchase it at rock-bottom prices. Although Lytton blamed the millions of deaths that resulted from the famine on "natural causes," it is clear that man-made structures and his own decisions as a powerful agent contributed heavily to these terrible consequences.[18]

This mixture of structures also highlights the distinction we made in chapter 7 between "acute" violence—physically destroying, maiming, and hurting people—and structural violence, which we defined as institutions and practices imposing systematic injustice on target groups. Imperialism is a transnational system of structural violence built on rules and practices that confer advantageous access to resources on the imperial power, its agents, and its citizens, and corresponding disadvantages on local communities and their agents and citizens. Yet as we have argued throughout this volume, "the system" alone does not determine outcomes. Lytton as an agent chose to prevent food aid from being distributed by the state or by private parties even though other agents—compassionate English citizens like Richard Grenville, the Duke of Buckingham, journalist William Digby, and the most famous nurse in the world, Florence Nightingale—struggled to open India to famine relief supplied through their official and social networks. The impact of structure on agency also is clear. Agents with charitable impulses were structurally blocked not only by rules but even more by Lytton as an agent and interpreter of these rules, and by another agent with vast structural resources, the British prime minister Benjamin Disraeli.[19] Without structures like railroads, the telegraph, an industrialized British military, and the British government in London, the harm that Lytton and Disraeli could have inflicted on Indians during the famine would have been far less, but with other agents in charge of these same powerful structures, the famine might never have occurred.[20]

The most prominent structure facilitating globalization in the nineteenth century and today is "the market," vast, interconnected, national and transnational systems of rules and practices that govern capitalist relations of production and exchange. The "incorporation" (absorption) of territories and populations into global capitalist networks takes place on many different fronts. Barriers to trade and investment set by protective local and national legal regimes are broken by treaties and laws, and by transportation and communication technologies that allow buyers and sellers to penetrate former backwaters. Transport technologies are critical to creating and maintaining integrated markets. Until railroads were built, most goods traded over long distances went by ship or barge, still the cheapest mode of transport.[21] Products from microeconomies in interior regions were isolated from towns and cities located on rivers and seacoasts, trapped by the high cost of getting goods from one place to another via human and animal transport over land. The result was many small subsistence markets, some market towns and fairs, and a few cosmopolitan centers such as we described in chapter 5.[22]

One prominent exception was the land route to Asia, over which camels carried packs of precious objects from East to West. "Precious" explains this trade. Silk, jewels, and spices could be transported long distances over land because of the high prices per unit of weight that sellers received for them, enough to buy food, water, and lodging for the men and beasts operating the trade route and still make a healthy profit. What determined whether a land route was economic was the cost of protection money that had to be paid to the warlords who controlled the territories the traders crossed. As long as most of Asia remained politically fragmented, there were too many warlords to make the land route profitable.

Genghis Khan's conquests and subsequent political consolidation allowed the land route to compete with the two sea routes between Europe and Asia. The availability of the land route also greatly increased the volume of Europe's trade with China—and with cities in between, such as Samarkand, which otherwise would not have been the crossroads of commerce and centers of culture that they became during this time.[23] Modern rulers of nation-states sought to integrate the economies in territories they controlled. Among the first steps to opening the interiors of consolidated realms was to improve transportation. This allowed rulers to subdue and pacify remote regions and, by stimulating trade, to increase the state's income.[24] Road systems and canals linked to navigable rivers made travel cheaper and faster. China's economy was constructed around market towns located on waterways, drawing agricultural produce from hinterland villages into larger networks of trade.[25] State-regulated monetary systems also boosted internal trade, along with taxation and the "invention" of the national debt, a system that mobilizes financial support to pay for larger and more active governments.[26] Increasingly, people were required to pay taxes in money and not "in kind"—corn or chickens or whatever else they produced. To get money to pay their taxes, peasants had to sell goods, their labor, and sometimes also their land, deepening the spread of market relations. For many peasants, market relations represented a great improvement over feudal dues in the form of forced labor and military service, and servile (unfree) status,[27] helping to explain the fervor with which groups like the Levellers embraced possessive individualism.

Railroads increased the integration of national markets and extended the reach of traders and investors into interior regions abroad. The role of railroads as tools of both imperialism and marketization is especially clear in sub-Saharan Africa, where most colonial-era rail lines ran from ports to regions in the interior rich in raw materials.[28] One consequence is that the socially fragmented territories of postcolonial states had few physical supports for creating national economies.[29] Railroad construction in developing areas brought other benefits to Europeans, providing a market for national steel companies after rail networks were substantially completed in their home countries.[30] It speeded up capital accumulation by the investors who financed these rail lines and sometimes by the investors' home governments, which felt compelled to take over the economies of countries unable to repay the cost of railroads and other goods and services they had received (whether they wanted them or not).[31]

The importance of railroads to the progress of nineteenth-century globalization has a twentieth-century parallel in the construction of highways and airports for motor vehicle and air travel. Not coincidentally, multinational oil companies were key agents of globalization during much of the twentieth century. Supplying fuel to consumer markets required cross-border transactions from the industry's beginnings.[32] Struggles between imperial powers often masked and were fueled by conflicts over who would control oil-producing regions. A classical example of cascading damage from these conflicts is the formation and subsequent history of the nation-state of Iraq. It was assembled by the victors of World War I from large segments of what had been three districts of the defeated Ottoman Empire: Baghdad, with its majority of Sunni Muslim Arabs; Basra, where the majority of the population is Shi'i Muslim Arab; and Mosul, where Iraqi oil was first discovered on territory occupied mostly by Sunni Muslim Kurds. The construction of this "multinational" state was masterminded by the British government, the "mandate power" in Iraq, which wanted to be sure that it would control the exploitation of Iraq's oil resources. In 1990, the goal of limiting Iraq's oil-market power was one of the several reasons offered by the United States–led coalition for its decision to liberate Kuwait in 1990 and 1991, and the control of Iraqi oil was a major objective of the U.S.-British invasion of Iraq in 2003.[33]

Access to mechanical modes of transport was widespread thanks to their commercial exploitation. Automobiles started off as toys for the very rich, becoming conveniences for the well-to-do, and finally finding their way into working-class life. As we described in chapter 2, cars became necessary adjuncts to a new lifestyle financed by the post–WW II "GI Bill of Rights." Car ownership enabled urban workers to live outside the city, changing housing patterns and stimulating real estate markets. Mobility also helped to "rationalize" labor markets, because workers could travel longer distances to jobs that paid higher wages or offered better working conditions. Favorable regulation enabled trucks to replace trains as long-distance carriers of products, and, following airline deregulation, lower prices made air transport of goods and people an economical alternative to other, slower, modes. People "voted with their feet"—or wheels and wings—leaving home and country to study abroad, enjoy vacations in exotic places, or join the military to see the world.

Railroads were key to moving supplies and troops to war zones in the U.S. Civil War and during WW I. Air transport rapidly became a more far-reaching and destructive element in the technology of violence. Aircraft carry troops and supplies to far-off fields of battle and deliver death directly by bombing and strafing enemy targets. Even motor vehicles are incorporated into warfare. Perhaps the most famous early story of the deployment of cars in battle tells of the September 1914 transport by Paris taxicabs of six thousand French reservists to the front during the first battle of the Marne. Since then, motor vehicles have become integral to war fighting. Tanks were used by Italy in its conquest of Libya during the 1920s. Armed (and armored) versions of what started out as trucks and road-building equipment, military "humvees" have made the transition back to consumer markets in the form of extra-large SUVs. Roads themselves are part of the technology of violence. The Kuwaitis built a road to carry military supplies to Iraq during its 1980–1988 war with Iran. The same road was used by Iraq to invade Kuwait two years after that war was over. In February 1991, the road attracted fleeing Iraqi soldiers trying to escape coalition forces liberating Kuwait, enabling fighter plane crews to incinerate Iraqi vehicles and personnel with murderous efficiency on what the press dubbed "the highway of death."

Globalization and Neighborhoods

Technology also is a major component of "bottom-up" globalization, speeding processes whose agents are individuals making choices about their own lives.

Space programs were inaugurated as part of the cold-war competition between the Soviet Union and the United States, and large corporations choke radio, TV, and the Internet with advertisements for their products. Yet individuals still manage to transform the products of all these activities into ideas and symbols with meaning for themselves. Images of the earth as seen from space were captured by cameras carried by satellites. These images evoked a new understanding of the planet as a unity, one that is finite, beautiful, and, in the vastness of space, small and vulnerable. The image of a fragile unitary earth was not what U.S. policy makers had intended to generate from the space program, but it occurred spontaneously and was reinforced by the products of mass culture we noted earlier. World music, international films, and televised sports also encouraged human beings to see themselves as participants in a global culture belonging to that precious blue planet. All of this fostered appreciation of systemic linkages that produce problems transcending state boundaries and jurisdictions. Technology analyst Clark Miller writes:

> Underpinning the construction of ideas about the ozone layer and the climate system is a dramatic change in people's conceptual frameworks. Until the 1970s, scientists and lay observers alike [thought of the] atmosphere in predominantly local terms. In 1941, for example, the first US government assessment of human-climate interactions defined climate as follows: "the climate of a place is merely a build-up of all the weather from day to day." . . . This . . . supports the notion that Boston and Miami have different climates. [In contrast] . . . the definition of climate adopted by the 1992 UN Framework Convention on Climate change . . . is an integrated, global system comprising "the totality of the atmosphere, hydrosphere, biosphere, and geosphere and their interactions." From this perspective, climate is not specific to an individual locale but rather encompasses the planet as a whole.[34]

One reason why we think of globalization as something new is that the process is more accessible today than it was in earlier eras. What we have called the democratization of globalization is made possible by commerce. Money, even more than family background or nationality, offers agency to billions of people. Small outlays can buy access to a worldwide virtual audience for one's ideas or complaints via Internet cafés. But democratization doesn't always produce understanding or appreciation of human difference. People turning on their television sets, suddenly confronted by images of the alien features, immoral sexual behavior, and disgusting cuisine of others who, twenty years ago, they might not have known even existed, are not always charmed by the novelty. With invasions of private, communal, and sacred spaces by students, tourists, and soldiers, and the economic changes imposed by trade regimes these once-sheltered people still might be unaware of, globalization has become pervasive. As it has, its contradictory effects become more obvious and more resented.

It is true that globalization operates as an engine of integration—the conventional image is "the global village." Forces as diverse as images of the earth as seen from space, the worldwide consumption of Coca-Cola, McDonald's, and Levi's, and the growing dependence of nearly everyone in the world on products and services produced somewhere else, give us the impression that the world is becoming smaller and people are becoming more like one another. This illusion of similarity is fostered by the structure of media industries, where oligopolistic competition homogenizes formats, although not necessarily coverage. Media analyst Naomi Sakr traces the business and personal links connecting the interests of media moguls like Bill Gates, Rupert Murdoch, and Silvio Berlusconi—people you've probably heard of—to others like Prince Alwaleed bin Galal, Leo Kirch, and Rafiq Hariri, whom you might not know about at all.[35] She argues that the global village metaphor might describe the relationship among elites who own shares in multiple media conglomerates, but its deceptive coziness hides the political connections that shape news and information coverage to suit the interests of the leaders and governments that regulate media in national markets. Although "CNN look-alikes" abound on satellite services, the product delivered to viewers varies according to the dictates of power holders in corporate boardrooms and national capitals. Even CNN produces one program for viewers overseas and another (more like FOX News) for home consumption.

This is because contact with foreigners in blue jeans—or turbans—often nourishes resentment. According to "the narcissism of little differences," distinctions of all sizes and kinds become sharper and more painful when contact is increased. Media producers react by shaping products to conform both to political pressures and to consumer demand. Divergences in news content from country to country are particularly evident during wars.[36] Even in more normal times, however, consumers everywhere like to see their country and themselves portrayed in a favorable light as compared to other countries and their citizens, and we should not be surprised that consumers choose media products that suit their preferences. Cultural pressures combined with a sense that "strangers are invading our space and taking our stuff" make contemporary interpersonal and international relationships more rather than less contentious, even among peoples who have lived side by side (but perhaps not cheek by jowl) for centuries.

The Amorality of Globalization

"Globalization" also describes the proliferation of private and relatively unpoliced networks for raising and transferring funds and mobilizing armies; such networks are also used for moving and selling both relatively benign products like Coca-Cola and deadly ones, like guns and cocaine. Globalization speeds up traffic in persons, the theft of ideas and identities, and the proliferation of sophisticated weapons and weapons systems formerly monopolized by states. States must adjust to a world in which they no longer are the sole proprietors of the means to inflict great violence. Although they continue to insist that they remain the sole *legitimate* wielders of violence, their legitimacy as well as their capacity are challenged directly by terrorists at home and abroad.

Political analyst Olivier Roy argues that globalization is integral to the creation of contemporary terrorists and their networks.[37] It produces "deracination," a term that refers to the results of transplanting people from familiar surroundings to strange new environments.[38] Deracination detaches such persons from the familiar social structures that used to protect them, connect them to family and friends, supply their needs and desires, and constrain their behavior; it places them in new structures that endanger their lives and shape their choices and behaviors differently. Deracination is the first stage in commodification, a process that transforms people into products. Deracination works by separating young persons from familiar settings and those responsible for their welfare, and making them into strangers dependent on entrepreneurs who want to transform their bodies and minds into commodities. Sex workers and terrorists are similar products of different kinds of transnational commodification networks. Sex tourists take advantage of deracination to gain cheap and ready access to the bodies of children and youth, and terrorist organizations use it to gain access to bodies and minds they can deploy in their strategic conflicts. Globalization provides the efficient and democratized transportation networks that serve both of these dark-side markets.

The commercial quality of globalization allows actors to buy access to networks that let them move resources and themselves quickly, cheaply, and easily from one jurisdiction to another. Carolyn Nordstrom tells how movie producers race large amounts of sophisticated equipment into war zones, where they can find young refugees to use—and use up—as victims in violent pornographic films.[39] Afghan war zones have been a destination for religious idealists since the late 1970s, and post-Saddam Iraq has become a new magnet for young persons who go there to fight the "Crusaders" and end up becoming terrorists. Indeed, contemporary terrorist movements get their strength from the ease with which individuals can cross national boundaries and find government allies whose interests coincide at least in part with their own. One example is the symbiotic relationship that existed between the Taliban government in Afghanistan and the al Qaeda network. The Taliban provided sanctuary and recruits for al Qaeda. In return, al Qaeda provided money and other assistance to a government whose policies had earned it the status of an international pariah and cut it off from normal channels of aid and assistance.[40]

Al Qaeda and other mass movements incorporating terrorist elements frequently are led by members of privileged social classes with vast political and economic resources. The social positions of Saudi Osama bin Laden and one of his close associates, Kuwaiti Sulaiman bu Ghaith, kept them alive and active despite their illegal activities by ensuring that they would be exiled rather than arrested and tried (and possibly executed) for their crimes. The bin Laden family's great wealth and its political connections in the United States as well as at home in Saudi Arabia, along with the financial contributions that mullahs such as Sulaiman could attract through appeals to the faithful and then transfer abroad under the guise of charity, contributed significantly to their successes.[41] These resources and the geographic mobility supplied by globalized transit networks increase the capacity of terrorist organizations to act.

Globalization is thought to be the primary engine of growth for "new social movements." These are relatively unstructured networks whose elements come together when an "opportunity structure"—a series of events, the appearance of a charismatic leader, a sudden influx of resources—allows people to take action with a reasonable hope for success.[42] As we discussed in chapter 5, many new social movements work to support human rights and environmental protection. Others fit descriptions suggested by analysts David Ronfeldt and John Arquilla, who argue that they are uniquely capable of "netwar." This is social struggle carried out by flexible, nonhierarchical coalitions of sometimes widely dispersed activists which come together for a particular purpose at a particular time and then disperse when that task has been completed.[43] An alternative view of globalization and revolutionary social movements is offered by Michael Hardt and Antonio Negri.[44] They see netwar positively, using a name coined by French philosopher Michel Foucault, "biopower," to describe modern technology in combination with human agents. In the Hardt and Negri view, such networks allow oppressed people to mobilize on their own behalf against "Empire," a worldwide combination of state and capitalist institutions—both networks and Empire being products of globalization.

The networks described by Hardt and Negri are available to every interconnected element: not just to Citibank but also to informal banks and agents that allow guest workers abroad to send money home cheaply and quickly to families residing in remote rural areas,[45] and to terrorists, thieves, and drug lords; not just to the rich and famous but also—especially—to the ordinary and anonymous, whose very lack of distinction allows them to move through the networks' channels unnoticed and still mostly unchecked. This point highlights both the key role of agents acting within structures, and how small differences in structures open possibilities for action to agents who are alert.

The amorality of networks as such and their dependence on the actions and ethics of agents is clearly illustrated in an example that compares India and Pakistan, two countries with a common heritage and a common border. *New York Times* columnist Tom Friedman describes Indians and Pakistanis as people who share "blood, brains and civilizational heritage" but the differences he finds show how little individual measures like "blood," or IQ, or "heritage" matter when structures interfere with persons being able to realize their full potentials. In India, "50 years of . . . democracy and secular education, and 15 years of economic liberalization," produced a nation in which religious violence is localized and, increasingly, anomalous.[46] This is true. But political scientist Ashutosh Varshney concludes that these different outcomes are explained less by different trade regimes than by differences in local civil societies.[47] Varshney presents a more complicated picture of India than Friedman does. Varshney's India is divided into regions. Some enjoy a functioning civil society that alerts the community to the possibility of violence and works purposefully to head it off—usually with some success. But others lack civil society structures, and this is where intergroup violence is far more common. People who live there have low levels of literacy, and there are few voluntary associations that cross religious lines.

Friedman argues that religion is a main reason for Pakistan's problems: "Across the border in Pakistan . . . 50 years of failed democracy, military coups and imposed religiosity have produced 30,000 madrassahs—Islamic schools, which have replaced a collapsed public school system and churn out Pakistani youth who know only the Koran and hostility toward non-Muslims."[48] But Varshney shows that authoritarian politics prevents the kind of citizen activism he finds in some parts of India from developing elsewhere. Storefront religious "education" and youth unemployment provide a fertile ground for terrorist organizers in socially impoverished areas of Hindu India, just as they do in most of Muslim Pakistan. As Varshney and development analyst Amartya Sen emphasize, the real explanation for differences in communal violence between parts of India and nearly all of Pakistan lies in the differences between economically healthy democratic communities whose populations have autonomous political and economic choices, and impoverished, authoritarian communities whose populations have very little autonomy or hope.[49]

Market Fundamentalism

Fundamentalist social movements that thrive in today's globalized environment are not merely "religious" in a theological sense. Economic "prophets" are in even better positions to propagate their doctrines and make them real by forcing changes in social practice. This is why Nobel laureate economist Joseph Stiglitz and billionaire investor George Soros call the ideas of these economic prophets "market fundamentalism."[50] Like religious fundamentalisms, market fundamentalism asserts the "inerrancy" (literal truth) of selectively drawn texts.[51] In his list of the sacred texts of market fundamentalists, Stiglitz includes Adam Smith's *The Wealth of Nations*, the writings of twentieth-century economists like W. A. Lewis and Simon Kuznets, and the speeches of British prime minister Margaret Thatcher and U.S. president Ronald Reagan. The market fundamentalist "religion" is sometimes called the "Washington Consensus" because of the dominance of Americans in the development and propagation of this ideology and the location of its primary institutions and leaders in Washington, D.C. Stiglitz writes,

> The Washington Consensus policies . . . were based on a simplistic model of the market economy, the competitive equilibrium model, in which Adam Smith's invisible hand works . . . perfectly. Because in this model there is no need for government—that is, free, unfettered, "liberal" markets work

perfectly—the Washington Consensus policies are sometimes referred to as "neo-liberal," based on "market fundamentalism," a resuscitation of the laissez-faire policies that were popular in some circles in the nineteenth century.[52]

A primary tenet of market fundamentalism is liberalization. We described this in earlier chapters as the removal of government participation, regulation, and oversight from financial markets, capital markets, and trade relations. Faith in liberalization is based on a single mention by Adam Smith in his classic book of an "invisible hand" guiding markets. Fundamentalists interpret the term as an analogue of providence (divine direction) and evidence that markets are inherently self-regulating, leading them to promote a state of affairs they also describe (as Stiglitz does in the quote above), as "laissez-faire"—freedom of contract.

The terms "liberal" and "laissez-faire" are not equivalent, however, and they impose contradictory demands on governments. Liberalization requires that governments refrain from regulation and market participants refrain from collusion that could interfere with market mechanisms. They should let the invisible hand do its work. A laissez-faire system assumes that private interests, from labor to capital, buyers, and sellers, can legitimately organize to pursue their own interests. Unions can strike as legitimately as business can divide markets or form oligopolies, and consumers can organize boycotts.[53] Fundamentalists and nonfundamentalists both oppose some kinds of laissez-faire behaviors, such as making and selling goods that are harmful to consumers, although they disagree on how best to stop this. But usually these interests diverge. Fundamentalists want to restrict labor organizing and collective action by consumers, while nonfundamentalists want environmental protection and an end to business concentration.

Privatization is another tenet of market fundamentalism. This refers to the conversion of state-owned and/or -managed producers of goods and services to private ownership and management. Belief in the inherent superiority of private enterprise as opposed to socially owned production grows out of a belief that markets are inherently efficient and always spring up to meet every human need.[54] Pressures for privatization reflect investors' desires to take over lucrative state-owned industries such as oil production, and necessary public services like drinking water delivery.[55] These promise large returns to their new owners from relatively small financial investments. A similar ethic underpinned privatization in the former Soviet Union, where mostly domestic and sometimes criminal interests snapped up the best investments at fire-sale prices.[56]

Market fundamentalists are better able than religious fundamentalists to get governments to adopt and enforce rules to transform their visions into reality. They occupy the commanding heights of powerful structures that reach beyond nationality and religion to encompass most of the earth. The term "Washington Consensus" reflects agreement among U.S. policy makers whose positions on liberalization and privatization are well known, and the people in charge of international financial institutions such as the International Monetary Fund, the World Bank, the World Trade Organization, and NAFTA. It even includes informal institutions like the G-5/G-7/G-8, a small group of varying numbers of leaders of the most economically powerful governments who meet regularly to "fine-tune" the global economy to suit their interests.[57] Through the "self-enforcing" mechanisms at their disposal, these organizations can force financially distressed governments to cut education and health services, and open markets to cut-price goods from abroad. The organizations are impervious to outcomes that include forcing thousands into destitution and undermining those governments' authority and ability to govern. Among the many examples that could be cited is Rwanda, which was forced to adopt "open market" and "structural adjustment" policies that impoverished its rural population and provided a platform for government officials to instigate a massive genocide against an ethnic minority.[58]

At their best, however, markets can be a force for economic democratization, insofar as what they define as good behavior is both fair and the same for everyone. The WTO ruled against the United States in 2003 for subsidizing some manufactured exports and authorized U.S. trading partners to impose tariffs to make up for the losses these subsidies imposed. If the WTO were to mandate the end of agricultural subsidies by the United States, Japan, and Western Europe, developing nations everywhere could sell their products abroad at competitive prices and make the money they need to increase living standards for their populations. But the WTO, NAFTA, and other global economic regimes are not yet sufficiently egalitarian to have these beneficial effects. All of them must expand their interest representation beyond business to include labor and consumers, change their rules to include environmental protection, and also change their own practices to make them more transparent and democratic.

The need for a change in NAFTA's infamous Chapter 11 is just one example. Writing in the *New York Times*, Joseph Stiglitz discusses the consequences of Chapter 11 on democracy and social justice in North America.[59] Under Chapter 11, as we noted earlier, a foreign investor is entitled to sue for damages if he believes he is harmed by local regulations. This is a problem, for several reasons. First, it gives special rights to foreigners that are not enjoyed by national investors. Second, these rights are enforced in an unfair way. The foreign investor does not have to take his case to a national court, which decides cases of national and local law in a public forum, but instead can go before special NAFTA tribunals that hear international trade cases in secret. Third, the party that is liable is the national government. This contravenes a basic tenet of federalism (all three NAFTA signatories are federal systems), which is that states and localities have the authority and right to regulate in their own jurisdictions. NAFTA gives incentives for national governments to supercede local regulations by justifying state quashing of local environmental and labor laws, along with local land-use regulations, as necessary to reduce the costs incurred as the result of industry challenges—and the costs could be very high: so far, foreign investors have filed suits in NAFTA tribunals asking for more than $13 billion in damages. Finally, the NAFTA system includes an additional inequality: localities have no right to sue in an international tribunal if they are harmed by the actions of foreign firms. This lets foreign firms operate under "moral hazard," a situation in which any gains from risky or careless behavior go to the agent, while any losses are borne by someone else. A foreign firm can block regulation intended to limit damages from its operations but is not itself liable for damages. As Stiglitz notes, U.S. businesses have tried to get a deal like this domestically but usually have been rebuffed by Congress or the courts. NAFTA gives them a free pass as long as they operate in Mexico or Canada. It gives similar free passes to Mexican and Canadian investors operating in the United States.

Globalization and Internationalization

The failure of reigning global economic institutions to incorporate protections for workers and the environment closes off the most favorable forum for developing international regulations in areas far more difficult to control than trade. As we noted earlier, the main source of leverage that international economic regimes like NAFTA and the WTO have at their disposal is "self-enforcement." Would-be members have to change their domestic regimes to conform to international standards. Countries with widely differing cultures and economies struggle to bring their institutions into line with WTO standards because they know they can lose significant economic benefits if they remain outside the system. We noted in chapter 5 that the connection between economic and political liberalization can be a force for democratization, showing how the lure of the WTO is encouraging cooperation among different political factions, each of which wants to open one or more aspects of the political economy, in Kuwait; a similar process is beginning in Saudi Arabia.[60] If existing trade regimes were to extend their standards to other aspects of the global economy, they could strengthen workers' rights—free trade could also be fair trade—and protect the environment.[61]

One example of a very important issue neglected by international trade regimes is public health. The establishment and enforcement of standards of best practice are especially important with regard to agriculture. Practices that leave chemical residues from pesticides and herbicides and bacterial contamination on foods endanger consumers around the world. Hepatitis A infections have become increasingly common in the United States where, by 2000, fully half of the reported cases were traced to vegetables irrigated or washed in sewage-contaminated water. Foreign imports are frequently cited as the sources of hepatitis A outbreaks, such as the one in the Pittsburgh area in 2003 that killed four persons and made more than six hundred others ill. But the problem is not only in foreign countries: reportedly half of the contamination in food products sold in the United States is homegrown.⁶² There are no international standards for testing foods destined for foreign markets, and many national agencies, such as the Food and Drug Administration in the United States, do inadequate analyses of samples of imported *and* domestically originating foods. Testing standards vary widely, and some results are not available until the food has already entered the distribution system.

Rapid technological change raises the stakes for ignoring the need for international standards for testing new foods and new food production techniques. The spread of bovine spongiform encephalitis, known popularly as "mad cow disease," brought this issue into prominence. The disease was first encountered in Britain in 1985, probably as the result of changes in animal feeding. Scientists now believe that mad cow disease originated with a genetic mutation whose effects were spread by the contamination of animal feed with brain and nerve tissue from afflicted animals.⁶³ Starting in the 1960s, vegetarian animals like cows began to be fed protein obtained from otherwise unmarketable body parts of slaughtered animals, including other cows. People were no more aware that the beef they were eating came from cows that had been fed animal remains than they were that the "meat by-products" listed on packages of sausage and other processed meat referred to the same thing.

The British government insisted that mad cow disease would not affect people, a position they were able to support for some time because it takes years for humans to present with symptoms. In 1996, ten cases of the human form (officially known as variant Jacob-Creutzfeld syndrome) were diagnosed, leaving the British government with no alternative but to admit that there was a connection between eating beef from "mad" cows and coming down with the disease. Experts estimate that between the time mad cow disease was first discovered and the time when the British government acted to halt the spread of infection, more than one million infected cows had been consumed in Britain, and an unknown number of others had been shipped abroad.⁶⁴ As more people became infected, some governments tightened their regulation of beef production, but industry pressures in major beef-producing countries like the United States and Canada ensured that, as in Britain before news of infected people hit the front pages, little was done.⁶⁵ In contrast, Japan was among the first countries to require that even the parts of a slaughtered animal be tracked and tested.⁶⁶

A different globalized disease threat from the food supply links the development of new viral diseases like SARS (severe acute respiratory syndrome) and epidemics of varieties of avian (bird) influenza (another viral disease) to unsanitary methods of raising animals for food and inadequate sanitation in their slaughter and preparation. Avian flu is a hazard for people because a few individuals do catch it, encouraging the virus to mutate in ways that contribute to its wider infectiousness in other human beings. Agricultural practice that failed to halt the spread of avian flu is thought to have triggered the great influenza epidemic of 1918–1919, which began near the end of WW I and killed an estimated twenty million persons; it also is associated with other notable influenza epidemics, such as the one in 1957–1958.[67] Diseases like SARS and influenza spread easily from person to person, making international travel a disease vector. This is how SARS spread so quickly to Europe and North America from Asia in the spring of 2003.

A disease that, like avian flu, can leap from animals to humans is a deadly danger. AIDS (acquired immune deficiency syndrome) is thought to have been caused by a virus leaping from African green monkeys to people, either because people ate the monkeys or via some other pathway. UN official and BBC correspondent Edward Hooper outlined another possible chain of transmission in his book *The River*, which traces the AIDS epidemic back to polio vaccine trials run in Central Africa and in prison populations in the United States.[68] Hooper's thesis is controversial, and the evidence remains unclear. The thesis also is morally daunting, explaining why people prefer to attribute the genesis of AIDS to "natural" causes. But, as with mad cow disease, resisting an open and rigorous investigation of all possible causes and links delays identifying and understanding how the disease came about and is transmitted, leading to further spread of the original disease and leaving unexplored possible pathways of contagion for new diseases.

An entirely different globalization problem related to food production has been identified by the U.S. National Research Council of the National Academy of Sciences. In a 2004 report, it pointed out that many measures currently used to prevent the escape of genetically engineered plants and animals into the wild are unproven and even ineffective. Genetic engineering is used not only to grow plants and animals with specific qualities, like resistance to a certain disease, but also to produce desirable products like pharmaceuticals. The report notes specific concerns with the escape of engineered genes placed into plants and animals used for food. In a manner similar to how viruses mutate when they move from one kind of host to another, engineered genes could spread from transgenic plants to wild ones. "Genes giving crops resistance to herbicides or insects might spread to weeds, making the weeds harder to eradicate. Pollen flow from corn engineered to produce a drug could allow the drug to get into corn destined for the food supply."[69] Corn in Mexico already has been contaminated by manufactured genes spread from the United States.[70] Here again, national regulation lags behind, leading to a need for international regulation and enforcement to avoid situations that could endanger everyone in the world.

A New World Order?

In a very basic sense, globalization, or the movement of human beings and their cultures across the planet, has been taking place for a very long time.[71] Yet it also is true that, under capitalism, globalization is taking place far more rapidly and through the spread of structures that increase human interdependence by many orders of magnitude. In their 1977 study, Robert Keohane and Joseph

Nye describe international interdependence as occurring along two dimensions.[72] The first they called "sensitivity," which refers to the rapidity and magnitude of responses in one country to events occurring elsewhere. The events that stimulated them to write their book were the energy crisis and oil revolution of the early 1970s, whose effects were rapidly translated into higher energy prices, economic recession, and rising foreign debt obligations around the world. In this example, sensitivity is measured by how efficiently the market operates as a transmission belt for economic signals—how quickly the hurt travels.

The other dimension of interdependence is "vulnerability." This is the ability of a country to defend itself against the domestic effects of outside events, and the speed with which this defense can be mobilized. Responses to vulnerability constitute "adjustment"—how states and populations change their behavior to diminish the pain and costs of sensitivity and perhaps to reduce sensitivity itself. The results of adjustment demonstrate differences in state capacity far better than the standard measures of stuff that some political scientists calculate when they look for power under lampposts (see chapter 3). In the context of vulnerability, state capacity would include being able to reconfigure the national political economy to adjust not just rapidly but also advantageously to external shocks. That ability rests on resources, but resources broadly defined—a list that includes flexibility, innovation, and resilience. These characteristics belong to human beings as well as to economies. People too show differences in their capacity to adjust to unanticipated change. Those who are active and alert may benefit from interdependence-caused upheavals, finding new opportunities when old structures are rocked on their foundations. Like globalization, the interdependence that it both cultivates and reveals is amoral—neither good nor bad in itself but available to be used for good or bad by agents as large as states and firms, and as small as persons, viruses, and even genes.

That having been said, interdependence also presents grave problems because it reduces the autonomy of states and makes their populations vulnerable to the actions of persons outside their control. Consequently, in addition to inflicting pain, interdependence intensifies competition as states, firms, and people struggle to displace the costs of adjustment onto agents other than themselves.[73] That trading partners did not receive equal benefits from trade was obvious to the rulers of early European nation-states, who chose mercantilism as their preferred policy. The philosophy behind mercantilism is that a state would be stronger if it exported more than it imported, thereby accumulating gold and other forms of commodity money allowing it to buy whatever it might need. As you can imagine, mercantilism restricted trade. Strong states imposed regulations to ensure that they would come out on top of whatever trade did take place. The series of British laws known as the Navigation Acts are an example of regulations that impose such a regime of punishment; they were drawn up to cripple trade with Britain's then-rival Holland and to wring the greatest profit for the mother country from British colonies in North

America. The colonists responded with energetic smuggling and, eventually, armed rebellion.

Neoclassical theories beloved by market fundamentalists say that trade benefits both parties if each one offers what it can produce most efficiently.[74] Yet "terms of trade"—how much of the things other countries produce that an exporting country can buy with what it earns on its overseas sales—tend both to be unstable and to favor the higher-value-added products that come primarily from developed countries. This means that even when trade regimes operate without mercantilist interference in the form of tariffs on imports or subsidies and other price supports for domestic products, inequalities persist and even grow. During the last rapid period of globalization, which ran from about 1850 to 1914 (with a little coda from about 1920 to 1930), domestic expansion kept the peace in Europe until the depression of the nineteenth century, which began in the early 1870s and lasted for more than twenty years. As domestic markets shrank, Europeans sought to expand their colonial possessions and wring even more from the ones they already had. At that time Africa was the least exploited world region, a place where amateur explorers sought the source of the Nile and some even preached the Gospel. Although Europeans held parts of western and South Africa, in the mid-1870s, 80 percent of the land in sub-Saharan Africa remained in the hands of local people.[75]

The need to replace falling profits with what could be squeezed from colonies and trade dependencies, like the ones Germany had created in neighboring Slavic regions, led to fierce competition for new colonies in that "empty" 80 percent of Africa. Europeans also sought cash by imposing regimes of punishment on borrowers slow to repay their foreign debts. Egypt had borrowed heavily to invest in cotton production during the U.S. Civil War, only to be hit by plummeting prices when cotton from the U.S. South returned to the world market after the war was over. Another desperate borrower was the steadily disintegrating Ottoman Empire, unable to put down independence movements in its Balkan possessions or protect its domestic economy from European traders. Yet the wealth torn from new African colonies and the large amounts of money siphoned from debtor nations were not enough to halt the growing economic and political rivalry among the European powers, a rivalry that persisted through two world wars.

The economic regimes adopted after WW II tried to rein in globalization, substituting for open trade and investment arrangements that limited both. But economic globalization could not be halted. It was extended through the operations of multilateral financial regimes like the IMF and the World Bank, cold war politics, the growing reach of multinational industries, and the evolution of an integrated economy in much of Western Europe. Even before the late-twentieth-century fall of the Soviet Union and the opening of Eastern Europe to trade and investment from the West, technological development and the deepening of capitalism had intensified interdependence. Countermovements, many presenting themselves as protectors of traditional values and exploited or humiliated populations, also were visible in the politics of nations from the United States to Afghanistan. These movements have since strengthened.

The question in many minds is whether the current round of globalization can be sustained through the development of representative international institutions and regulatory regimes, or will instead collapse in depression and war as earlier globalizing regimes did. The processes we are talking about are not exactly cyclical, so there is no reason to believe that collapse and war are inevitable. Technology, as we have emphasized throughout this book, has expanded steadily and in a direction that allows more people to become directly engaged in influencing international structures and events. Agents in addition to governments began independent and interdependent engagement in diplomacy, institution-building, and conflict resolution during the nineteenth-century wave of globalization.[76] This capacity is even greater today.

We think that a mobilized and vibrant civil society is a necessary condition for system transformation in the direction of plurality, democracy, and cooperation in a globalized world. But we understand that system transformation could change the relationship between people and states in undemocratic ways, toward the normalization of social fragmentation—deracination—and political and economic dominance by a tightly organized, secretive, and exploitive elite. The latter would put us back on the road to global war.

This is why agents are extremely important. Structures, including economic cycles, have their own logic. But structures are malleable. Alert agents who understand structures' constraints, processes, and opportunities can take effective action if they choose. What is needed is accurate information, a space of appearance, and a commitment to citizen activism. In the last chapter, we suggest some ways for agents to take advantage of opportunities to alter structures to suit their needs and desires.

10

People Matter

The discovery of society is, indeed, the anchor of freedom.

—Karl Polanyi

nd, so, we arrive at our last chapter. Throughout this book, we have tried to offer a framework for thinking about global politics in terms of the people who comprise the world. We have argued—persuasively, we hope—that it is the social individual who is at the heart of global politics and, indeed, is both its architect and building block. We have offered stories and explanations about how individuals act in response to the conditions they find and how they attempt to change those conditions. We have tried to frame the possibilities of agency in relation to what sometimes appear as overwhelmingly complex structures and processes. And we have tried to combine a certain amount of idealism with what we believe is an accurate realism. In this chapter, we turn from description, explanation, and analysis to action, and discuss how *you* can be an agent in global politics.

We begin with what might be called the "human enterprise." The political world is both united and divided, integrated and fragmented, but all of it is organized around complex relations and interactions among people. While it is conventional to think about such relations and interactions as somehow contained within states, drawing national boundaries is only one aspect of the human enterprise, and to focus on that obscures more than it reveals. The human enterprise is social *and* cultural *and* economic, but, most of all, it is political, and in the broadest sense. Politics shapes every one of its myriad forms.

But politics is not simple. Throughout this book, we have tried to emphasize that politics is about the power to make decisions and choices with and for people. Power is not one dimensional, and yet, although it is possible to accumulate some tools of power (such as weapons), the most important manifestations of power and politics cannot be stockpiled. This is because power enlists people in reproducing that which *is*, while it also enlists people in striving for what *could be*. Politics, in other words, is rooted in acting together with others conscious of what power can help to make possible.

Countering this vision is a recent history during which those "in power" have struggled to minimize or eliminate what Sheldon Wolin has called "the political," that is, action that threatens to destabilize the social order that puts them at the top.[1] In Hannah Arendt's formulation, they are struggling to prevent the emergence of something really new.[2] Critical decisions and choices are left to "experts"—economists, scientists, and analysts—who proffer "rational" proposals that leave little to be decided except, perhaps, how much should be spent. The result is a machine inside which individuals perform specific functions but have little say about whether it ought to be switched on or off, or what it ought to be doing if it is switched on.

Is it possible to develop a "theory of global politics" out of all of this, a framework that is descriptive, analytical, and action-oriented? Can we find ways to describe the world as it is without conveying the message that this is how things must always be? We think so. That is why the social individual is at the center of our theory rather than the state or the multinational corporation. Remember that the social individual lives and acts within a complex web of social relations and institutions, some of which appear "natural" and others of which do not. Our task, therefore, is not to do away with states or corporations or international organizations or NGOs. Instead, we should re-form our research problem into one of understanding how these institutions emerged through the activities of social individuals.

The Human Enterprise

The *American Heritage Dictionary of the English Language* offers the following definition of "enterprise": "1. An undertaking, especially of some scope, complication and risk; readiness to venture; boldness; initiative; 2. A business; industrious effort, especially when directed toward making money."[3] Fans of *Star Trek* and its many spin-offs will recognize that the first definition—"to boldly go where no one has gone before"—is a basic characteristic not simply of individuals but even more of humanity's many and diverse societies.[4] The second definition might seem more apt as a description of the economic dimension of globalization, and the objectives of those who drive and benefit from it: "making money." Together, the two definitions offer some useful insights into what we are calling "the human enterprise."

Coming down from the trees to the savannah and relying on wits rather than speed or camouflage were pretty bold undertakings when humans first appeared in Africa many millennia ago. Whether this shift in habitat and habits was due to climate change, neural evolution, or something else, it resulted in what might be thought of as the first glimmerings of politics. Members of human groups had to act socially to avoid predation and starvation, and they had to make decisions in order to survive and reproduce. Out of such prototypical "political" organizations emerged the tribes, cities, kingdoms, empires, and states of recorded human history. How many different forms of social and political organization were tried? How was it possible to get large numbers of people to go along? And what determined the kind of world we see around us today?

No one knows with certainty the answers to these or any other questions about how our world came about. It seems logical to argue that the activities of Sir Edward Grey, described in chapter 1, had an effect on the way Britain fought in WW I. But can we be sure that, in the absence of Grey, the war would have been avoided or taken a different turn? It is just as easy to assume that something else would have triggered German insecurity, or that the outcome of the war would have been more or less the same even if England had not come to the aid of Belgium, or if it had come into the war at a much later date. We might imagine a different British history, one in which some king or another dodged a knife or sword, with the result that Edward Grey became a chimney sweep rather than a foreign minister. The question is whether and how this might matter.

If we believe that "great men" (and, occasionally, a "great woman") make history because they control the levers that can move mountains, then the human enterprise looks very much like the product of a very few people out of the billions who have lived on earth. Yet if this were true, political change would look different. It would be slower, because "great men (and women)" want to preserve their own power by the way they control the levers that can move mountains. It might be faster if greatness were simply the result of talent or position and anyone with energy and connections could seize the day and make the world her oyster. But as it is: complicated, contested, and constantly changing in many different directions, the human enterprise is probably more like an iceberg than an ice cube—from where you stand you can see the tip, but, underneath, there is a lot more substance. Yet the iceberg metaphor still doesn't capture the quality of the submerged 90 percent of the human enterprise. A single molecule of water trapped in an iceberg can only hope and wait until external conditions change and it is freed. A person may be constrained, but she is not trapped. She can use her wits to free herself.

Even so, as we have made clear throughout this book, social individuals are not the autonomous atoms of classical liberalism. From its inception, and notwithstanding Hobbes's mythic State of Nature, the success of the human enterprise has depended on sociality rather than autonomy, interdependence rather than independence. Sociality in the sense of cooperation and coordination through time and space makes possible the complex societies in which we live today, including the organized violence and systemic injustices that we are able to visit on one another. What is key here is what we might call the *differential complexity* of those societies—not social relations as such or the institutions that comprise them, but the extent to which complex organization has made it possible for some people and societies to dominate others.

We have no illusions about this: domination is something that is not likely to end during our lifetimes or yours, and perhaps will not even end during the lifetime of the human species. We do not see this as a matter of human nature, as Hobbes and many others have claimed, but as a consequence of the social structures and organizations within which we live. What, then, is possible? What might we do to transform things as they are into things that are more to our liking? If we cannot do away completely with injustice, poverty, hunger, and violence, can we at least make them less pervasive and, especially, less harmful? Questions such as these push us to ask, "What is the purpose of the human enterprise, anyway?" If we could define a purpose, perhaps we could begin to think about what we might do.

Unfortunately, there is no easy answer to that question, either. Those who are deeply religious or spiritual have no trouble finding a purpose in life, although, for many of them, that purpose seems to be to get through it as quickly as possible and move on to a better existence somewhere else. For those whose understanding of life begins and ends right here on earth, an answer to the question of life's purpose is fundamentally different. In the absence of God (or gods) or some notion of a universal teleology (a heaven or nirvana where we will go at the end of our material existence), we are left on our own to devise a purpose.

Both religious and nonreligious people have hierarchies of values, sets of ideals and goals that are not quite so cosmic as *the* purpose of life but still move us as individuals and communities to cherish and invest in them because we see them as good and worthy of struggle. Over the past two hundred years or so, one such purpose has been conceived primarily in terms of nation-states, via nationalism, in the struggle to achieve national independence and recognition. Nationalism seems stronger than ever, even though there is a growing sense that the future of all of humanity is, more or less, yoked together.

How about the pursuit of happiness and improvement? The Enlightenment introduced the secular concept of progress into the human lexicon, and, since then, it has become a goal of many societies. Looking from one perspective, progress is moving right along. Many of the world's people are better off than most people were a century ago: they live longer, eat more, own more, and have more comfortable lives. For them, progress has been a material benefit as well as an idea. For others, however, not that much has changed, and, tragically, we can identify many places and situations where people are worse off today than they were a hundred years ago.

This leads to the question of how far progress can progress. To the point that no one is hungry and everyone has access to clean and plentiful water? To the point that everyone has a bicycle? A car? To the point that everyone lives as well as the average North American or European? Even these sketchy images of progress reveal tensions between human desire and the earth's carrying capacity. Progress for the already developed world by itself may be too much for the earth to sustain. If everyone were to enjoy the same lifestyle and standard of living as North Americans and Europeans, the consequences would be disastrous.[5] So, perhaps the purpose of the human enterprise cannot be progress if that means high levels of material consumption.

An alternative objective might be to ensure that every person can live a full and satisfying life in which neither poverty nor injustice forecloses opportunities for her to reach for her heart's desires. This is what Amartya Sen argues, and it does not seem to be an unreasonable program.[6] More to the point, it is eminently achievable with a relatively modest global expenditure of a few hundred billion dollars per year for food and clean water, health care, and education. This is not a large sum compared to the trillion or more spent on military forces by all countries. But even this modest objective is unlikely to be undertaken through the existing states system. Countries with money to spend refuse to spend much of it on things that do not serve their interests, and those without money have had only marginal success persuading the others to use their wealth for the benefit of the less fortunate.[7] Yet even if economic "have-nots" were to control other tools of influence, it is not clear that this would be a positive development. Imagine a group of poor countries holding rich ones hostage with the threat of nuclear attack: What might be the outcome of that?

The difficulty of accomplishing such projects obscures another, more important question: Who is to decide what the program will be? For that matter, by what right would someone, or some group of people, countries, or businesses, make such a decision for everyone else? Deciding together, after all, is what politics is all about, and, it must be said, what the human enterprise ought to be about. Politics has done much, in concert with culture and economics, to shape that enterprise, its diversity, and its conflicts. No one should expect or seek a unity of purpose, because anyone's purpose would, in all likelihood, clash with the purposes of billions of others. As we suggest in the next section, however, at least one of the major projects underway in the world does seek to impose such unity, not surprisingly, through the *elimination* of politics.

Power and Politics

In chapter 3 we discussed power at some length. There, you will recall, we tried to illustrate that power is not merely force or stuff, although that is what most people talk about when they speak of power. Power is fundamentally the ability to get things done, to influence and persuade, to convince people that a particular project is worth doing and that they ought to join in. Think about that for a moment. As analysts from Arendt to Foucault emphasize, power is not a thing, and it cannot be accumulated or stockpiled. Rather, it is better understood as a relation, that is, something that requires two or more people to create. While many people on both the Right and the Left feel uncomfortable thinking about power, because they believe it is useful only to abuse or oppress others, in fact, power is essential to the human enterprise. It is not power-over, but power-with plus power-to and power-as-if, that make the human enterprise and its riot of projects, good and bad, constructive and destructive, possible. And, because power is so central to those projects, power must also be, of necessity, about politics.

Think about some of the examples and cases offered in earlier chapters of this book. Hitler conceived of a project—a repulsive one, to be sure—that relied not only on force but also on relational power. The German people did have a sense of themselves as a nation, although their concept of nationhood was incomplete and flawed. At the same time, even the small, preunification German statelets had little experience with politics, although some, especially Prussia, had a long experience of force. Hitler's appeals to the German *volk* struck one of the nerves connecting Germans to one another and, drawing on the "productive network that runs through the whole social body,"[8] mobilized them in support of the Nazi regime. Whether the people had any awareness in 1933 of where the Third Reich would go in 1939 (to war) and 1941 (to the Holocaust) is difficult to say, notwithstanding Daniel Goldhagen's arguments. But once bound into a "social body," individuals and groups found it exceptionally difficult to escape the demands of a regime built from both peer pressure and state sanctions—force—as was the case in Nazi Germany.

Regimes of power based on peer pressure and state sanctions are actually quite common. They are revealed by the routinized beliefs and social practices in which we all engage, often quite unthinkingly. No matter how aware we might be of having been socialized into accepting any number of beliefs and practices as "natural," and no matter how hard we might resist them, it is difficult to escape them entirely. Consider gender and patriarchy. Our society is steeped in gender roles whose "naturalized" forms are reinforced through advertising, political campaigns and controversies, and even social movements. Each generation of women and men feels enormous implicit and explicit pressure to conform to the era's gender stereotypes.

But naturalization is a continuing process. During the 1990s, the prospect of gay rights was a surefire way to mobilize the Christian Right base and get Republican candidates elected in the United States. Despite the results of the 2004 U.S. presidential election, however, the "usual suspects" did not get an unambiguous result from their introduction of constitutional amendments to prohibit gay marriage on ballots in swing states. Quiet naturalization of gay relationships is proceeding. More people "coming out" to parents and friends, and the incorporation of gay characters into popular-culture artifacts like *Queer Eye for the Straight Guy*, have made gays seem less scary. What social conservatives thought was their power to reinforce the status quo and make homosexuality seem alien, even deadly, to the social body is dissolving as spaces of appearance become more inclusive.

There are other examples of positive and progressive trends in politics. Think, for example, of the International Campaign to Ban Land Mines (ICBL), a project that was initiated in Canada and grew into a global social movement consisting of more than thirteen hundred groups in ninety countries.[9] At the outset of the project, no one believed that it would be possible to get governments to sign on to an international convention prohibiting the use of antipersonnel mines. Yet, between 1992 and 1997, a convention was formulated, signed, and ratified into international law, all within a relatively short time, as these things go. (The United States and Finland are the only rich countries that have not signed the agreement.) Diana, Princess of Wales, is remembered even by people who aren't very interested in royalty for using her celebrity to naturalize this fight, and the ICBL and its coordinator, Jodi Williams, received the Nobel Peace Prize in 1997.

Here, we see how power-to is productive, creating both knowledge and discourse. Williams and her colleagues, famous and not, managed to tap into a kind of global awareness, an "episteme," if you will, of people dedicated to a broad range of causes—"human rights, humanitarian, children, peace, disability, veterans, medical, humanitarian mine action, development, arms control, religious, environmental and women's groups"[10]—all of whose members shared an idea of what was necessary to eliminate one source of random and meaningless violence against innocent civilians. Working together, these individuals and groups were able to educate, lobby, and pressure legislators, policy makers, and bureaucrats to support the treaty.[11] In the process, they also created a community that crosses national boundaries, one composed of a wide diversity of people, ideas, and loyalties, yet united by the shared exercise of the power of an emerging global "social body."

Politics Disappears

Unfortunately, as the case of Nazi Germany illustrates, negative forms of power persist. They are exercised through repression and, even more effectively, through attempts to do away with politics entirely. This is a mostly subtle process, one that constrains alternatives by suppressing opposition, substituting expertise for political choice, and changing rules to move authority outside of politics. Take, for example, economic policy, in which decisions are based on the application of economic models and principles to "aggregates," but ignore the outcomes for real individuals whose jobs are "rationalized" away and whose investments are "restructured" into failure and loss.[12] Such expert recommendations acquire an illusory sheen of science as experts tell us that their models and principles, if applied properly, always provide "correct" answers. We don't think the answers are necessarily correct; we even question the questions. One question that is sometimes asked of economists is: "How much should we spend on guns as opposed to butter?" This question presumes that there is an absolute trade-off between the size of a country's military forces and the amount that can be spent on consumer goods, welfare services, and so on. Of course, any sum of money spent on a gun cannot be used to purchase butter directly, but the makers of guns, who are paid handsomely for their products, find themselves with much higher incomes with which to buy everything from butter to yachts. Meanwhile, the makers of "butter"—in the sense of providers of education, health care, roads, scientific research, and other social goods—have less income, and many lose their jobs, while basic services are cut back and the living standard of the people declines. It's not only what we buy and how much we spend but also who profits from what we buy that is the story here.

The guns-versus-butter trade-off tends to be framed as a stark choice between "security" and "consumption." The concrete meaning of both is left unarticulated other than in extraordinary cases. For example, the current debate about U.S. "security" from terrorist attacks is fueled by divisions within the defense policy community over the threat presented by terrorist organizations like al Qaeda and its many spin-offs, and the former Iraqi regime. Diplomats, defense analysts, and individuals charged with formulating and implementing security policy have spoken publicly about their concern that the U.S. war on Iraq has taken resources away from antiterrorism efforts, pointing to the minimal attempts to eliminate the Taliban and terrorist groups, and to pacify Afghan warlords whose drug industries help to finance them.[13] Even "consumption" could bear some deconstruction.[14] Scientific research, education, and health care could just as appropriately be defined as capital outlays, investments in greater productivity in the future. By suppressing the guns-versus-butter debate, or casting it in a format that replaces content with buzzwords, the enemies of democracy remove these important issues from politics. The World Bank and International Monetary Fund routinely impose structural adjustment programs (SAPs) on countries that seek financial support for major projects or help in rolling over their international debts. As we discussed in previous chapters, SAPs impose specific spending restrictions on governments, especially when it comes to social welfare, health, and education programs, while encouraging expenditures on items such as infrastructure, more efficient revenue collection programs, tourist facilities, and tax rebates for foreign investors. Experts guarantee that these policies will lead to economic growth, but they ignore the costs of increasing the misery index of the population as a whole. The people, in any case, have no say about the provisions of SAPs or whether their governments should adopt them. These kinds of prescriptive measures are not restricted to poor, developing countries; similar medicines are hawked in wealthy countries.[15]

When people and politicians argue that decisions must be made on a "scientific basis" and not be left to the dictates of politics, what are they really saying? Not that they would accept a scientist's judgment about what ought to be done, but rather that they would like an expert to support what they want. What such claimants seek are authoritative propositions that eliminate the possibility of political debate. After all, we tend not to argue if a biologist says, "It is absolutely certain that shortly after you ingest large quantities of sodium cyanide, you will die!"

Two examples illustrate this point. About twenty-five years ago, an economist named Arthur Laffer devised a model that, he claimed, showed that a major reduction in U.S. tax rates would lead to increased tax collections by the Internal Revenue Service. How could this be? Less is less, right? Not according to the Laffer Curve, which is based on the following logic. High marginal tax rates—that is, the percentage of incremental income going to taxes as income levels increase—remove incentives for people to earn more. After all, if 95 percent of your income above $500,000 goes to taxes, that means that from every additional $100,000 earned you would keep only $5,000, which hardly makes a difference to your overall earnings. So why bother?

Assume, however, that the marginal tax rate is reduced to 40 percent. Now you get to keep $60,000, which isn't peanuts. And this motivates you to work harder and earn more, let's say $300,000. Now, you get $180,000, and the IRS receives $120,000. Because people will work harder and earn more, tax revenues will rise. Not only that, but the wealthy will invest those additional funds in productive activities that will provide jobs and additional income. Everyone wins!

Ronald Reagan was elected president in 1980. He and his colleagues so strongly believed in this "expert" analysis that they took office determined to get a drastic tax cut through the U.S. Congress. And they did. But tax revenues did not rise as expected—apparently, high earners didn't really want to work more—and the federal government began running record deficits. Even worse, Reagan also inaugurated major increases in military spending while he insisted that budget cuts be made in social programs for the general welfare because the United States couldn't afford to pay for them. On the basis of incorrect expertise, in other words, policy decisions were made without much political debate.[16]

Climate change, or "global warming," is the other example. Climate change appears to be taking place as a result of high volumes of greenhouse gas emissions into the earth's atmosphere from cars, trucks, planes, factories, and power plants. Although scientists disagree about how much warming will take place, which countries will be most affected, and how rapidly they will be affected, there is a broad consensus that global climate change is already occurring or will occur during this century. Few scientists dispute the data on which these conclusions are based, and almost none argue that human-caused climate change is impossible.[17]

The United States is only weakly committed to doing anything about climate change. Action initially would be costly and, more to the point, it would require significant changes in government policy and citizen behavior. The Clinton administration did little; the George W. Bush administration has done even less, rejecting every proposal to reduce greenhouse gas emissions. They cite high levels of uncertainty inherent in climate predictions, and assert that doing anything would incur enormous costs and injure the American economy. The White House points to a handful of experts who disagree with the broad consensus to support its claim that "more research is needed" before a change in policy would be warranted. Polar ice sheets have begun to melt, but until the oceans flood coastal Florida and the Gulf Stream that warms Europe stops flowing northward, we are unlikely to see a shift in this position. By then, of course, it will be too late to reverse these trends. Yet expert advice is claimed as a justification for these very controversial decisions—and we need to remember that refusing to do something is every bit as much a decision as choosing to take action.

Over the past few decades, the "logic of the market" has invaded the realm of politics to the extent that decisions about many issues no longer are open to broad debate. How many times have you heard that "the market is more efficient and effective than government"? Or that public services should be turned over to the private sector, which can provide the same benefits for less money and still make a profit? Or that the decision about whether or not to implement a particular policy should depend on the ratio of benefits to costs? Statements such as these are saying, in effect, "Let the (capitalist) market do it."

Of course, the market may be good at providing things, such as cereal, computers, and cars. It might provide services such as street cleaning and garbage collection at lower rates than city government can. But we should be asking ourselves how the same services can be provided by a profit-making organization for less than it would cost for a nonprofit to provide them. And that question has answers. One way to reduce the cost of city services is through contracting, which means that city workers lose jobs paying good wages and providing health insurance and other benefits. (Most replacement workers—such as the hourly workers hired by a contractor to pick up the garbage—earn lower wages and receive no benefits.)[18] Another way is to reduce the services themselves. In our example, that means fewer garbage pickups. The idea that an inherently higher-cost operation (profits are a cost) can supply anything more cheaply than a lower-cost operation is silly. The real story here is who pays—taxpayers? Workers? Householders? We never ask that question.

Some services cannot be left to the market at all because markets simply fail to provide them. Research on drugs for illnesses that afflict very few people—so-called orphan drugs—is rarely supported by private firms because, even if they are successful and find something effective, they won't make much money on producing it for sale to just a few people. Despite the need, such drugs are not supplied without socially provided intervention such as publicly funded research and subsidies to drug companies. Socially supplied intervention also might make sense in markets that otherwise provide too much—think of fiber-optic cable and telecom services generally—leading to plummeting prices, bankruptcy, investor losses, unemployment, and a waste of the resources used to build redundant plants and equipment.

The ethics of relying on economic criteria as the basis for choosing a public policy also should be considered. If an expert says that lowering air pollution levels will cost $10 million but save only five lives, does that mean we shouldn't bother?[19] (Some people—besides insurance actuaries, whose job it is to decide how much a lost life is worth—actually do think this way.) Self-interest also is an ethically suspect basis for making public policy. What if the president's budget advisor argues that a particular social service for the poor will cost $10 billion a year, but a $10 billion tax cut for the rich will garner more votes (because the poor tend not to vote, and the rich tend to contribute heavily to political campaigns): Does that mean that votes are worth more than the welfare of the poor, or that it is OK to subvert the electoral process to suit the interests of a particular candidate or party?

Again, and even in the case of the election example, politics disappears from the equation. Politics is not merely deciding how much money will be spent, where it will go, and who will pay, especially if those decisions are little more than signing off on some "expert's" recommendation. Politics is debating about what kind of society we would like to live in and how we should go about trying to make it happen. Should we spend our money on weapons or welfare? Should we lower taxes or improve public schools and ensure that all our citizens have health care? Should we give foreign aid to a country to make its youth available to fight our wars, or should we finance opportunities for education that would allow them to grow into adults able support themselves and their families? Those kinds of debates rarely happen, because the forms of power circulating through the social body lead people to accept the status quo as "natural" and as difficult, if not impossible, to change. We elect leaders on the basis of what they promise, but often we discover afterward that they have little intention of fulfilling those promises and are, in any case, busy reinforcing negative power to keep citizens out of the decision-making process. Decisions are made, but politics plays a very little part.

What Can Be Done?

At this point in many texts on global politics, you probably would be treated to a long list of things that ought to be done: reduce military spending, fund family planning, provide education (especially for women), foster sustainable development, protect biodiversity and human rights, democratize, eliminate agricultural subsidies, and on and on. We too believe these are useful and even necessary steps, but, as the old nursery rhyme says, "If wishes were horses, then beggars would ride." Making a list of what we'd like to see doesn't accomplish anything if there is little inclination on the part of those who benefit from the status quo to let these things happen, much less make them happen. You also might be told that voting, communicating with legislators, joining public interest organizations, and putting pressure on officials is the way to get governments to change their policies. Sometimes, as in the example of the movement to support corporate divestment from South Africa during the 1980s, these actions work. More often, however, they do not—the "political" system resists.

Furthermore, there is only a finite amount of material resources in the world, and a limit to the number of people who are in a position to volunteer to help the poor, the oppressed, the environment, and so on. Most people are interested in making a living, being comfortable and happy, and getting on with their lives. Their interest in changing the world is limited, for some because they see no reason to change it and for others because to make even some of the improvements we and others suggest seems like an impossible dream.

This points to another difficulty. So many things that ought to be changed are linked together that treating them individually might make things worse. For example, enlarging the area of arable land to increase food supplies might require water for irrigation to be supplied from deep aquifers. More food could be produced, but drawing down the water table in one place can cause wells and springs to go dry elsewhere. If the water we exploit is fossil water, deposited in tiny amounts over thousands of years, that solution is not only the source of new problems but also has a limited life span if consumption exceeds replenishment. Similarly, building a dam to generate environmentally clean hydroelectric power erases downstream communities whose lands will be flooded after the dam is built. It also reduces the amount of water available to people downstream. Each party in these examples can make legitimate claims. There is no inherently "right" solution to such "conflicts of interest."

We believe that the primary reason problems like these tend to be decided by "experts" lies in the general belief that people do not matter where the "big things" are concerned. When IMF advisors go to a poor country on a mission to fix national finances, they don't go there to make people miserable. Yet because their fix-it focus is under the lamppost, in areas where progress is easy to measure—imports and exports, budget deficits, foreign reserves, grain production, social expenditures, and so on—that's often what they do. People as such never appear on the books, except as sources of tax revenues and sinks for social service expenditures. "Welfare" is a central concern, of course, but it is welfare in the aggregate—growth. People—the social individuals of real life—are irrelevant.

Michel Foucault, whose views of power we discuss throughout this book, calls this approach to problem solving "governmentality." Governmentality is not about politics; rather, it is about management, about ensuring and maintaining the "right disposition of things" in the territory that is being governed or ruled. As Foucault puts it, governmentality is "the ensemble formed by institutions, procedures, analyses and reflections, the calculations and tactics that allow the exercise of this very specific albeit complex form of power, which has as its target populations, as its principal form of knowledge, political economy, and as its essential technical means apparatuses of security."[20]

Governmentality is effected through "bio-politics," another term from Foucault that we've encountered before. According to Mitchell Dean, bio-politics "is concerned with matters of life and death, with birth and propagation, with health and illness, both physical and mental, and with the processes that sustain or retard the optimisation of the life of a population." Dean writes,

> Bio-politics must then also concern the social, cultural, environmental, eco-nomic and geographic conditions under which humans live, procreate, become ill, maintain health or become healthy, and die. From this perspec-tive bio-politics is concerned with the family, with housing, living and work-ing conditions, with what we call "lifestyle," with public health issues, patterns of migration, levels of economic growth and the standards of living. It is concerned with the bio-sphere in which humans dwell.[21]

Even here, and with the best of intentions, people are imagined as groups to be dealt with rather than as agents able and entitled to participate in charting their own destinies.

What Are *We* to Do?

So, to introduce some reflexivity into Lenin's famous question, what are we to do?[22] When we answer this question, our first impulse is to focus on affecting policy. We assume that public opinion as well as scientific and other forms of knowledge are tools of persuasion and change. But, as Deborah Stone has pointed out, "public policy" is not about politics. It is about accomplishing particular ends in a rational (read "market-oriented" or "administrative") man-ner. For policy makers enmeshed in an ethic of governmentality, social goals are already known. All that matters is how to achieve them most efficiently and with the least resistance. Stone looks to Plutarch to highlight this distinction: "They are wrong who think that politics is like an ocean voyage or a military campaign, something to be done with some end in view, or something which levels off as soon as that end is reached. It is not a public chore, to be got over with; it is a way of life."[23]

What *we* regard as politics is not the exercise of power-over. We do not even subscribe to the definition found in most texts on social problems, which says that politics is about distribution or who gets what share of the pie. We think that politics is about *constitution*, about how, and to what ends, power is to be used. As we saw earlier in this book, power has multiple facets. It can be used not only to persuade or coerce but also to construct and produce. In prac-tising politics, we seek to do more than bribe or reward others for supporting our project. We want to create communities of obligation made up of commit-ted persons at all stages, so that the realized outcome will reflect all of our needs, recognize everyone's status, and generate productive outcomes that are just and beneficial for both people and nature.

Politics is about engagement with the principles and conditions of life, and the explicit processes whereby people make decisions collectively and act on them. Politics does not have to involve "global" strategies with grand objec-tives; indeed, it is such grand approaches that, as often as not, produce unin-tended consequences and failure.[24] It is less important to think big than to act, to decide with others of like mind (or those who can be persuaded), to become political as a way of life rather than to treat politics as a spectator sport with yourself in the audience rather than on the stage.

Foucault argues that power is constitutive of contemporary social relations. The (post)modern subject—each of us—is a product of power, power that is diffused in "capillary" fashion throughout human civilizations and societies. Foucault also pointed out that power is productive. As he famously writes,

> If power were never anything but repressive, if it never did anything but say no, do you really think one would be brought to obey it? What makes power hold good, what makes it accepted, is simply the fact that it doesn't only weigh on us as a force that says no, but that it traverses and produces things, it induces pleasure, forms knowledge, produces discourse. It needs to be considered as a productive network that runs through the whole social body, much more than as a negative instance whose function is repression.[25]

Although Foucault was nowhere very explicit about how power, in his understanding, could be directed against the "productive network" of governmentality, we have seen throughout this book and in our lives that power can "traverse and produce things." This does not involve rearranging parts of the web so as to create different arrangements of governmentality (reform), or destroying it so as to create a chaos out of which a new system might arise (revolution). Rather, it is about generating, through politics, new or different webs of power.

To put this another way, power "produces" the subject, and it also produces ruptures in the web of governmentality. Most ruptures are small discontinuities that are hardly noticeable at first. Think of the housewives who went back into the job market despite the pressures from 1950s family ideology, or the decision of gay women and men to come out to their parents and friends so that the world could see them as persons, not monsters. Like a spider's web, the human social web also can tolerate many such small ruptures. These are of no real concern to a spider until her web falls apart, after which she spins a new one. What happens as such ruptures accumulate in the webs of governmentality is an open question. Usually "the system" changes, and in unpredictable ways. Although the web-of-governmentality metaphor is only approximate, it still suggests something about politics, power, and action. Power must be applied and practice altered within the micropolitical spaces of contemporary life, in the realm that, in Hannah Arendt's words, "rises directly out of acting together."[26]

As we have shown throughout this book, Arendt has much to say about politics, power, and action that is germane here. In *The Human Condition*, she notes,

> What first undermines and then kills political communities is loss of power and final impotence; and power cannot be stored up and kept in reserve for emergencies, like the instruments of violence, but exists only in its actualization. . . . Power is actualized only where word and deed have not parted company, where words are not empty and deeds not brutal, where words

are not used to veil intentions but to disclose realities, and deeds are not used to violate and destroy but to establish relations and create new realities.[27]

Where can such politics take place? In the "space of appearance," according to Arendt, which "comes into being wherever men [*sic*] are together in the manner of speech and action, and [it] therefore predates and precedes all formal constitution of the public realm and the various forms of government, that is, the various forms in which the public realm can be organized."[28] For Arendt, politics could take place only through the *polis*, the self-conscious political body first constituted in ancient Greece and inherent in any human community that seeks to realize its potential for speech and action.

> The *polis*, properly speaking, is not the city-state in its physical location; it is the organization of the people as it arises out of acting and speaking together, and its true space lies between people living together for this purpose, no matter where they happen to be. . . . [A]ction and speech create a space between the participants which can find its proper location almost any time and anywhere.[29]

This particular conception of the *polis* is an interesting one, for it suggests that although space is fundamentally important, place is not an essential concomitant to politics and action. We shall return to this point below, but first want to consider how politics conducted in spaces of appearance can create something new, an alternative that does not reproduce the relations of power that constitute governmentality and its subjects.

From inside spaces of appearance, democracy becomes radically different from the diluted representational form we normally see it as taking. We contribute our own voices to creating the power to act, perhaps the most important step in resisting governmentality and recognizing how limiting it really is. We also realize the indeterminacy of action. Anyone who has been fortunate enough to live in Iowa during a presidential election year knows how much the final decision of a caucus depends on who comes, what she says, and how she says it. The outcome of politics is not the cut-and-dried affair it appears to be from in front of the television set. Yet how can we know what democratic politics is if we have never participated in it? How can we comprehend what is missing from our "democratic" systems if we have not experienced democratic politics? And how can we challenge the marketization of politics if we think only about the monetary cost of decision making and not about the disposition of power?

Governmentality is about management, but politics and action as we envision them here are not. Management seeks to suppress diversity and dissent. Politics as speech is inevitably contentious. It brings conflicting interests into the foreground, letting everyone know what those interests are and how each interest might be affected by politics as action. It challenges governmentality, one of whose preoccupations is to remove accountability and thereby responsibility from decision making. Speech and action challenge exactly those principles, practices, and policies that seek to "manage" both populations and nature even as they undermine and destroy them. Politics and action offer a different way of thinking about and acting for people and nature. Governmentality is about order; politics and praxis are not.

The flowering of social movements over the past two decades, although not without problems and contradictions, suggests that new spaces for political life are constructed continuously. The creation of these political spaces results from the productive use of power generated by relationships of action and commitment among social individuals. It is by now a cliché to claim that human institutions are "social constructions," although this claim still is regarded by some as tantamount to a threat to rationality and by others as the sheer denial of "reality."[30] Such defensiveness is most likely to come from those whose vocation approximates protection of authority. It grossly misunderstands the concept of social construction but, nevertheless, reflects awareness of the implications of Arendt's—and Thomas Jefferson's—ideas about democratic politics acquiring widespread currency.

The concept of "political space" is a fairly old one,[31] although it has been given many meanings. In the interstate realm, political space is treated as "full" yet anarchic, lacking rules and therefore requiring the imposition of "order" by great powers or hegemons. The nation-state, of course, is the archetypal political space in our time. Even within "international regimes," institutionalized politics has been, for the most part, restricted to practices considered legitimate on the territory of each political actor—and therefore implicitly located in a place rather than existing as a space. When "politics" is defined as encompassing only practices permitted by the structures that organize and constrain political space (rules, beliefs, laws, acts, agencies, etc., created and disciplined through dominating power) in particular places (nation-states), other forms of political practice are marginalized and may even be suppressed by force.

Social movements that challenge institutionalized practices—especially those like labor movements during the late nineteenth and early twentieth centuries,[32] the environmental movement, peace movements during wars, and indigenous rights and antiglobalization movements—are by definition without a legitimizing framework and, for that reason, are castigated by opponents as unrepresentative, illegal, and even traitorous. Over time, some become legitimate (e.g., labor unions) or are co-opted into institutionalized politics (e.g., the German Greens). Some of the issues and organizations that emerge from them are institutionalized through bureaucratized nongovernmental organizations, thereby becoming integral to governmentality. So far, we seem to be saying that the best ideas of novel movements just turn into "normal" politics.

But that is not all. Engendering these unauthorized political spaces and movements shines a bright light on the inadequacies of institutionalized politics. Social movements are not the product of rational calculations of self-interest, and this is their great strength. If they were "rational," they could be anticipated, obstructed, and co-opted by the defenders of the faith. But because they are based on principled commitment to action that is inherently independent of a unitary construction of self-interest, their logic is opaque to the practitioners of institutionalized politics. As a result of the collective action of social individuals, united not by contract but by commitment, such movements have objectives but no cost-benefit calculus. The satisfaction they offer cannot be reduced to those countable things we might find under a lamppost. Given legal and social constraints on the production of political spaces, how do social individuals create and move into them, and how do they generate support and legitimacy for their projects? How are social individuals constrained, limited, or marginalized by political projects and spaces already in existence? What enables some but not others to open political space and launch their political projects?

In established contexts governed by patterned rules, relations, and behaviors, social individuals seeking agency bring two kinds of resources to bear on their project; let us call them "social" and "material." Social resources include intellectual arguments, social capital, and structural knowledge, often called "local knowledge," which embraces the personalities, institutions, rules, and distribution of resources in a particular political space. Material resources include authority, wealth, and offers of benefit. "Getting things done" requires being able to field both types of resources according to the "rules" for action. Having devised an objective or a project, social individuals in a space of appearance map out a strategy. As we implied earlier, this plan is rarely worked out completely because it has to be responsive to changing conditions, including the ideas and goals of new entrants into the space of appearance.

Such a strategy uses the two forms of resources (social and material) to mobilize supporters through intellectual argumentation and the dissemination of benefits and promises. Most analyses of social action, especially economistic ones, focus on the latter because material effects are easier to observe and measure. Even so, as Arendt emphasizes, intellectual resources in the form of "speech" are at least as important. Yet ultimately, as Norman Long points out,

> Effective agency . . . requires organizing capacities; it is not simply the result of possessing certain persuasive powers or forms of charisma. . . . *[A]gency (and power) depend crucially upon the emergence of a network of actors who become partially, though hardly ever completely, enrolled in the "project" of some other person or persons.* . . . It becomes essential, therefore, for social actors to win the struggles that take place over the attribution of specific social meanings to particular events, actions and ideas.[33]

As the discussion in chapters 2 and 3 emphasized, we are especially concerned here with the ways in which power-over "produces" isolated individuals—objects of governmentality—and, therefore, does not produce agents engaged in politics. We also are concerned about the ways in which persons might use power productively to emancipate themselves as social subjects.

Most of the international relations and international political economy (IPE) literature concentrates on the structural power wielded by and inherent in the dominating institutions that cluster underneath the lamppost. Conventional questioners look only where the light is brightest and regard the penumbra as both uninteresting and unimportant. As one moves away from the lamppost, the light decreases, and so, it appears, does power. This may be why discussions of international politics always contrast "states" with "other" actors, ask whether those others possess any juridical power, and dismiss them when it becomes clear that they do not.[34]

But productive power—what Mary Ann Tétreault and Robin Teske argue is a "function of the distribution and strategic location of capacities"[35]—has an entirely different character. It is, first of all, relational, in that social bonds connecting individuals play a major role in their constitution: productive power appreciates how emotions and bonds marginalized by juridical power and dismissed by liberalism are actually constitutive of human life. Second, productive power operates in the microspaces of everyday life, not through domination but rather through the *respect* that individuals give to one another and the *empathy* and *love* they have for one another. Finally, productive power is useful: the individual can apply it to resist and undermine structures of domination.

It is in this context that we can ask, "Who acts?" For inhabitants of the world of IR and IPE that question is a relatively simple one. Their ready answer obscures not only the complexity of the unit to which action is ascribed (to them this already is limited to the state or the individual) but also the very meaning of the term "action." The denizens of IR and IPE often note that, strictly speaking, corporate organizations such as the state do not "act" in the generally understood meaning of the term, which, at its simplest, is based on an image of a rational actor choosing among alternative paths to reach a single objective.[36] Nonetheless, it also is evident that corporate behavior is not the sum of the individual behaviors of those who make up the corporate organization. Historically, we have elided (papered over) this difficulty by "assuming the spherical cow,"[37] that is, by pretending and behaving as though we could interpret actions by a corporate body the same way that we interpret the actions of individuals.

What we lose as a result of clinging to that spherical cow is both an appreciation of the complexity of individual action and any conception of non-individual social action. Here is where the notion of "social agency" becomes central. We envision social agency as a product of the histories and social relations of each person who acts, alone and together. This is not a contradiction in terms because, just as no one is an isolated individual, no one acts in isolation from others. The social contexts of each person are products of complicated histories and relations with other persons and, of course, with structures. Such relationships remain important throughout the individual's life, even though they shift and change as a person lives longer and gains more experience.

The location of each social individual in global politics is the result of such unique social histories. They unfold among social relationships that differ according to culture and position, making possibilities for agency that, although they are similar, are never identical. Think of marriage. If you were to marry J, you would have a life that would be similar in some ways and yet different in others from the life you'd have if you were to marry N. Another element in shaping agency is more broadly systemic, arising from the dynamism of the global politics and political economy, which makes some types of change virtually ubiquitous but, at the same time, differently expressed and having different impacts depending on the cultures and peoples responding to them.[38] Only by mapping out the life choices and trajectories of particular social individuals in a range of different social contexts can we begin to comprehend the complexity both of global politics and those conditions experienced by the social individuals we select. What a people-centered analysis would look like in practice is less than evident (and is a project in progress), but here is an imagined example that draws on elements from some of Ronnie D. Lipschutz's earlier work.[39]

One illustration of productive power is the watershed organization. Consider groups in the Mattole River Valley of Northern California that have organized to protect the river's watershed.[40] They are much like thousands of similar groups in the United States and around the world that have similar concerns about the environment. Almost unheard of in 1985, twenty years later such groups are everywhere. Although each focuses on a single stream or river, together they share an epistemic vision of the place of watersheds in the local and global environment. These organizations look much like standard NGOs applying standardized techniques and practices to solve environmental problems. Yet, there is reason to think that few of the practicing watershed groups really are standard. They all share the view that their creek, stream, or river is central to where they live, and merits more attention and care than it is getting. At the same time, these groups are different in their political cultures, their economies, their watersheds, and their projects.

Governments are not insensitive to local concerns about watersheds, especially where they are required by law to clean them up and keep them clean. Responsible agencies are also aware of the role watershed groups can play in furthering governmental goals. These apparently similar interests create openings where power-with and power-as-if can be realized. In many places "official" state-sanctioned watershed projects have been launched; in others, independent groups have been given a role to play in official programs.[41] Yet few state agencies charged with water-related responsibilities are entirely comfortable with the independent groups, which tend to be more radical, less manageable, more impulsive, and less systematic than bureaucrats and technocrats. The independent groups are not impressed by private property rights. They have no respect for the legal niceties and procedures of the regulatory process. They do not pay adequate attention to scientific principles and evidence.

They are *too political.*

"Too political" is code for the creation of a space of appearance in which people can engage in politics and practice. People experience what is possible in these spaces, and they learn that action is a form of productive power. They find that politics is not only the pursuit of shared interests, as social movement theorists generally describe it,[42] or the mobilization of resources, as social movement theorists believe it should be.[43] They understand it as the application of power to produce. *People choose. People decide.* This is an experience that institutionalized political processes—voting, lobbying, e-mailing representatives—never offer. It is one that illuminates the possibilities of politics in its raw, elemental form.[44] Thus, it is disruptive and aggravating—but it is also productive. It is not a "solution" to a problem but a means of engaging with what exists and moving toward what should be.

Engagement can start with even smaller tears in the web of governmentality. So much of what we think of as normal is just what "everybody says." The most powerful tool of propaganda is to repeat without ceasing what people are supposed to believe, and the most effective weapon against it is to say something different. This is why Arendt says that "speech" and "action" are equivalent. In politics, they are. As Eric Wolf puts it,

> The construction and maintenance of a body of ideological communications is . . . a social process and cannot be explained merely as the formal working out of an internal cultural logic. The development of an overall . . . "design for living" is not so much the victory of a collective cognitive logic or aesthetic impulse as the development of redundancy—the continuous repetition, in diverse instrumental domains, of the same basic propositions regarding the nature of constructed reality.[45]

Being "too political" means challenging those "same basic propositions" wherever we find them to be mean, unfair, and false. It means speaking out, asking different questions—not just "What is the most efficient way to do this or that?" but "Why are we doing this or that, and what are we not doing because we are doing these other things?" It means stepping forward to say "I don't agree," and even "I'm not sure." Dissent is another name for diversity among ideas. At its most fundamental, dissent offers the possibility that what "everybody knows" might not be correct. To say that the way things are is not the way they have to be, or ought to be, is to create a space of appearance where politics can happen.

Being "too political" ruptures the web of governmentality, but, like tears in the spider's web, most are small ruptures and are not very conspicuous. No one in Washington or São Paulo, in Delhi or Beijing, cares very much about watershed groups causing small ruptures nearby. They don't care very much about what people are saying to planning boards or in town meetings or in student governments. They have important problems to worry about, thank you. No one loses sleep worrying that such small tears in the fabric of governmentality threaten the stability of the republic or the kingdom or the union. At most, they might be a nuisance for municipal and civic sensibilities. (But who, in the capitals of the world's great nation-states, cares about that?) They are hardly a threat to civilization.

But perhaps they are.

After all, if governmentality is about management, politics as we envision it here is not. Indeed, politics challenges the very basis of governmentality. It challenges exactly those principles, practices, and policies that seek to "manage" problems by managing populations in a way that keeps people out of the process. Speech and action offer a different way to build a life, one that grows out of association, coming together to engage in a common enterprise. Speech and action create politics, spaces of appearance in which people have the power to make the world. People matter!

Notes

Chapter 1

1. Thomas Hobbes, *Leviathan*. This volume was first published in 1651 and is widely available in many different editions.

2. Christine Di Stefano, "Masculinity as Ideology in Political Theory: Hobbesian Man Considered," *Women's Studies International Forum* 6 (1983): 638.

3. Nicholas G. Onuf, *World of Our Making: Rules and Rule in Social Theory and International Relations* (Columbia: University of South Carolina Press, 1989).

4. Robert Cox, *Production, Power and World Order* (New York: Columbia University Press, 1987).

5. An example of an almost purely structural approach can be found in Kenneth N. Waltz, *Theory of International Politics* (Reading, Mass.: Addison Wesley, 1979). One that depends heavily on agency can be found in Ian Kershaw, *Hitler, 1889–1936: Hubris* (New York: Norton, 1991) and *Hitler, 1936–45: Nemesis* (New York: Norton, 2000).

6. Anthony Giddens, *The Nation-State and Violence, Volume Two of a Contemporary Critique of Historical Materialism* (Berkeley: University of California Press, 1987), 11.

7. Giddens, *The Nation-State and Violence*, 13.

8. Philip Greven, *Spare the Child: The Religious Roots of Punishment and the Psychological Impact of Physical Abuse* (New York: Vintage, 1990).

9. Waltz, *Theory of International Relations*.

10. Some of these Eurocentric preconceptions are discussed in J. M. Blaut, *The Colonizer's Model of the World: Geographical Diffusionism and Eurocentric History* (New York: Guilford, 1993). See also www.tpub.com/content/USMC/mdpub1_1/css/mdpub1_1_28.htm.

11. Some of these theories are discussed and "deconstructed" in Edward W. Said, *Orientalism* (New York: Vintage, 1979).

12. Clifford Geertz, *Negara: The Theatre State in Nineteenth-Century Bali* (Princeton, N.J.: Princeton University Press, 1980).

13. Robert Kaplan, *The Ends of the Earth* (New York: Random House, 1996), 91–100, draws on these theories of Marx and Wittfogel.

14. Blaut, *The Colonizer's Model*.

15. Scholars who advocate this theory include Spencer R. Weart, *Never at War: Why Democracies Will Not Fight One Another* (New Haven, Conn.: Yale University Press, 1998); and Bruce Russett and John R. Oneal, *Triangulating Peace: Democracy, Interdependence,*

and International Organizations (New York: Norton, 2001). For a statement by the president, see William Jefferson Clinton, "Confronting the Challenges of a Broader World," in U.S. Department of State, Bureau of Public Affairs, *Dispatch* 4, no. 39 (1993): 3.

16. Joanne Gowa, *Ballots and Bullets: The Elusive Democratic Peace* (Princeton, N.J.: Princeton University Press, 1999).

17. Ido Oren, "The Subjectivity of the 'Democratic' Peace," *International Security* 22, no. 2 (Fall 1995).

18. Niall Ferguson, *The Pity of War: Explaining World War I* (New York: Basic Books, 1999).

19. Ferguson, *The Pity of War*, 81. Ferguson cites Zara S. Steiner as another historian who takes this position.

20. Ahmad Rashid, *Taliban* (New Haven, Conn.: Yale Nota Bene, 2001); Chalmers Johnson, *Blowback: The Costs and Consequences of American Empire* (New York: Metropolitan Books, 2000). The Stinger missile story is discussed in detail in Alan J. Kuperman, "The Stinger Missile and U.S. Intervention in Afghanistan," *Political Science Quarterly* 114, no. 2 (1999): 219–63.

21. Herman Schwartz, *States versus Markets: The Emergence of a Global Economy*, 2nd ed. (New York: St. Martin's, 2000).

22. Peter Uvin, *Aiding Violence: The Development Enterprise in Rwanda* (West Hartford, Conn.: Kumarian, 1998).

23. Ferguson, *The Pity of War*, 59.

24. Jane J. Mansbridge, *Beyond Adversary Democracy* (Chicago: University of Chicago Press, 1983).

25. Daniel Jonah Goldhagen, *Hitler's Willing Executioners: Ordinary Germans and the Holocaust* (New York: Knopf, 1996).

26. See the detailed overview of this literature in Ron Rosenbaum, *Explaining Hitler* (New York: Harper Perennial, 1999).

27. Eric R. Wolf, *Envisioning Power: Ideologies of Dominance and Crisis* (Berkeley: University of California Press, 1999).

28. Wolf, *Envisioning Power*, 211.

29. Kershaw, *Hitler, 1889–1936: Hubris*.

30. Rosenbaum, *Explaining Hitler*.

31. Elaine Scarry, *The Body in Pain: The Making and Unmaking of the World* (New York: Oxford University Press, 1985).

32. Michel Foucault, *Discipline and Punish: The Birth of the Prison*, translated by Alan Sheridan (New York: Vintage, 1995).

33. Greven, *Spare the Child*, 19–20.

34. Giddens, *Consequences*.

35. See Anthony Lewis, "Making Torture Legal," *New York Review of Books*, July 15, 2004, 4, 6, 8; and Mark Danner, "The Logic of Torture," *New York Review of Books*, June 24, 2004, 70–74.

36. Scarry, *The Body in Pain*, 29.

37. Sereno Dwight, quoted in Greven, *Spare the Child*, 21.

38. Stanley Cohen, *States of Denial: Knowing about Atrocities and Suffering* (Cambridge, U.K.: Polity, 2000).

39. See the appendix on "Newspeak" in George Orwell's novel *1984*.

40. Cohen, *States of Denial*, 294.

41. Cohen, *States of Denial*, 293–94, emphasis in the original.

42. Nikki R. Keddie and Richard Yann, *Roots of Revolution: An Interpretive History of Modern Iran* (New Haven, Conn.: Yale University Press, 1981); Haideh Moghissi, *Populism and Feminism in Iran: Women's Struggle in a Male Defined Revolutionary Movement* (New York: St. Martin's, 1995).

Chapter 2

1. Nicholas Abercrombie, Stephen Hill, and Bryan S. Turner, *Sovereign Individuals of Capitalism* (London: Allen and Unwin, 1986); C. B. Macpherson, *The Political Theory of Possessive Individualism: Hobbes to Locke* (London: Oxford University Press, 1964).

2. Hedley Bull, *The Anarchical Society: A Study of Order in World Politics* (New York: Columbia University Press, 1977).

3. John Locke, *Two Treatises of Government*, edited by Peter Laslett (Cambridge: Cambridge University Press, 1988); Jean-Jacques Rousseau, *The Social Contract: An Eighteenth-Century Translation*, edited by Charles Frankel (New York: Hafner, 1947).

4. J. A. L. Singh and Robert M. Zingg, *Wolf-Children and Feral Man* (Hamden, Conn.: Archon Books, 1966); John Bowlby, *A Secure Base: Parent-Child Attachment and Healthy Human Development* (New York: Basic Books, 1988).

5. Immanuel Wallerstein and Joan Smith, "Household as an Institution of the World Economy," in *Creating and Transforming Households: The Constraints of the World-Economy*, edited by Joan Smith and Immanuel Wallerstein (Cambridge: Cambridge University Press, 1992), 7.

6. Wallerstein and Smith, "Household."

7. Eric Wolf, *Europe and the People without History* (Berkeley: University of California Press, 1982), 90–94.

8. Gayle Rubin, "The Traffic in Women: Notes on the Political Economy of Sex," in *Toward an Anthropology of Women*, edited by Rayna R. Reiter (New York: Monthly Review, 1975), 157–210.

9. Laura Gowing, "Secret Births and Infanticide in Seventeenth-Century England," *Past and Present* 156 (August 1997): 87–115; Carol Patemen, "'God Hath Ordained to Man a Helper': Hobbes, Patriarchy and Conjugal Right," in *Feminist Interpretations and Political Theory*, edited by Mary Lyndon Shanley and Carol Pateman (University Park: Pennsylvania State University, 1991), 53–74; Amy Dru Stanley, *From Bondage to Contract: Wage Labor, Marriage, and the Market in the Age of Slave Emancipation* (New York: Cambridge University Press, 1998).

10. Maureen Dowd, "The Doctor Is Out," *New York Times*, January 15, 2004, A-33; Katha Pollitt, "Judy, Judy, Judy," *Nation*, February 16, 2004; Jodi Wilgoren, "On the Campaign Trail, Teresa Heinz Kerry's Specialty Is Straight Talk," *New York Times*, July 15, 2004, A16.

11. Vance Packard, *The Hidden Persuaders* (New York: D. McKay, 1957); Richard Wightman Fox and T. J. Jackson Lears, eds., *The Culture of Consumption: Critical Essays in American History, 1880–1980* (New York: Pantheon Books, 1983).

12. William Irwin, Mark T. Conard, and Aeon J. Skoble, eds., *The Simpsons and Philosophy: The D'oh! of Homer* (Chicago: Open Court, 2001); Mark Poster, *Critical Theory of the Family* (New York: Seabury, 1978).

13. William H. Chafe, *The American Woman: Her Changing Social, Economic, and Political Roles, 1920–1970* (New York: Oxford University Press, 1972).

14. Fred W. McDarrah, Gloria S. McDarrah, and Timothy S. McDarrah, *Anarchy, Protest, and Rebellion: And the Counterculture That Changed America* (New York: Thunder Mouth's, 2003); Richard M. Fried, *Nightmare in Red: The McCarthy Era in Perspective* (New York: Oxford University Press, 1991); John Shelton Reed, *Whistling Dixie: Dispatches from the South* (New York: Harvest Books, 1992).

15. *Migration and the Labour Market in Asia: Recent Trends and Policies* (Paris: Organization for Economic Cooperation and Development, 2002); Caitlin Flanagan, "How Serfdom Saved the Women's Movement, *Atlantic Monthly* 293, no. 2 (March 2004): 109–28.

16. Susan Faludi, *Backlash: The Undeclared War against American Women* (New York: Crown, 1991).

17. Thomas Frank, *What's the Matter with Kansas* (New York: Metropolitan Books, 2004); Carolyn Gallaher, *On the Fault Line: Race, Class, and the American Patriot Movement* (Lanham, Md.: Rowman & Littlefield, 2003).

18. That is: 1.5 billion households $\times$ 4 hours/day $\times$ 365 days/year $\times$ \$6/hour = \$13.1 trillion.

19. John Agnew, "Representing Space: Space, Scale and Culture in Social Science," in *Place/Culture/Representation*, edited by James Duncan and David Ley (London: Routledge, 1993), 262.

20. Amartya Sen, *Development as Freedom* (New York: Anchor, 1999), 8.

21. Or, as Henry Kissinger once said, "Power is the great aphrodisiac." Quoted in the *New York Times*, January 19, 1971. A potential partner's income prospects are also an aphrodisiac. See Barbara Ehrenreich, *Hearts of Men: American Dreams and the Flight from Commitment* (New York: Doubleday Anchor, 1984).

22. But, see Ellen Meiksins Wood, *The Origin of Capitalism: A Longer View* (New York: Verso, 2002).

23. Francis Fukuyama, *Trust: Social Virtues and the Creation of Prosperity* (New York: Free Press, 1995); also Ehrenreich, *Hearts of Men*.

24. Fred L. Block, *The Origins of International Economic Disorder: A Study of United States International Monetary Policy from World War II to the Present* (Berkeley: University of California Press, 1977).

25. Lisa Jardine, *Worldly Goods: A New History of the Renaissance* (New York: Norton, 1998).

26. The flooding of the market with diamonds became a major problem in the 1990s, a direct outcome of African wars, as warlords would sell "conflict diamonds" to raise money for more weapons. See, for example, William Reno, *Warlord Politics and African States* (Boulder, Colo.: Rienner, 1998).

27. Of course, diamonds remain a store of wealth only as long as their price is high. Over time, the value of a particular piece of jewelry may increase because of its artistic value, but most of the diamond jewelry one sees advertised in the media is mass produced and overpriced, and has little long-term value.

28. Sidney Tarrow, *Power in Movement: Social Movements and Contentious Politics*, 2nd ed. (Cambridge, U.K.: Cambridge University Press, 1998).

29. Mancur Olson, *The Logic of Collective Action* (Cambridge, Mass.: Harvard University Press, 1965).

30. Milton Friedman and Rose Friedman, *Free to Choose* (New York: Harcourt Brace Jovanovich, 1980). See also Ronnie D. Lipschutz, *Regulation for the Rest of Us?* (London: Routledge, forthcoming).

31. Olson, *Logic of Collective Action*.

Chapter 3

1. Kenneth Waltz, *Theory of International Relations* (Reading, Mass.: Addison-Wesley, 1970); Robert Dahl, "The Concept of Power," *Behavioral Science* 2 (1957): 201–18.

2. Michael Barnett and Raymond Duvall, *Power and Global Governance* (Cambridge: Cambridge University Press, 2004).

3. See, for example, Hannah Arendt, *The Human Condition: A Study of the Central Dilemmas Facing Modern Man* (Garden City, N.Y.: Doubleday, 1959); and Hannah Arendt, *On Revolution* (New York: Compass Books, 1965).

4. Robin L. Teske, "The Butterfly Effect," in *Conscious Acts and the Politics of Social Change,* edited by Robin L. Teske and Mary Ann Tétreault (Columbia: University of South Carolina Press, 2000), 107–23.

5. Arendt, *The Human Condition,* 177–78.

6. C. Vann Woodward, *Reunion and Reaction: The Compromise of 1877 and the End of Reconstruction* (Boston: Little, Brown, 1966); David W. Blight, *Race and Reunion: The Civil War in American Memory* (Cambridge, Mass.: Belknap, 2001).

7. Ruth Whiteside, "Justice Joseph Bradley and the Reconstruction Amendments" (Ph.D. diss., Rice University, May 1981), chap. 6.

8. Clare Dyer, "Confidential Tobacco Documents Enter Public Domain," *British Medical Journal* 316 (April 18, 1998): 1185, at http://bmj.bmjjournals.com/cgi/content/full/316/7139/1185/c (accessed October 2004).

9. Other examples are given in Douglas Starr's book *Blood: An Epic History of Medicine and Commerce* (New York: Knopf, 1998), which deals with wrongful injury lawsuits brought against companies and organizations that collected and knowingly distributed blood products contaminated with HIV. *New York Times* reporters found similar successful resistance by the U.S. beef industry to regulations preventing sick animals from being used for food and even to testing for "mad cow disease" before it was discovered in the tissues of one obviously ill animal whose meat entered the food chain before the test results were reported. See, for example, Christopher Drew, Elizabeth Becker, and Sandra Blakeslee, "Despite Warnings, Industry Resisted Safeguards," *New York Times,* December 28, 2003, 19; and chapter 9 of this volume.

10. Although Bosnia had separated from Yugoslavia and been recognized as an independent country, United Nations members spoke and behaved as though they believed it was still part of Yugoslavia, by that time consisting only in Serbia and Montenegro, and therefore Yugoslavia's to do with as it wished.

11. Howard Ball, *Prosecuting War Crimes and Genocide: The Twentieth-Century Experience* (Lawrence: University Press of Kansas, 1999). For more information on the ICC, see www.iccnow.org/.

12. Václav Havel, "Kosovo and the End of the Nation-State," translated by Paul Wilson, *New York Review of Books,* June 10, 1999, 4, 6.

13. Václav Benda, et al., "Parallel Polis; or an Independent Society in Central and Eastern Europe: An Inquiry," *Social Research* 55 (1988): 211–26.

14. Jiřina Šiklová, "Women and the Charta 77 Movement in Czechoslovakia," in Teske and Tétreault, 270.

15. Diane M. Duffy, "Finding Power in a Hegemonic Environment: Lessons on Surviving and Thriving from Five Women's Organizations in Poland," in *Partial Truths and the Politics of Community,* edited by Mary Ann Tétreault and Robin L. Teske (Columbia: University of South Carolina Press, 2003), 238–62.

16. That the capture of the "occupied territories" was accidental is the thesis of Michael B. Oren's book *Six Days of War: June 1967 and the Making of the Modern Middle East* (New York: Oxford University Press, 2002).

17. Amos Elon, "War without End," *New York Review of Books*, July 15, 2004, 26–29.

18. Different models of the balance of power are discussed in Inis Claude, *Power and International Relations* (New York: Random House, 1962); and in Karl Polanyi, *The Great Transformation* (New York: Farrar and Rinehart, 1944), esp. 259–62.

19. Robert Gilpin, *War and Change in World Politics* (New York: Cambridge University Press, 1981).

20. Niall Ferguson, *The Pity of War: Explaining World War I* (New York: Basic Books, 1999); George Frost Kennan, *The Fateful Alliance: France, Russia, and the Coming of the First World War* (New York: Pantheon Books, 1984). Ferguson goes on to point out that, despite having a lot more stuff, Germany's opponents almost lost the war—another reason to take balance-of-power theory with a grain of salt.

21. Hedley Bull, Andrew Hurrell, and Stanley Hoffmann, *The Anarchical Society*, 3rd ed. (New York: Columbia University Press, 2002).

22. Norman Angell, *The Great Illusion: A Study of the Relation of Military Power in Nations to Their Economic and Social Advantage* (1910; reprint, New York: Garland, 1972); Edward Hallett Carr, *The Twenty-Years' Crisis, 1919–1939* (1939; reprint, New York: Perennial, 1964).

23. Joseph A. Schumpeter, *Business Cycles: A Theoretical, Historical, and Statistical Analysis of the Capitalist Process* (New York: McGraw-Hill, 1939); also, *Imperialism and Social Classes*, translated by Heinz Norden (New York: Kelley, 1951).

24. Paul Kennedy, "The Tradition of Appeasement in British Foreign Policy, 1865–1939," in *Strategy and Diplomacy, 1870–1945* (London: George Allen and Unwin, 1983), 13–40.

25. The United States participated in the negotiation of the Versailles Treaty, which marked the formal resolution of World War I. However, the Senate refused to ratify the treaty, and the United States did not participate effectively as a strategic partner in the peace.

26. John Maynard Keynes, *The Economic Consequences of the Peace* (New York: Penguin Reprint, 1995).

27. Jason A. Beckett, "Interim Legality: A Mistaken Assumption? An Analysis of Depleted Uranium Munitions under Contemporary International Humanitarian Law," *Chinese Journal of International Law* 3, no. 1 (2004): 87–134; also Katheine Stapp, "Experts Warn of Radioactive Battlefields in Iraq," InterPress News Service, September 13, 2003, at www.kurd.org.

28. These revised rules have been sharply criticized by international financiers and Nobel laureates for their terrible effects on postcommunist and postcolonial countries. See, for example, George Soros, *George Soros on Globalization* (New York: PublicAffairs Press, 2002); and Joseph E. Stiglitz, *Globalization and Its Discontents* (New York: Norton, 2002).

29. Alan J. Kuperman, "The Stinger Missile and U.S. Intervention in Afghanistan," *Political Science Quarterly* 114, no. 2 (1999): esp. 249–53.

30. James William Gibson, *The Perfect War: The War We Couldn't Lose and How We Did* (New York: Vintage, 1988).

31. Taylor Branch, *Parting the Waters: America in the King Years, 1954–63* (New York: Daedalus Books, 1988); Diane McWhorter, *Carry Me Home: Birmingham, Alabama; The Climactic Battle of the Civil Rights Revolution* (New York: Simon and Schuster, 2001).

32. Eva Fogelman, *Conscience and Courage: Rescuers of Jews during the Holocaust* (New York: Anchor Books, 1994).

33. Evgenia Ginzberg, *Into the Whirlwind*, translated by Paul Stevenson and Manya Harari (London: Harvill, 1999); and *Within the Whirlwind*, translated by Ian Boland (New York: Harcourt Brace Jovanovich, 1981).

34. Ginzburg, *Within the Whirlwind*, 354.

35. Charles Tilly, "War Making and State Making as Organized Crime," in *Bringing the State Back In*, edited by Peter Evans, Dietrich Rueschemeyer, and Theda Skoçpol (New York: Cambridge University Press, 1985), 169–91.

36. Michael Walzer, *The Revolution of the Saints* (Cambridge, Mass.: Harvard University Press, 1965).

37. Jane J. Mansbridge, *Beyond Adversary Democracy* (Chicago: University of Chicago Press, 1983).

38. Kevin Phillips, *Wealth and Democracy: A Political History of the American Rich* (New York: Broadway Books, 2002).

39. Hamid Zageneh, e-mail communication to Mary Ann Tétreault, July 22, 2002.

40. Alejandro Colás, *International Civil Society* (Cambridge, U.K.: Polity, 2002); also Darrow Schecter, *Sovereign States or Political Communities? Civil Society and Contemporary Politics* (Manchester, U.K.: Manchester University Press, 2000); and Teske and Tétreault, *Conscious Acts*.

41. John M. Cotter writes about the use of rock and roll to attract new members to skinhead organizations. See "Sounds of Hate: White Power Rock and Roll and the Neo-Nazi Skinhead Subculture," *Terrorism and Political Violence* 11, no. 2 (Summer 1999): 111–40.

Chapter 4

1. Katherine Boo, "The Churn: Creative Destruction in a Border Town," *New Yorker*, March 29, 2004, at www.newyorker.com/printable/?fact/040329fa_fact (accessed July 21, 2004).

2. John Agnew, "Representing Space: Space, Scale and Culture in Social Science," in *Place/Culture/Representation*, edited by James Duncan and David Ley (London: Routledge, 1993), 262.

3. These data can be found in the statistical tables in both the annual *Human Development Report* published by the UN Development Programme (www.undp.org/) and the *World Development Report* published by the World Bank (www.worldbank.org/).

4. René Girard, *Violence and the Sacred*, translated by Patrick Gregory (Baltimore: Johns Hopkins University Press, 1977).

5. Eric R. Wolf, *Envisioning Power: Ideologies of Dominance and Crisis* (Berkeley: University of California Press, 1999).

6. Wolf, *Envisioning Power*.

7. Peter Drahos with John Braithwaite, *Intellectual Feudalism* (New York: Norton, 2003).

8. Jürgen Habermas, *Legitimation Crisis*, translated by Thomas McCarthy (Boston: Beacon, 1975).

9. This "labor theory of surplus value" is disputed by neoclassical economists,

who argue that the value of any good is set merely by the local prevailing wage plus other variable and fixed costs. Profit represents the risk premium to capital and has no relationship to the value of labor inputs.

10. This would be the case even if the coconuts were obtained for free, since there are costs involved in transport, time, and building and operating the stand.

11. See, for example, Vance Packard, *The Hidden Persuaders* (New York: McCay, 1957); Michael Dawson, *The Consumer Trap: Big Business in American Life* (Urbana: University of Illinois Press, 2003).

12. Eric R. Wolf, *Europe and the People without History* (Berkeley: University of California Press, 1982), 79–88.

13. Ellen Meiksins Wood, *The Origins of Capitalism: A Longer View* (London: Verso, 2002), chap. 5.

14. Wolf, *Europe*, 91.

15. Robert D. Putnam, *Bowling Alone: The Collapse and Revival of American Community* (New York: Simon and Schuster, 2000); Francis Fukuyama, *Trust: Social Virtues and the Creation of Prosperity* (New York: Free Press, 1995).

16. Putnam, *Bowling Alone*, 19.

17. Mark Rupert, *Producing Hegemony: The Politics of Mass Production and American Global Power* (Cambridge: Cambridge University Press, 1995).

18. Fred L. Block, *The Origins of International Economic Disorder: A Study of United States International Monetary Policy from World War II to the Present* (Berkeley: University of California Press, 1977).

19. Robert A. Pollard, *Economic Security and the Origins of the Cold War, 1945–1950* (New York: Columbia University Press, 1985); Ronnie D. Lipschutz, *When Nations Clash: Raw Materials, Ideology and Foreign Policy* (New York: Ballinger/Harper and Row, 1989).

20. Rupert, *Producing Hegemony*.

21. Rupert, *Producing Hegemony*; also Leo Panitch, "The New Imperial State," *New Left Review* (March–April 2000): 5–20.

22. Habermas, *Legitimation Crisis*.

23. Joseph Schumpeter, "The Process of Creative Destruction," in *Capitalism, Socialism, and Democracy* (New York: Harper and Row, 1975), 81–86; also Boo, "The Churn."

24. See Ronnie D. Lipschutz, *After Authority: War, Peace and Global Politics in the 21st Century* (Albany, N.Y.: SUNY Press, 2000), chap. 2.

25. Mary Kaldor, *The Imaginary War: Understanding the East-West Conflict* (Oxford, U.K.: Blackwell, 1990).

26. For an undertheorized discussion of this transformation, see Lipschutz, *After Authority*, chap. 2. A more detailed analysis can be found in Enrico Augelli and Craig Murphy, *America's Quest for Supremacy and the Third World: A Gramscian Analysis* (London: Pinter, 1988).

27. For a historical discussion of this process, see James R. Kurth, "The Political Consequences of the Product Cycle: Industrial History and Political Outcomes," *International Organization* 33, no. 1 (Winter 1979): 1–34; Robert H. McGuckin, "Can Manufacturing Survive in Advanced Countries?" *Executive Action* (Conference Board) 93 (March 2004), at www.conference_board.org/pdf_free/EAReports/A_0093_04_EA.pdf (accessed July 26, 2004).

28. It no longer makes sense to speak simply of rich and poor countries. Within the former, there are growing numbers of poor and immigrants who, while not so

badly off as their counterparts in the developing countries, have only limited access to goods and services. Within the latter, there are growing numbers of rich and powerful who, while not so well off as their counterparts in the industrialized countries, have high levels of access to goods and services. The term "Global South" recognizes that poverty is a structural phenomenon of global extent.

29. Katherine Boo, "The Best Job in Town," *New Yorker*, July 5, 2004, 54–69.

30. See Ronnie D. Lipschutz, *Global Environmental Politics: Power, Perspectives, and Practice* (Washington, D.C.: Congressional Quarterly, 2003), chap. 3.

31. Stephen Gill, "Globalization, Market Civilization and Disciplinary Neo-Liberalism," in *Power and Resistance in the New World Order*, edited by Henk Overbeek (Houndsmill Basingstoke, U.K.: Palgrave Macmillan): 116–42; also Henk Overbeek, *Restructuring Hegemony in the Global Political Economy* (London: Routledge, 1993).

32. See Lipschutz, *Global Environmental Politics*, 63–68.

33. Kenneth P. Thomas, *Competing for Capital: Europe and North America in a Global Era* (Washington, D.C.: Georgetown University Press, 2000).

34. Boo, "Best Job in Town."

35. See, for example, Anthony Giddens, *The Consequences of Modernity* (Stanford, Calif.: Stanford University Press, 1990).

36. J. Gary Taylor and Patricia J. Scharlin, *Smart Alliance: How a Global Corporation and Environmental Activists Transformed a Tarnished Brand* (New Haven, Conn.: Yale University Press, 2004); Edmund Conway, "Battle Lines Draw for Banana Wars Two," *money .telegraph*, July 3, 2004, at www.telegraph.co.uk/money/main.jhtml?xml = /money/ 2004/07/03/ccban03.xml&s Sheet = /money/2004/07/03/ixcoms.html (accessed July 22, 2004).

37. Amartya Sen, "How to Judge Globalism," *American Prospect*, January 1, 2002, at www.prospect.org/print/V13/1/sen-a.html (accessed July 22, 2004). See also Amartya Sen, *Development as Freedom* (New York: Knopf, 1999).

38. Amartya Sen, "Food for Thought," *Guardian*, March 31, 2001, at www.guardian .co.uk/saturday_review/story/0,3605,465796,00.html (accessed July 22, 2004).

39. Karl Polanyi, *The Great Transformation* (1944; reprint, Boston: Beacon, 2001).

40. Giddens, *Consequences of Modernity*.

Chapter 5

1. The outline of the change from the ancient to the medieval world comes from Henri Pirenne, *Mohammed and Charlemagne* (Mineola, N.Y.: Dover, 2001).

2. María Rosa Menocal, *The Ornament of the World: How Muslims, Jews, and Christians Created a Culture of Tolerance in Medieval Spain* (Boston: Little, Brown, 2002).

3. Pirenne, *Mohammed and Charlemagne*, 235.

4. Charles Petit-Dutaillis, *The Feudal Monarchy in France and England from the Tenth to the Thirteenth Century*, translated by E. D. Hunt (New York: Harper Torchbooks, 1964). For a brief sketch of the struggles of the heirs of Louis the Pious, see Stuart Airlie, "Private Bodies and the Body Politic in the Divorce Case of Lothar II," *Past and Present* 161 (November 1998): 5–6.

5. Lucette Valensi, *The Birth of the Despot*: *Venice and the Sublime Porte*, translated by Arthur Denner (Ithaca, N.Y.: Cornell University Press, 1993); Lisa Jardine and Jerry

Brotton, *Global Interests: Renaissance Art between East and West* (Ithaca, N.Y.: Cornell University Press, 2000).

6. Leo Braudy, *From Chivalry to Terrorism: War and the Changing Nature of Masculinity* (New York: Knopf, 2003), 59.

7. Barbara Tuchman, *A Distant Mirror: The Calamitous Fourteenth Century* (New York: Ballentine Books, 1987). Janet L. Abu-Lughod traces the spread of plague along fourteenth-century trade routes in *Before European Hegemony: The World System A.D. 1250–1350* (New York: Oxford University Press, 1989); see especially the map on 173. Even earlier epidemics have been traced to trade and war. See, for example, Pirenne, *Mohammed and Charlemagne*, 95–96.

8. Joseph Strayer, *On the Medieval Origins of the Modern State* (Princeton, N.J.: Princeton University Press, 1970), 26–41.

9. Michael Herb, "Taxation and Representation," *Studies in Comparative International Development* 38, no. 3 (Fall): 3–31.

10. Jardine and Brotton, *Global Interests*.

11. Abu-Lughod, *Before European Hegemony*, 181.

12. Abu-Lughod, *Before European Hegemony*, 59.

13. Aziz al-Azmeh, *Muslim Kingship: Power and the Sacred in Muslim, Christian and Pagan Polities* (London: I. B. Tauris, 1997).

14. For the story of this interesting parallel to the more recent clash between (king) Bill Clinton and (archbishop) Kenneth Starr, see Airlie, "Private Bodies and the Body Politic in the Divorce Case of Lothar II."

15. This process is laid out in detail by James C. Scott in *Seeing Like a State: How Certain Schemes to Improve the Human Condition Have Failed* (New Haven, Conn.: Yale University Press, 1998).

16. Donna J. Guy, " 'White Slavery,' Citizenship and Nationality in Argentina," in *Nationalisms and Sexualities*, edited by Andrew Parker, Mary Russo, Doris Sommer, and Patricia Yaeger (New York: Routledge, 1992): 201–17.

17. Robert Frost, "The Death of the Hired Man," *Collected Poems of Robert Frost* (New York: Halcyon House, 1939).

18. Caroline Bynum, *Holy Feast and Holy Fast: The Religious Significance of Food to Medieval Women* (Berkeley: University of California Press, 1987); W. J. Sheils and Diana Wood, eds., *Women in the Church*, Studies in Church History, vol. 27 (Oxford: Oxford University Press, 1990).

19. Braudy, *From Chivalry to Terrorism*, 63–80.

20. Isaiah Berlin, "Two Concepts of Liberty," in *Four Essays on Liberty* (Oxford: Oxford University Press, 1969), 118–72.

21. C. B. Macpherson, *The Political Theory of Possessive Individualism: Hobbes to Locke* (Oxford: Oxford University Press, 1964).

22. Karl Polanyi, *The Great Transformation* (New York: Farrar and Rinehart, 1944).

23. Garry Wills, *Under God: Religion and Politics in America* (New York: Simon and Schuster, 1990).

24. Cynthia Weber, *Simulating Sovereignty: Intervention, the State and Symbolic Exchange* (Cambridge: Cambridge University Press, 1995).

25. P. W. Singer, *Corporate Warriors: The Rise of the Privatized Military Industry* (Ithaca, N.Y.: Cornell University Press, 2003), chap. 2. See also Patrick Radden Keefe, "Iraq: America's Private Armies," *New York Review of Books*, August 12, 2004, 48–50. A different perspective on this evolution can be found in Braudy, *From Chivalry to Terrorism*.

26. Robert Jackson, *Quasi-states: Sovereignty, International Relations and the Third World* (Cambridge: Cambridge University Press, 1990). Individuals have the same problem with negative liberty—the lack of equality limits the exercise of liberty.

27. Václav Havel, "Kosovo and the End of the Nation-State," *New York Review of Books,* June 10, 1999, 4, 6.

28. T. H. Marshall, "Citizenship and Social Class," in *"Citizenship and Social Class" and Other Essays* (Cambridge: Cambridge University Press, 1950), 1–85.

29. Kurt Burch, *"Property" and the Making of the International System* (Boulder, Colo.: Rienner, 1998).

30. Richard Newhauser, *The Early History of Greed* (Cambridge: Cambridge University Press, 2000). Also, Albert O. Hirschman, *The Passions and the Interests: Political Arguments for Capitalism before Its Triumph*, 20th anniversary ed. (Princeton, N.J.: Princeton University Press, 1997).

31. John Brewer, *War Money and the English State, 1688–1783* (New York: Harper-Collins, 1989); James MacDonald, *A Free National Deep in Debt: The Financial Roots of Democracy* (New York: Farrar, Straus and Giroux, 2003).

32. Michael Walzer, *Revolution of the Saints* (Cambridge, Mass.: Harvard University Press, 1965); also Max Weber, *The Protestant Ethic and the Spirit of Capitalism*, translated by Talcott Parsons (New York: Charles Scribner's Sons, 1958).

33. For example, Kenneth N. Waltz, *Theory of International Relations* (Reading, Mass.: Addison-Wesley, 1979).

34. Mary Ann Tétreault, "Pleasant Dreams: The WTO as Kuwait's Holy Grail," *Critique: Critical Middle Eastern Studies* 12, no. 1 (Spring 2003): 75–93.

35. Reactions to globalization are explored in Harold James, *The End of Globalization: Lessons from the Great Depression* (Cambridge, Mass.: Harvard University Press, 2001).

36. This is the viewpoint reflected in Peter J. Taylor, *Modernities: A Geohistorical Interpretation* (Minneapolis: University of Minnesota Press, 1999).

37. Jackson, *Quasi-states*, chap. 2.

38. William Reno, *Warlord Politics and African States* (Boulder, Colo.: Rienner, 1999), esp. chap. 3; Jill Crystal, *Oil and Politics in the Gulf: Rulers and Merchants in Kuwait and Qatar* (New York: Cambridge University Press, 1990). For a discussion of reasons behind the unexpected stability of the Gulf oil monarchies, see Michael Herb, *All in the Family: Absolutism, Revolution, and Democracy in the Middle Eastern Monarchies* (Albany, N.Y.: SUNY Press, 1999).

39. For examples from sub-Saharan Africa, see Jean-François Bayart, Stephen Ellis, and Béatrice Hibou, *The Criminalization of the State in Africa* (Bloomington: Indiana University Press, 1999). The concept of protected spaces is developed in Mary Ann Tétreault, "Civil Society in Kuwait: Protected Spaces and Women's Rights," *Middle East Journal* 47, no. 2 (Spring 1993): 178–91.

40. See Misha Glenny's 1995 interview with Iso Rusi, editor in chief of the Albanian language weekly *Lobi*, at http://foro.estudiosbalcanicos.org/archivo/koha/1995/Dig67.txt (accessed July 28, 2004).

41. Clea Koff, *The Bone Woman: A Forensic Anthropologist's Search for Truth in the Mass Graves of Rwanda, Bosnia, Croatia, and Kosovo* (New York: Random House, 2004), 262.

42. A good introduction to modern civil society can be found in John Keane, "Despotism and Democracy: The Origins and Development of the Distinction between Civil Society and the State, 1750–1850," in *Civil Society and the State*, edited by John Keane

(London: Verso, 1988): 35–71. That civil society is fundamentally international is the thesis of Alejandro Colás, *International Civil Society: Social Movements in World Politics* (Cambridge U.K.: Polity, 2002).

43. Niall Ferguson, *The House of Rothschild: Money's Prophets, 1798–1848* (New York: Penguin, 1999); Herman M. Schwartz, *States versus Markets: History, Geography, and the Development of the International Political Economy*, 2nd ed. (New York: St. Martin's, 2000).

44. Edmund S. Morgan, "America's First Great Man," *New York Review of Books* 44, no. 10 (June 12, 1997), at www.nybooks.com/articles/1161. See also Richard S. Dunn and Laetitia Yeandle, eds., *The Journal of John Winthrop, 1630–1649* (Cambridge, Mass.: Belknap, 1996); and Edmund S. Morgan, *The Puritan Dilemma: The Story of John Winthrop* (Boston: Little, Brown, 1958).

45. John Winthrop, quoted in Morgan, "America's First Great Man."

46. J. G. A. Pocock, ed., *Three British Revolutions, 1641, 1688, 1776* (Princeton, N.J.: Princeton University Press, 1980); Jack A. Goldstone, "The English Revolution: A Structural-Demographic Approach," in *Revolutions: Theoretical, Comparative, and Historical Studies*, edited by Jack A. Goldstone (New York: Harcourt, Brace, Jovanovich, 1986), 88–104; Lawrence Stone, "The Revolution over the Revolution," *New York Review of Books* 39, no. 11 (1992): 47–52.

47. Colás, *International Civil Society*.

48. See, for example, Aryeh Neier, *Taking Liberties: Four Decades in the Struggle for Rights* (New York: Public Affairs, 2003); Abigail Abrash, "Let Freedom Ring: Recharging and Consolidating 'Inside the Beltway' Activism," in *Partial Truths and the Politics of Community*, edited by Mary Ann Tétreault and Robin L. Teske (Columbia: University of South Carolina Press, 2003): 211–37; Michael Ignatieff, "The Rights Stuff," *New York Review of Books* 49, no. 10 (June 13, 2002), at www.nybooks.com/articles/15465.

49. Ignatieff, "The Rights Stuff."

50. Roger Howard, "America's Dubious Ally," Institute for War and Peace Reporting, Oxford, U.K., May 19, 2003, at www.kurd.org.

51. For example, see any issue of the *World Development Report*, an annual publication of the United Nations.

52. For a range of critiques, see Gilbert Rist, *The History of Development: From Western Origins to Global Faith*, translated by Patrick Camiller (London: Zed Books, 1997); Amartya Sen, *Underdevelopment as Freedom* (New York: Doubleday Anchor, 2000); George Soros, *George Soros on Globalization* (New York: Public Affairs, 2002); Joseph E. Stiglitz, *Globalization and Its Discontents* (New York: Norton, 2002).

53. Kevin Phillips, *Wealth and Democracy: A Political History of the American Rich* (New York: Broadway Books, 2002).

54. For a recent example, see Don Van Natta Jr. and Neela Banerjee, "Top G.O.P. Donors in Energy Industry Met Cheney Panel," *New York Times*, March 1, 2002, A1, A15.

55. For examples, see Garry Wills, *Papal Sin: Structures of Deceit* (New York: Doubleday, 2000), on the Catholic Church; Ken Auletta, "Vox Fox," *New Yorker*, May 26, 2003, 58–66, 68–73, on the leadership of Fox News; John Cassidy, "The Investigation," *New Yorker*, April 7, 2003, 54–62, 64–73, on corrupt investment bankers and advisors; and James B. Stewart, "Spend! Spend! Spend!" *New Yorker*, February 17–24, 2003, 132–39, 141–47, on Tyco's CEO, Dennis Koslowski.

56. Singer, *Corporate Warriors*; also Ken Silverstein, *Private Warriors* (London: Verso, 2000).

57. Keefe, "America's Private Armies."

58. Keefe, "America's Private Armies"; also Singer, *Corporate Warriors*; Reno, *Warlord Politics*.

59. Karen Ordahl Kupperman, *Indians and English: Facing Off in Early America* (Ithaca, N.Y.: Cornell University Press, 2000)—but the natives did not let this happen without a fight. See Linda Colley, *Captives: The Story of Britain's Pursuit of Empire and How Its Soldiers and Civilians Were Held Captive by the Dream of Global Supremacy, 1600–1850* (New York: Pantheon, 2002).

Chapter 6

1. Irving Janis, *Groupthink: Psychological Studies of Policy Decisions and Fiascoes* (Boston: Houghton Mifflin, 1982); U.S. Senate, Select Committee on Intelligence, *Report on the U.S. Intelligence Community's Prewar Intelligence Assessments on Iraq*, July 7, 2004, 272–83, 357–65 (note that portions of the latter have been blacked out for security reasons), at http://intelligence.senate.gov/iraqreport2.pdf (accessed July 23, 2004).

2. Eric R. Wolf, *Europe and the People without History* (Berkeley: University of California Press, 1982), chap. 3

3. James C. Scott, *Seeing Like a State: How Certain Schemes to Improve the Human Condition Have Failed* (New Haven, Conn.: Yale University Press, 1998).

4. Donna J. Guy, *White Slavery and Mothers Alive and Dead: The Troubled Meeting of Sex, Gender, Public Health and Progress in Latin America* (Lincoln: University of Nebraska Press, 2000); Rhacel Salazar Parreñas, *Servants of Globalization: Women, Migration and Domestic Work* (Stanford, Calif.: Stanford University Press, 2001); Dennis Altman, *Global Sex* (Chicago: University of Chicago Press, 2001).

5. Benedict Anderson, *Imagined Communities: Reflections on the Origins and Spread of Nationalism* (London: Verso, 1991).

6. Chalmers Johnson, *The Sorrows of Empire: Militarism, Secrecy, and the End of the Republic* (New York: Metropolitan Books, 2004), 24.

7. According to Walker Conner, at least 90 percent of a state's population must be of a single ethnic group for it to qualify as an actual nation-state; see Walker Conner, *Ethnonationalism: The Quest for Understanding* (Princeton, N.J.: Princeton University Press, 1994).

8. Charles Tilly, "War Making and State Making as Organized Crime," in *Bringing the State Back In*, edited by Peter B. Evans, Dietrich Rueschemeyer, and Theda Skoçpol (Cambridge: Cambridge University Press, 1985), 169–91.

9. Anderson, *Imagined Communities*.

10. Basil Davidson, *The Black Man's Burden: Africa and the Curse of the Nation-State* (New York: Times Books, 1992).

11. Philip Gourevitch, *We Wish to Inform You That Tomorrow We Will Be Killed with Our Families: Stories from Rwanda* (New York: Farrar, Straus and Giroux, 1998); Mahmood Mamdani, *When Victims Become Killers: Colonialism, Nativism, and the Genocide in Rwanda* (Princeton, N.J.: Princeton University Press, 2001); Linda Melvern, *Conspiracy to Murder: The Rwandan Genocide* (London: Verso, 2004).

12. For an especially harrowing example see Peter Landesman, "A Woman's

Work," *New York Times Magazine,* September 15, 2002, 82–89, 116, 125, 130, 132, 134. This article is about Pauline Nyiramasuhuko, Rwanda's minister of rape.

13. Sandra Halperin, *In the Mirror of the Third World: Capitalist Development in Modern Europe* (Ithaca, N.Y.: Cornell University Press, 1997); Sandra Halperin, *War and Social Change in Modern Europe: The Great Transformation Revisited* (Cambridge: Cambridge University Press, 2004).

14. Karl Polanyi, *The Great Transformation* (Boston: Beacon, 1944, 2001); Halperin, *War and Social Change.*

15. Garry Wills, *"Negro President": Jefferson and the Slave Power* (Boston: Houghton Mifflin, 2003).

16. Keller Morton, *Regulating a New Economy: Public Policy and Economic Change in America, 1900–1933* (Cambridge, Mass.: Harvard University Press, 1990). Today, rule by experts has replaced regulatory administration; see chap. 10, as well as Ulrich Beck, *Risk Society: Towards a New Modernity* (Beverly Hills, Calif.: Sage, 1992), and Timothy W. Luke, *Capitalism, Democracy, and Ecology: Departing from Marx* (Urbana: University of Illinois Press, 1999), chap. 2.

17. Amy Dru Stanley, *From Bondage to Contract: Wage Labor, Marriage and the Market in the Age of Slave Emancipation* (Cambridge: Cambridge University Press, 1998); Cynthia Enloe, *Bananas, Beaches and Bases* (Berkeley: University of California Press, 1990); Fatima Mernissi, *Islam and Democracy: Fear of the Modern World,* translated by Mary Jo Lakeland (Reading, Mass.: Addison-Wesley, 1992).

18. V. Spike Peterson, "An Archeology of Domination: Historicizing Gender and Class in Early Western State Formation" (Ph.D. diss., Department of Political Science, American University, 1988).

19. See, for example, Luigi Cavalli-Sforza, *Genes, Peoples, and Languages,* translated by Mark Seielstad. (New York: North Point, 2000).

20. Stephen Jay Gould, *The Mismeasure of Man* (New York: Norton, 1981).

21. David Brion Davis, "The Terrible Cost of Reconciliation," *New York Review of Books,* July 18, 2002, 50–52. It is not that this is a new strategy for eliding class differences. Aristotle made similar observations in *Politics,* asserting the superiority of Greek men over "barbarians" and persons he insisted were "slaves by nature," including women.

22. Martin Pratt and Janet Allison Brown, eds., *Borderlands under Stress* (The Hague: Kluwer Law International, 2000); Carlos G. Vélez-Ibáñez, *Border Visions: Mexican Cultures of the Southwest United States* (Tucson: University of Arizona Press, 1996).

23. Linda Gordon, *The Great Arizona Orphan Abduction* (Cambridge, Mass.: Harvard University Press, 1999).

24. Nationality and citizenship in Mexico remain fluid and contested concepts. See www.mexconnect.com/mex_/dt/dtdualcitizenship.html and http://migration.ucdavis .edu/mn/more.php?id=1491_0_2_0 (accessed August 14, 2004).

Chapter 7

1. We make this argument in spite of the rhetoric used by the Bush administration to describe a policy it calls a "war against terrorism."

2. Wolfgang Schivelbusch, *The Culture of Defeat: On National Trauma, Mourning, and Recovery,* translated by Jefferson Chase (New York: Metropolitan Books, 2003), 5.

3. Thucydides, *The Peloponnesian War*. There are many editions of this work, which is over twenty-five hundred years old, and it has attracted famous translators. One of the earliest English translations was prepared by our old friend Thomas Hobbes.

4. Immanuel Kant, "Perpetual Peace"; Karl von Clausewitz, *On War*. Both are widely available in many different editions.

5. See, for example, W. Michael Reisman and Chris T. Antoniou, eds., *The Laws of War: A Comprehensive Collection of Primary Documents on International Laws Governing Armed Conflict* (New York: Vintage, 1994).

6. Anatol Rapoport, introduction to *On War*, by Carl von Clausewitz (New York: Penguin, 1968), 19.

7. The Americans also had substantial assistance from France, including French forces and, even more important, a great deal of French money. See Simon Schama, *Citizens: A Chronicle of the French Revolution* (New York: Knopf, 1989), 25–26, 38–40, 47–49, 61. Schama argues that French financial support for the American Revolution undermined the state and helped bring on the French Revolution in 1789.

8. Schivelbusch, *Culture of Defeat*, 107–12.

9. The literature on this long and bitter war is enormous. Useful examples that reveal the strange combination of limited and total war from the American perspective include Leslie Gelb and Richard K. Betts, *The Irony of Vietnam: The System Worked* (Washington, D.C.: Brookings, 1979); Jeffrey Record, *The Wrong War: Why We Lost in Vietnam* (Annapolis, Md.: Naval Institute Press, 1998). For examples from the Vietnamese perspective, see Truong Nhu Tang, *A Viet Cong Memoir* (New York: Vintage, 1985); Tam Vu, "People's War against Special War"; and Le Tan Danh, "The South Vietnam National Front for Liberation during the Period from 1961 to 1965," both in *Vietnamese Studies* 11, "The Failure of 'Special War'" (Hanoi: English language reprint, n.d.). Works that focus on the disjunction explicitly include Tom Mangold and John Penycate, *The Tunnels of Cu Chi* (New York: Berkeley, 1985); and James William Gibson, *The Perfect War: The War We Couldn't Lose and How We Did* (New York: Vintage, 1988).

10. Noel Perrin, *Giving Up the Gun: Japan's Reversion to the Sword, 1543–1879* (Boulder, Colo.: Shambhala, 1980).

11. Zygmunt Bauman, *Modernity and the Holocaust* (Ithaca, N.Y.: Cornell University Press, 2000); Irving Louis Horowitz, *Taking Lives: Genocide and State Power* (New Brunswick, N.J.: Transaction Books, 1980). The "body count" amassed between 1900 and 1987 by states that targeted specific populations for extermination, a period that omits notorious genocidal campaigns in Bosnia and Rwanda, along with smaller-scale efforts in Kosovo, Uganda, Burundi, Chechnya, and elsewhere, reached about 169,198,000 persons. See R. J. Rummel, *Death by Government* (New Brunswick, N.J.: Transaction Books, 1994).

12. Mary Ann Tétreault and Harry W. Haines, "Postmodern War and Historical Memory" (paper presented at the annual meeting of the International Studies Association, Montreal, March 2004).

13. Simon Chesterman, ed., *Civilians in War* (Boulder, Colo.: Rienner, 2001).

14. Theda Skoçpol, *Protecting Soldiers and Mothers: The Political Origins of Social Policy in the United States* (Cambridge, Mass.: Belknap, 1995).

15. Washington Headquarters Services, Directorate for Information Operations and Reports, U.S. Department of Defense Records, "Principal Wars in Which the US Participated: US Military Personnel Serving and Casualties," table 2-23, at www.cwc.lsu.edu/cwc/other/stats/warcost.htm (accessed August 8, 2004).

16. This is the message of psychiatrist Jonathan Shay in two books about American veterans and combat trauma: *Achilles in Vietnam: Combat Trauma and the Undoing of Character* (New York: Touchstone, 1994); and, with Max Cleland and John McCain, *Odysseus in America* (New York: Scribner, 2002).

17. Elaine Showalter, "Male Hysteria," in *The Female Malady: Women, Madness, and English Culture, 1830–1980* (New York: Penguin, 1987). Showalter argues that part of the resistance to admitting that men could experience "hysteria" was that it denied the masculinity of war as an enterprise. The other reason was that officers were afraid that if men could get out of combat by claiming mental illness, practically everyone would do it. The latter, of course, is the premise of Joseph Heller's famous WW II novel, *Catch-22*.

18. Jason Epstein, "Always Time to Kill," *New York Review of Books*, November 4, 1999, at www.nybooks.com.

19. P. W. Singer, *Corporate Warriors: The Rise of the Privatized Military Industry* (Ithaca, N.Y.: Cornell University Press, 2003), 53.

20. This ultimately self-destructive legacy of war is the main text of Chris Hedges's book *War Is a Force That Gives Us Meaning* (New York: PublicAffairs, 2002). It afflicts women as well as men. Compare Lynda Van Devanter, *Home before Morning* (New York: Warner Books, 1983); and Philip Caputo, *A Rumor of War* (New York: Holt, Rinehart and Winston, 1977).

21. Charles Tilly, "War Making and State Making as Organized Crime," in *Bringing the State Back In*, edited by Peter Evans, Dietrich Rueschemeyer, and Theda Skoçpol (New York: Cambridge University Press, 1985), 169–91.

22. Tilly, "War Making"; also Frederic C. Lane, "The Economic Meaning of War and Protection," in *Venice and History: The Collected Papers of Frederic C. Lane* (Baltimore: Johns Hopkins University Press, 1966).

23. Robert Gilpin, *War and Change in World Politics* (New York: Cambridge University Press, 1981).

24. See Kevin Phillips, *American Dynasty: Aristocracy, Fortune, and the Politics of Deceit in the House of Bush* (New York: Viking, 2004); and Ron Suskind, *The Price of Loyalty: George W. Bush, the White House, and the Education of Paul O'Neill* (New York: Simon and Schuster, 2004). A similar analysis of cold war resource redistribution can be found in Kees van der Pijl, *The Making of an Atlantic Ruling Class* (London: Verso, 1984).

25. Kenneth N. Waltz, *Man, the State, and War: A Theoretical Analysis* (New York: Columbia University Press, 1965).

26. Kenneth N. Waltz, *Theory of International Relations* (Reading, Mass.: Addison Wesley, 1979), 18.

27. Various ways to interpret what is meant by "balance of power" are analyzed in Karl Polanyi, *The Great Transformation* (New York: Farrar and Rinehart, 1944), 259–64.

28. Robert Jervis, *Perception and Misperception in International Politics* (Princeton, N.J.: Princeton University Press, 1976).

29. The results of an exhaustive literature survey seeking evidence of cultures without war are reported in Joshua S. Goldstein, *War and Gender* (New York: Cambridge University Press, 2001), chap. 1.

30. Thomas Hobbes, *Leviathan* (Chicago: Encyclopedia Britannica, 1952), 86.

31. Hans J. Morgenthau, *Politics among Nations: The Struggle for Power and Peace*, 5th ed. (New York: Knopf, 1973).

32. George W. Bush, "The National Security Strategy of the United States," White House, Washington, September 17, 2002, at www.whitehouse.gov/nsc/nss.html (accessed March 3, 2004).

33. Former U.S. treasury secretary Paul O'Neill says that even at the first meeting of the principals of the Bush National Security Council on January 30, 2001, "it was about Iraq," while, by February 2001, the Defense Intelligence Agency was "mapping Iraq's oil fields and . . . listing companies that might be interested in leveraging the precious asset." Ron Suskind, *The Price of Loyalty* (New York: Simon and Schuster, 2004), 75, 96.

34. Robert Gilpin, *War and Change in International Politics* (New York: Cambridge University Press, 1981); Robert O. Keohane and Joseph S. Nye, *Power and Interdependence: World Politics in Transition* (Boston: Little, Brown, 1977). The most spirited defense of the soft version of hegemonic stability theory can be found in Robert O. Keohane, *After Hegemony: Cooperation and Discord in the World Political Economy* (Princeton, N.J.: Princeton University Press, 1984), and below in the text.

35. Keohane, *After Hegemony*, 34.

36. Martha Nussbaum, "Kant and Stoic Cosmopolitanism," *Journal of Political Philosophy* 5, no. 1 (March 1997): 2; emphasis in the original.

37. Nussbaum, "Kant and Stoic Cosmopolitanism," 3.

38. Nussbaum, "Kant and Stoic Cosmopolitanism."

39. Nussbaum, "Kant and Stoic Cosmopolitanism."

40. *Kant: Political Writings*, 2nd ed., edited by Hans Reiss, translated by H. B. Nisbet (Cambridge: Cambridge University Press, 1994), 93–130.

41. *Kant: Political Writings*, 104.

42. J. Ann Tickner, *Gender in International Relations: Feminist Perspectives on Achieving Global Security* (New York: Columbia University Press, 1992); V. Spike Peterson, *A Critical Rewriting of Global Political Economy: Integrating Reproductive, Productive, and Virtual Economies* (London: Routledge, 2003).

43. Chris Hables Gray, *Postmodern War: The New Politics of Conflict* (New York: Guilford, 2003), 245.

44. These are discussed in Gray, *Postmodern War*, and in James William Gibson, *Warrior Dreams: Paramilitary Culture in Post-Vietnam America* (New York: Hill and Wang, 1994). See also James Der Derian, *Virtuous War: Mapping the Military-Industrial-Media-Entertainment Network* (Boulder, Colo.: Westview, 2001).

45. Tétreault and Haines, "Postmodern War."

46. Fairness and Accuracy in Reporting (FAIR), "What a Difference Four Years Makes: Why U.N. Inspectors Left Iraq—Then and Now," October 2002, at www.fair.org/extra/0210/inspectors.html (accessed August 13, 2004).

47. W. Lance Bennett, *News: The Politics of Illusion*, 4th ed. (New York: Longman, 2001); also Pierre Bourdieu, *On Television*, translated by Priscilla Parkhurst Ferguson (New York: New Press, 1998).

48. Daniel C. Hallin, "The Media, the War in Vietnam, and Political Support: A Critique of the Thesis on an Oppositional Media," *Journal of Politics* 46, no. 1 (February 1984): 2–24.

49. Terese A. Thompson, "The Political and Ideological Context of Broadcast News: CBS Nightly News Coverage of Eastern Europe" (M.A. thesis, Old Dominion University, 1991). In an example from popular culture, *Rambo, First Blood*, Rambo's captors in Vietnam look suspiciously like Japanese and Germans in WW II. See Ronnie

D. Lipschutz, *Cold War Fantasies: Film, Fiction, and Foreign Policy* (Lanham, Md.: Rowman & Littlefield, 2001), 146–47.

50. Jürgen Habermas, *The Structural Transformation of the Public Sphere: An Inquiry into a Category of Bourgeois Society*, translated by Thomas Burger with Frederick Lawrence (Cambridge, Mass.: MIT Press, 1991).

51. The three Gulf Wars are: Iran-Iraq (1980–1988), Kuwait (1990–1991), and the ongoing war that began in March 2003.

52. Steven Kull (principal investigator) et al., "Misperceptions, the Media and the Iraq War," Program on International Policy Attitudes and Knowledge Networks, October 2, 2003, at www.pipa.org/OnlineReports/Iraq/Media_10_02_03_Report.pdf (accessed February 13, 2004).

53. Compare, for example, Susan Sontag, "Looking at War," *New Yorker*, December 9, 2002, 82–98; Douglas Kellner, *The Persian Gulf TV War* (Boulder, Colo.: Westview, 1992), 160. Philip Taylor also finds video-game analogues in coverage of the second Gulf War (1990–1991), a situation that Mary Ann Tétreault calls "Nintendo war." See Philip M. Taylor, *War and the Media: Propaganda and Persuasion in the Gulf War* (Manchester, U.K.: Manchester University Press, 1993).

54. See, for example, Bill Katovsky and Timothy Carlson, *Embedded: The Media at War in Iraq* (Guilford, Conn.: Lyons, 2003).

55. Robert Jervis, "Cooperation under the Security Dilemma," *World Politics* 30, no. 2 (January 1978): 167–214; also Ronnie D. Lipschutz, *After Authority: War, Peace, and Global Politics in the 21st Century* (Albany, N.Y.: SUNY Press, 2000), 33–62.

56. Economist Mehrdad Valibeigi, personal communication to Mary Ann Tétreault, September 2003.

57. This is one of the discoveries made by a young marine who wrote about it in the context of his GW II experiences. See Anthony Swofford, *Jarhead: A Marine's Chronicle of the Gulf War and Other Battles* (New York: Scribner, 2003).

58. Vera Brittain, *Testament of Youth* (New York: Seaview Books, 1980). Originally published in 1933.

59. Brittain, *Testament of Youth*, 637–38.

60. Hedges, *War Is a Force*, 184–85.

Chapter 8

1. Presidential claims regarding the torture and abuse of prisoners at Iraq's Abu Ghraib prison, and protests by the families of soldiers charged with these activities, illustrate the widely held notion that injustice is committed by "bad apples." See, for example, Eric Scmitt, "Army Report Says Flaws in Detention Didn't Cause Abuse," *New York Times*, July 23, 2004, at www.nytimes.com/2004/07/23/politics/23abus.html?th (accessed July 23, 2004). For discussions of this point, see Anthony Lewis, "Making Torture Legal," *New York Review of Books* 51, no. 12 (July 15, 2004); and Mark Danner, "The Logic of Torture," *New York Review of Books* 51, no. 11 (June 24, 2004).

2. Peter Singer, "Famine, Affluence, and Morality," *Philosophy and Public Affairs* 1 (1972): 229–44.

3. This is a contested viewpoint. The moral competence of charities to deliver assistance to the suffering is very much in doubt, according to William Shawcross, *The Quality of Mercy: Cambodia, Holocaust, and the Modern Conscience* (New York: Simon and

Schuster, 1984); and Peter Uvin, *Aiding Violence: The Development Enterprise in Rwanda* (West Hartford, Conn.: Kumarian, 1998).

4. Shawcross, *Quality of Mercy*; and Uvin, *Aiding Violence*.

5. Garrett Hardin, "Life Boat Ethics: The Case against Helping the Poor," *Psychology Today*, September 1974, 126.

6. See Eric Ross, *The Malthus Factor* (London: Zed, 1998).

7. Thomas Robert Malthus, *An essay on the principle of population; or, A view of its past and present effect on human happiness; with an inquiry into our prospects respecting the future removal or mitigation of the evils which it occasions* (1778; reprint, London: printed for J. Johnson by T. Bensley, 1803).

8. Hardin, "Life Boat Ethics."

9. John Rawls, *A Theory of Justice* (Cambridge, Mass.: Harvard University Press, 1971).

10. Martha Nussbaum, "The Enduring Significance of John Rawls," *Chronicle of Higher Education*, July 20, 2001, B7; Peter Berkowitz, "John Rawls and the Liberal Faith," *Wilson Quarterly* (Spring 2002) at http://wwics.si.edu/index.cfm?fuseaction=wq .print&essay_id=8468&stoplayout=true; Susan Moeller Okin, *Justice, Gender and the Family* (New York: Basic Books, 2001); Brian C. Anderson, "The Antipolitical Philosophy of John Rawls," *Public Interest* (Spring 2003) at www.findarticles.com/p/articles/ mi_m0377/is_2003_Spring/ai_100388979; Michael Sandel, *Liberalism and the Limits of Justice* (Cambridge: Cambridge University Press, 1983); Iris Marion Young, *Justice and the Politics of Difference* (Princeton, N.J.: Princeton University Press, 1990).

11. See, for example, Thomas W. Pogge, *World Poverty and Human Rights* (Cambridge, U.K.: Polity, 2002).

12. Isaiah Berlin, *Four Essays on Liberty* (London: Oxford University Press, 1969).

13. United Nations, Department of Public Information, "Fiftieth Anniversary of the Declaration of Human Rights," 1998, at www.un.org/rights/50/decla.htm (accessed July 23, 2004).

14. United Nations, "International Covenant on Civil and Political Rights," July 7, 1994, at www.hrweb.org/legal/cpr.html (accessed July 23, 2004).

15. United Nations, "International Covenant on Economic, Social, and Cultural Rights," July 7, 1994, at www.hrweb.org/legal/escr.html (accessed July 23, 2004).

16. Amnesty International, www.amnesty.org; Human Rights Watch, www.hrw .org.

17. Amartya Sen, *Development as Freedom* (New York: Anchor, 2000).

18. Sen, *Development as Freedom*, 36.

19. Sen, *Development as Freedom*, 18.

20. Sen, *Development as Freedom*, esp. chaps. 8 and 9.

21. Ashutosh Varshney, "Ethnic Conflict and Civil Society: India and Beyond," *World Politics* 53, no. 3 (April 2001): 262–98.

22. John Isbister, *Capitalism and Justice: Envisioning Social and Economic Fairness* (Bloomfield, Conn.: Kumarian, 2001), 15. This is one of the best introductions available to the problems of distributive and social justice.

23. Isbister, *Capitalism and Justice*, 14.

24. Philippe Van Parijs, quoted in Isbister, *Capitalism and Justice*, 16.

25. Isbister, *Capitalism and Justice*, 70–71.

26. Isbister, *Capitalism and Justice*, chap. 5.

27. As John F. Kennedy said, "Success has many fathers [*sic*]; failure is an orphan."

28. Remember, if Bill Gates is drinking in a bar with fifty bums, they are, on average, all billionaires.

29. Howard Ball, *The Bakke Case: Race, Education, and Affirmative Action* (Lawrence: University of Kansas Press, 2000).

30. Nancy Fraser, "Social Justice in the Age of Identity Politics: Redistribution, Recognition, Participation" (lecture given at the Wissenschaftszentrum Berlin für Sozialforschung, December 1998), at http://skylla.wz_berlin.de/pdf/1998/i98_108.pdf (accessed July 23, 2004).

31. Actually, Singer's position is a good deal more complex than this, for he is primarily concerned with minimizing pain and suffering, and uninterested in the welfare or fate of those who lack awareness of pain, including not only lower forms of life but also certain humans without sensory awareness. On Marx's view, see "On *the Jewish Question*," *Deutsch-Franzosische Jahrbucher*, February 1844, at www.marxists.org/archive/marx/works/1844/jewish_question/ (accessed July 23, 2004).

32. Chris Brown, *International Relations Theory: New Normative Approaches* (New York: Columbia University Press, 1992), esp. chap. 2.

33. See, for example, Charles Jones, *Global Justice: Defending Cosmopolitanism* (Oxford: Oxford University Press, 1999), esp. chaps. 2–4.

34. Onora O'Neill, *Bounds of Justice* (Cambridge: Cambridge University Press, 2000), chap. 10.

35. O'Neill, *Bounds of Justice*, 199.

36. Arlo Guthrie, "Alice's Restaurant," copyright 1966, 1967 (renewed) by Appleseed Music, Inc., all rights reserved.

37. Raymond A. Winbush, ed., *Should America Pay? Slavery and the Raging Debate over Reparations* (New York: Amistad, 2003).

38. Assume one million slaves working ten hours per day, three hundred days per year, for two hundred years, being paid minimum wage (in current dollars). Total wages would exceed $3.5 trillion in today's dollars.

39. Hardin, "Life Boat Ethics," 126.

40. Carol S. Robb, *Equal Value: An Ethical Approach to Economics and Sex* (Boston: Beacon, 1995), 145.

41. Thorstein Veblen, "The Beginning of Ownership," *American Journal of Sociology* 4, no. 3 (November 1898): 352–65, at http://socserv2.socsci.mcmaster.ca/~econ/ugcm/3ll3/veblen/ownersh (accessed July 23, 2004).

42. O'Neill, *Bounds of Justice*, 140, 141.

Chapter 9

1. Joseph E. Stiglitz, *Globalization and Its Discontents* (New York: Norton, 2002), 9.

2. James H. Mittelman, "The Dynamics of Globalization," in *Globalization: Critical Reflections*, edited by James H. Mittelman (Boulder, Colo.: Rienner, 1997), 3.

3. Harris Collingwood, "The Sink-or-Swim Economy," *New York Times Magazine*, June 8, 2003, 42–45.

4. Karl Marx and Friedrich Engels, *The Communist Manifesto* (New York: Pocket Books, 1964), 63.

5. Karl Polanyi, *The Great Transformation* (New York: Farrar and Rinehart, 1944), 159.

6. Anthony Giddens, *Runaway World: How Globalization Is Reshaping Our Lives* (London: Routledge, 1999), 33–34.

7. Plague transmission followed market routes worldwide in the Middle Ages. See Janet Abu-Lughod, *Before European Hegemony: The World System, A.D. 1250–1350* (New York: Oxford University Press, 1989), 173–74; Christopher Dyer, *Making a Living in the Middle Ages: The People of Britain, 850–1520* (New Haven, Conn.: Yale University Press, 2002), 271–77.

8. Eric R. Wolf, *Europe and the People without History* (Berkeley: University of California Press, 1982).

9. Mike Davis, *Late Victorian Holocausts: El Niño Famines and the Making of the Third World* (London: Verso, 2001). Davis looks at societies dominated by foreigners. Where native populations adjusted on their own, without the assistance to local elites that characterized adjustment in imperial dependencies, those local elites could occasionally be beaten back. See Dyer, *Making a Living*, 286–93.

10. For the political economy of the Irish potato famine, see Herman M. Schwartz, *States versus Markets: History, Geography, and the Development of the International Political Economy*, 2nd ed. (New York: St. Martin's, 2000); and www.people.Virginia.EDU/~eas5e/Irish/Famine.html. It should be noted that "Irish" landlords were mostly British, putting Ireland among the imperial dependencies referred to above. For the El Niño famines, see Davis, *Late Victorian Holocausts*. Davis stresses the importance of globalization in the spread of famine during these droughts. One example is that areas not served by railroads had lower food prices because there was no alternative external market, while regions connected by rail experienced skyrocketing prices even if their crops were not affected by drought. The integration of Ireland into European markets had the same effect.

11. Edmund Burke questioned the operation of the British East India Company in 1783, challenging assertions of its financial soundness and the involvement of court and Parliament in skimming profits from its activities. "Ninth Report of the Select Committee," June 25, 1783, in *The Writings and Speeches of Edmund Burke*, vol. 5, *India: Madras and Bengal, 1774–1785*, edited by P. J. Marshall (Oxford: Oxford University Press, 1985).

12. Linda Colley, *Captives: The Story of Britain's Pursuit of Empire and How Its Soldiers and Civilians Were Held Captive by the Dream of Global Supremacy, 1600–1850* (New York: Pantheon, 2002), chap. 9; John S. Galbraith, "The 'Turbulent Frontier' as a Factor in British Expansion," *Comparative Studies in Society and History* 2, no. 2 (1960): 150–68. We saw a similar loss of command and control in chapter 5, when we looked at the Massachusetts Bay Company. In that case, the crown found itself the unwitting (and unwilling) sponsor of a democratic political regime. It took fifty years for Britain to reimpose "normal" authoritarian rule in Massachusetts, given the command and control technologies of that time.

13. By then, the BEIC controlled all of India and was training local troops—Sepoys—to augment its need for military manpower. "The mutiny . . . began . . . when Indian soldiers who had been placed in irons for refusing to accept new cartridges were rescued by their comrades. The greased cartridges had to be bitten off before use, and the manufacturers had [packed them in a mixture of the] fat of beef and pork—repulsive to both Hindus and Moslems." See www.hyperhistory.com/online_n2/civil_n2/histscript6_n2/sepoy.html. Also see Christopher Hibbert, *The Great Mutiny of 1857* (New York: Viking, 1978); and Colley, *Captives*.

14. "Palace and Mosque: Islamic Art from the Victoria and Albert Museum," National Gallery of Art, Washington, D.C., July 18, 2004–February 6, 2005.

15. The classic work in this field is Theodor Adorno, "The Culture Industry: Enlightenment as Mass Deception," in *Dialectic of Enlightenment*, edited by Max Horkheimer and Theodor Adorno (New York: Herder and Herder, 1972), 120–67.

16. Barbara Jenkins, "Creating Global Hegemony: Culture and the Market," in *Rethinking Global Political Economy: Emerging Issues and Unfolding Odysseys*, edited by Mary Ann Tétreault, Robert A. Denemark, Kenneth P. Thomas, and Kurt Burch (London: Routledge, 2003), 65–85. Also, Ien Ang, *Watching Dallas: Soap Opera and the Melodramatic Imagination*, translated by Della Couling (London: Methuen, 1985).

17. A striking example is the authorship of the 1948 United Nations Declaration of Human Rights, which was drafted by a five-person committee chaired by Eleanor Roosevelt, the former first lady. The other members were John Humphrey, a Canadian attorney; René Cassin, a Jewish disabled veteran of WW II; Peng-chun Chang, a Chinese philosopher and playwright; and Charles Malik, a Greek Orthodox philosopher from Lebanon.

18. Davis, *Late Victorian Holocausts*, chap. 1.

19. Davis, *Late Victorian Holocausts*, 36, 43–44.

20. On the joint contributions of agents and structures to structural violence, see Johan Galtung, *Human Rights in Another Key* (Cambridge, U.K.: Polity, 1994), 27–38.

21. The very first econometric model was constructed to explain the limitations that transportation imposed on land rents and the location of production around a central market. See *Von Thünen's Isolated State: An English Edition of Der Isolierte Staat by Johann Heinrich von Thünen*, edited by Peter Hall, translated by Carla M. Wertenberg (Oxford: Pergamon, 1966).

22. *Von Thünen's Isolated State*. See also Schwartz, *States versus Markets*, chaps. 1–2.

23. Abu-Lughod, *Before European Hegemony*, 175–82.

24. The connection between national economic integration and state finance was a matter of great controversy, and, outside of England, it proceeded both slowly and in fits and starts. See, for example, Simon Schama, *Citizens: A Chronicle of the French Revolution* (New York: Knopf, 1989), chap. 2.

25. Barrington Moore, *The Social Origins of Dictatorships and Democracies: Lord and Peasant in the Making of the Modern World* (Boston: Beacon, 1966).

26. James Macdonald, *A Free Nation Deep in Debt: The Financial Roots of Democracy* (New York: Farrar, Straus and Giroux, 2003); also John Brewer, *The Sinews of Power: War and the English State, 1688–1783* (London: HarperCollins, 1989).

27. The leadership of peasants in spreading market relations in feudal Britain is one of the theses of Dyer's *Making a Living*.

28. Adam Hochschild, *King Leopold's Ghost* (Boston: Houghton Mifflin, 1999).

29. We thank geographer Bernard Logan for this point (personal communication with Mary Ann Tétreault).

30. James R. Kurth, "The Political Consequences of the Product Cycle: Industrial History and Political Outcomes," *International Organization* 33, no. 1 (Winter 1979): 1–34.

31. Davis reports that the British made the Indians pay the full cost of Britain's occupation of India. Stanley Karnow reports a similar policy by the French in Vietnam—see his *Vietnam: A History* (New York: Penguin, 1997). Africans were even more brutally exploited. Hochschild tells how King Leopold of Belgium extracted the costs of looting the Congo from native Africans; Edward Hooper reports that the Belgian government was paid by entrepreneurs developing polio vaccines for the right to test

the vaccines on the native peoples, a token of the status of the Congo as an "estate" of the Belgian government rather than an autonomous entity. See Edward Hooper, *The River: A Journey to the Source of HIV and AIDS* (Boston: Little, Brown, 1999).

32. See, for example, Anthony Sampson, *The Seven Sisters: The Great Oil Companies and the World They Shaped* (New York: Viking, 1975); also Robert W. Tolf, *The Russian Rockefellers: The Saga of the Nobel Family and the Russian Oil Industry* (Stanford, Calif.: Hoover Institute, 1977).

33. Phebe Marr, *The Modern History of Iraq* (Boulder, Colo.: Westview, 1985); Mary Ann Tétreault, "Independence, Sovereignty, and Vested Glory: Oil and Politics in the Second Gulf War," *Orient* 34, no. 1 (March 1993): 87–103; interview by Terry Gross of Charles Lewis, director of the Center for Public Integrity, on *Fresh Air*, National Public Radio, June 17, 2003.

34. Clark A. Miller, "The Globalization of Human Affairs: A Reconsideration of Science, Political Economy, and World Order," in Tétreault, Denemark, Thomas, and Burch, *Rethinking Global Political Economy*, 216–17.

35. Naomi Sakr, *Satellite Realms: Transnational Television, Globalization, and the Middle East* (London: I. B. Tauris, 2001), esp. chap. 3.

36. Mary Ann Tétreault and Harry W. Haines, "Postmodern War and Historical Memory" (paper presented at the annual meeting of the International Studies Association, Montréal, March 2004); also W. Lance Bennett, *News: The Politics of Illusion*, 4th ed. (New York: Longman, 2001); also Pierre Bourdieu, *On Television*, translated by Priscilla Parkhurst Ferguson (New York: New Press, 1998).

37. Olivier Roy, "Bin Laden et ses frères," *Politique International* 93, 67–81; "Bin Laden: An Apocalyptic Sect Severed from Political Islam," *East European Constitutional Review* 10, no. 4 (Fall): 108–14.

38. Olivier Roy, "Changing Patterns among Radical Islamist Movements," *Brown Journal of World Affairs* 6, no. 1 (Winter/Spring 1999): 109–20; also Roy, "Bin Laden et ses frères."

39. Carolyn Nordstrom, *Girls and Warzones* (Uppsala, Sweden: Life and Peace Institute, 1997); see also *Shadows of War: Violence, Power, and International Profiteering in the Twenty-first Century* (Berkeley: University of California Press, 2004).

40. Ahmad Rashid, *Taliban* (New Haven, Conn.: Yale Nota Bene, 2000).

41. Rashid, *Taliban*; also Mary Ann Tétreault, "International Relations," in *Understanding the Contemporary Middle East*, edited by Deborah J. Gerner (Boulder, Colo.: Rienner, 2000), 129–60; Craig Unger, "Saving the Saudis," *Vanity Fair*, October 2003, 162, 164–66, 175–76, 178–79.

42. David S. Meyer, "Protest Cycles and Political Process: American Peace Movements in the Nuclear Age," *Political Research Quarterly* 47, no. 3 (1993): 451–79; and "Social Movements: Creating Communities of Change," in *Conscious Acts and the Politics of Social Change*, edited by Robin L. Teske and Mary Ann Tétreault (Columbia: University of South Carolina Press, 2000), 35–55.

43. David Ronfelt and John Arquilla, "Networks, Netwars, and the Fight for the Future," *First Monday* 6, no. 10 (2001), at www.firstmonday.org/issues/issue6_10/ronfeldt/index.html (accessed June 2002). This is the same kind of activity that nonviolent—and legal—groups pursue, such as the coalition Let Freedom Ring, mentioned in chapter 5, which held demonstrations protesting China's human rights record during the 1997 state visit of the president of China to the United States.

44. Michael Hardt and Antonio Negri, *Empire* (Cambridge, Mass.: Harvard University Press, 2000).

45. Kirin Aziz Chaudhrey, *The Price of Wealth: Economies and Institutions in the Middle East* (Ithaca, N.Y.: Cornell University Press, 1997), 241–50. These little financial organizations are primary targets of antiterrorism efforts, even though larger sums are transferred internationally through far larger enterprises.

46. Thomas Friedman, "Where Freedom Reigns," *New York Times*, August 14, 2002, A29.

47. Ashutosh Varshney, "Ethnic Conflict and Civil Society: India and Beyond," *World Politics* 53, no. 3 (April 2001): 362–98.

48. Varshney, "Ethnic Conflict."

49. Amartya Sen, *Underdevelopment as Freedom* (New York: Doubleday Anchor, 2000).

50. Stiglitz, *Globalization and Its Discontents*; George Soros, *George Soros on Globalization* (New York: PublicAffairs, 2002).

51. Sen agrees, and argues that this involves systematic misinterpretation and suppression of all but a narrow segment from the canonical works of Adam Smith—see *Underdevelopment as Freedom*, 271–72.

52. Stiglitz, *Globalization and Its Discontents*, 13, 74, 78, quote from 74.

53. See Polanyi, *The Great Transformation*, 148. Such contradictions permeate formal clashes between proponents of these two incompatible tenets. For a recent example, see Ken Auletta, *World War 3.0: Microsoft and Its Enemies* (New York: Random House, 2001), which looks at the contradiction as it affects antitrust regulation.

54. Polanyi, *The Great Transformation*, 148.

55. Tony Clarke, "Priming the Pump: The Emerging Debate over Water Privatization in North America," *Cross Border Perspectives*, November 2002, at www.maxwell.syr.edu/campbell/XBorder/Clarke%20oped.pdf (accessed September 2003).

56. Janine R. Wedel, *Collision and Collusion: The Strange Case of Western Aid to Eastern Europe, 1989–1998* (New York: St. Martin's, 1998).

57. PBS's *Frontline* showed how the 1995 decision by the G-7 to change the dollar-yen exchange rate touched off the Asian economic crisis. *Frontline*, "The Crash," broadcast June 29, 1999. Transcript at www.pbs.org/wgbh/pages/frontline/shows/crash/etc/script.html (accessed January 2004).

58. Peter Uvin, *Aiding Violence: The Development Enterprise in Rwanda* (West Hartford, Conn.: Kumarian, 1998).

59. Joseph Stiglitz, "The Broken Promise of NAFTA," *New York Times*, January 6, 2004, A27.

60. Lawrence Wright, "The Kingdom of Silence," *New Yorker*, January 5, 2004, 70.

61. But for a more skeptical view, see Ronnie D. Lipschutz, *Regulation for the Rest of Us?* (London: Routledge, forthcoming).

62. Sandra G. Boodman, "Raw Menace: Major Hepatitis A Outbreak Tied to Green Onions," *Washington Post*, November 25, 2003, HE01; and also see www.agriculturelaw.com/archive/nov03.html.

63. Susan Lindquist, "From Mad Cows to Nanoscale Technology" (Trinity University Distinguished Scientist Lecture, San Antonio, April 5, 2004).

64. John Darnton, "Britain Ties Deadly Brain Disease to Cow Ailment," *New York Times*, March 21, 1996, A1, A7.

65. On resistance to regulation in the United States after the discovery of an infected cow in the state of Washington in December 2003, see Lynette Clemetson, "U.S. Officials Say Suspect Beef Went to a Wider Region," *New York Times*, December 29, 2003,

A1, A11; Glen Justice, "For Cattle Industry, A Quick Response Years in the Making," *New York Times*, January 1, 2004, A1, A14; Eric Schlosser, "The Cow Jumped over the U.S.D.A.," *New York Times*, January 2, 2004, A19.

66. "Japan Deems Beef Standards Lax in Canada and U.S." *New York Times*, January 20, 2004, D3.

67. Robert G. Webster, "Influenza: An Emerging Disease," *Emerging Infections Diseases* 4, no. 3 (July–September 1998), at www.cdc.gov/ncidod/eid/vol4no3/webster .htm (accessed January 2004).

68. Hooper, *The River*. The oral vaccine was grown in a culture medium derived from primate tissue.

69. Andrew Pollack, "No Foolproof Way Is Seen to Contain Altered Genes," *New York Times*, January 21, 2004, A10.

70. Carol Kaesuk Yoon, "Genetic Modification Taints Corn in Mexico," *New York Times*, October 2, 2001, at www.biotech_info.net/mexico_corn.html.

71. One account of globalization across the millennia can be found in Luigi Luca Cavalli-Sforza, *Genes, Peoples, and Languages* (New York: North Point, 2000).

72. Robert O. Keohane and Joseph S. Nye, *Power and Interdependence: World Politics in Transition* (Boston: Little, Brown, 1977).

73. For how this worked after the oil revolution, see Mary Ann Tétreault, *Revolution in the World Petroleum Market* (Westport, Conn.: Quorum Books, 1985).

74. This is David Ricardo's famous theory of comparative advantage.

75. Adam Hochschild, *King Leopold's Ghost: A Story of Greed, Terror, and Heroism in Colonial Africa* (Boston: Houghton Mifflin, 1999), 28, 42.

76. This trend was visible as early as the nineteenth century, but nongovernmental agents were appreciably smaller in capacity and reach as compared to states than at least a few such agents are today. See Craig N. Murphy, *International Organization and Industrial Change: Global Governance since 1850* (Cambridge, U.K.: Polity, 1994).

Chapter 10

1. Sheldon Wolin, "Fugitive Democracy," in *Democracy and Difference*, edited by Seyla Benhabib (Princeton, N.J.: Princeton University Press, 1996), 31–45.

2. Hannah Arendt, *On Revolution* (New York: Viking, 1963).

3. *American Heritage Dictionary of the English Language* (Boston: Houghton Mifflin, 1981), 436.

4. Lewis Mumford, *The Human Prospect* (London: Secker and Warburg, 1955), and *The Transformations of Man* (New York: Harper, 1956).

5. Bill McKibben, *The End of Nature* (New York: Anchor, 1999).

6. Amartya Sen, *Development as Freedom* (New York: Knopf, 1999).

7. Karen Walch, "Feminist Ideas on Cooperation and Self-Interest for International Relations," in *Partial Truths and the Politics of Community*, edited by Mary Ann Tétreault and Robin L. Teske (Columbia: University of South Carolina Press, 2003), 161–78.

8. Michel Foucault, *Power/Knowledge*, translated by Colin Gordon (New York: Pantheon, 1980), 119.

9. International Campaign to Ban Land Mines, at www.icbl.org.

10. International Campaign to Ban Land Mines.

11. Margaret Keck and Kathryn Sikkink, *Activists Beyond Borders: Advocacy Networks in International Politics* (Ithaca, N.Y.: Cornell University Press, 1998).

12. Katherine Boo, "The Churn: Creative Destruction in a Border Town," *New Yorker*, March 29, 2004, at www.newyorker.com/printable/?fact/040329fa_fact (accessed July 21, 2004).

13. See, for example, Richard A. Clarke, *Against All Enemies: America's War on Terror* (New York: Free Press, 2004). Clarke worked on antiterrorism policy in the Reagan, Bush One, Clinton, and Bush Two administrations. A prominent policy analyst who teaches at the U.S. Air War College has published very similar views. See Jeffrey Record, *Dark Victory: America's Second War against Iraq* (Annapolis, Md.: Naval Institute Press, 2004). The most blistering of these critiques comes from a CIA analyst: Anonymous, *Imperial Hubris: Why the West Is Losing the War on Terror* (Washington, D.C.: Brassey's, 2004).

14. Ronnie D. Lipschutz, *Global Environmental Politics: Power, Perspectives, and Practice* (Washington, D.C.: Congressional Quarterly, 2003), chap. 3.

15. For example, see Mark D. Harmon, *The British Labour Government and the 1976 IMF Crisis* (New York: St. Martin's, 1997).

16. David A. Stockman, *The Triumph of Politics: How the Reagan Revolution Failed* (New York: Harper and Row, 1986).

17. Intergovernmental Panel on Climate Change, *Climate Change 2001: Synthesis Report* (Geneva: IPCC Secretariat/World Meteorological Organization, 2001), at www.ipcc.ch/pub/un/syreng/spm.pdf (accessed July 26, 2004).

18. The literature on replacement jobs is large and growing. See, for example, Rich Reinhold, "How Laid Off Workers Fared in Their Reemployment Efforts," *Illinois Labor Market Review* 4, no. 1 (Spring 1998), at http://lmi.ides.state.il.us/lmr/article1.htm (accessed August 20, 2004).

19. A current controversy in the United States pits health economists against health advocates as to whether "a vaccine that could save the lives of nearly 3,000 people, many of them teenagers, from deaths caused" by bacterial meningitis will be provided because the cost to the government is estimated at $3.5 billion, or "more than $1 million a life spared, far more than health officials are normally willing to spend." See Gardiner Harris, "Panel Reviews New Vaccine That Could Be Controversial," *New York Times*, October 27, 2004, A12.

20. Michel Foucault, "Governmentality," in *The Foucault Effect: Studies in Governmentality*, edited by Graham Burchell, Colin Gordon, and Peter Miller, 87–104; quote on 102 (Chicago: University of Chicago Press, 1991).

21. Mitchell Dean, *Governmentality: Power and Rule in Modern Society* (London: Sage, 1999), 99.

22. Vladimir Ilyich Lenin, *What Is to Be Done? Burning Questions of Our Movement* (New York: International, 1929). In Russian, the phrase is "*Shto delat?*" and it has appeared in the titles of works by Tolstoy, Chernyshevsky, and others.

23. Deborah Stone, *Policy Paradox: The Art of Political Decision Making* (New York: Norton, 1997), 26.

24. James C. Scott, *Seeing Like a State: How Certain Schemes to Improve the Human Condition Have Failed* (New Haven, Conn.: Yale University Press, 1999).

25. Foucault, *Power/Knowledge*, 119.

26. Hannah Arendt, *The Human Condition*, 2nd ed. (Chicago: University of Chicago Press), 198.

27. Arendt, *The Human Condition*, 200.

28. Arendt, *The Human Condition*, 199.

29. Arendt, *The Human Condition*, 198.

30. See, for example, Bruno Latour, *Pandora's Hope: Essays on the Reality of Science Studies* (Cambridge, Mass.: Harvard University Press, 1999), chap. 2.

31. One discussion of "political space" can be found in Robin L. Teske, "Political Space: The Importance of the Inbetween," in *Conscious Acts and the Politics of Social Change,* edited by Robin L. Teske and Mary Ann Tétreault (Columbia: University of South Carolina Press, 2000), 72–90.

32. Even earlier than that—in medieval Britain, for example—unskilled workers were not permitted to associate. They couldn't form workers' organizations groups or even meet together regularly as a social club or a religious fraternity. The power of association to generate politics and the desire of status quo forces to repress that power explain why the right of association is part of the First Amendment to the U.S. Constitution, a position that announces its bedrock importance to democratic life. On medieval restrictions on associations in Britain see Christopher Dyer, *Making a Living in the Middle Ages: The People of Britain, 850–1520* (New Haven, Conn.: Yale University Press, 2002), 316.

33. Norman Long, "From Paradigm Lost to Paradigm Regained? The Case for an Actor-Oriented Sociology of Development," in *Battlefields of Knowledge: The Interlocking of Theory and Practice in Social Research and Development*, edited by Norman Long and Ann Long (London: Routledge, 1992), 23–24.

34. Ronnie D. Lipschutz, *After Authority: War, Peace and Global Politics in the 21st Century* (Albany, N.Y.: SUNY Press, 2000), chap. 8.

35. Mary Ann Tétreault and Robin L. Teske, "Framing the Issues," in Teske and Tétreault, *Conscious Acts*, 6.

36. This observation is laid out with great elegance in Graham Allison's classic work, *Essence of Decision: Explaining the Cuban Missile Crisis* (Reading, Mass.: Addison Wesley, 1972).

37. The joke is rather too long to tell here. Suffice it to say that it involves a physicist modeling a cow's failure to produce milk by "assuming a spherical cow." See John Harte, *Consider a Spherical Cow: A Course in Environmental Problem Solving* (Los Altos, Calif.: Kaufman, 1985).

38. That globalization has effects that produce reactions in the form of religious social movements is the premise of a set of case studies in Mary Ann Tétreault and Robert A. Denemark, eds., *Gods, Guns, and Globalization: Religious Radicalism and International Political Economy*, vol. 13, *The International Political Economy Yearbook* (Boulder, Colo.: Rienner, 2004).

39. Especially Ronnie D. Lipschutz, *Global Civil Society and Global Environmental Governance* (Albany, N.Y.: SUNY Press, 1996).

40. See Lipschutz, *Global Environmental Politics*, chap. 4.

41. Lipschutz, *Global Environmental Politics*.

42. Mancur Olson, *The Logic of Collective Action* (Cambridge, Mass.: Harvard University Press, 1965).

43. Sidney Tarrow, *Power in Movement: Social Movements and Contentious Politics*, 2nd ed. (Cambridge: Cambridge University Press, 1998); Doug McAdam, John D. McCarthy, and Meyer N. Zald, *Comparative Perspectives on Social Movements: Political*

Opportunities, Mobilizing Structures, and Cultural Framings (Cambridge: Cambridge University Press, 1996).

44. Chantal Mouffe, *The Democratic Paradox* (London: Verso, 2000).

45. Eric R. Wolf, *Europe and the People without History* (Berkeley: University of California Press, 1982), 388.

Index

About the Authors

Mary Ann Tétreault is the Una Chapman Cox Distinguished Professor of International Affairs at Trinity University in San Antonio. Her research and teaching interests include war and peace studies, Middle East politics, gender and politics, and U.S. foreign policy. Among her recent books are: *Gods, Guns, and Globalization: Religious Radicalism and International Political Economy* (International Political Economy Yearbook, vol. 13), coedited with Robert A. Denemark; *Rethinking Global Political Economy: Emerging Issues, Unfolding Odysseys*, coedited with Robert A. Denemark, Kenneth P. Thomas, and Kurt Burch (2003); *Feminist Approaches to Social Movements, Community, and Power*, vol. 2, *Partial Truths and the Politics of Community*, coedited with Robin L. Teske (2003); and *Stories of Democracy: Politics and Society in Contemporary Kuwait* (2000).

Ronnie D. Lipschutz is professor of politics and associate director of the Center for Global, International and Regional Studies at the University of California, Santa Cruz. He is also chair of the politics Ph.D. program at UCSC. His primary areas of research and teaching include international politics, global environmental affairs, U.S. foreign policy, globalization, international regulation, and film, fiction, and politics. His most recent books include *Regulation for the Rest of Us? Globalization, Governmentality, and Global Politics* (forthcoming, 2005*); Global Environmental Politics: Power, Perspectives, and Practice* (2004); *After Authority: War, Peace, and Global Politics in the 21st Century* (2000); and *Cold War Fantasies: Film, Fiction, and Foreign Policy* (2001).